MW01174873

Do You Think You Will Break?

Stretching Head, Hips and Heart in My Search for Happiness

Robin Patino

Creative Journeys Publishing
Easton, Pennsylvania

Grateful acknowledgment is made for permission to reprint lyrics from the
following songs:
Warning Shots by Thievery Corporation
Drive by Incubus
Change by Luka Blom
Walk On by U2
#9 Dream by John Lennon
Carry On Wayward Son by Kansas
Believe by Lenny Kravitz
I'm Free by Soup Dragons
Yahweh by U2
Salima by Jehro
I Know by Jude
You Gotta Be by Des'ree
Walk On by U2

Copyright © 2011 by Robin Patino. All rights reserved. No part of this book,
either in part or in whole, may reproduced by any mechanical, photographic,
or electronic process, or in the form of a phonographic recording; nor may it be
stored in a retrieval system, transmitted, or otherwise be copied for public or
private use—other than "fair use" as brief quotations embodied in articles and
reviews—without prior written permission of the publisher.

646-770-2363
www.robinpatino.com

Copyright © 2012 Robin Patino
All rights reserved.

ISBN: 0-6155-5271-4
ISBN-13: 9780615552712

Dedication

With love and gratitude to my family

—especially my Mom and Dad—

who have always been exactly what I needed.

Contents

Foreword

The Five Layers of the Body (*Koshas*)
Don Stapleton, Ph.D.

The *koshas,* or five layers of the body, comprise the self that undergoes the process of yoga. Robin Patino's brilliant book perfectly illustrates how the process works through personal stories about her own experiences of healing through yoga.

The journey of awakening into expanded consciousness begins when we ask ourselves the classic yogic question "Who am I?" The first thing we notice in answering that question is that we each live in a self-contained physical body, separate from the others. Like a peanut in the center of a chocolate coated M&M, the physical body is the most dense, solid form of energy. Consisting of the material elements of earth, water, fire, and air, the *anna-maya-kosha* of physical body is "home base" for the other subtler layers of the self.

But the physical body is more than a sum of its essential material elements. The body is animated by energy or *prana,* called the *prana-maya-kosha* in yoga philosophy. Accessing the workings of prana happens by connecting our mental awareness to the tides of sensation as they ebb and flow through various regions of the body. In observing sensations as they pulse through the body, the life force within our physical organism registers on the screen of our mental awareness. This level of the self, the *mana-maya-kosha* or "ego-mind," is what we call our personality and is made up of our thoughts and emotions. It arises out of the sense of "I" as a separate self that is responsible for fulfilling the biological imperative of securing the survival needs of the organism. By comparing this moment, this "now," with all past moments for information, the ego-mind learns how and when to move toward life-sustaining experiences and when and how to avoid pain, injury, illness, or death.

An axiom in yoga states that where the mind goes, prana flows. The ego-mind maintains its role by directing prana to act through the body to fulfill the body's survival imperatives. Beliefs about the goodness of one experience over another give rise to our perceived reality: our interpretations of how the world works and our place within it. Emotions arise from the ego-mind as well: the feelings we experience around getting or not getting, being included or not included, feeling secure or threatened are all energetic responses that we sense and feel in the body in reaction to events in the world in and around the individual self. Our feelings and emotions motivate us to take appropriate action to satisfy the needs of our personalities.

None of us could survive without a healthily functioning ego-mind. Try to cross a street without being able to judge how fast a truck is coming toward you and you will appreciate the way the ego-mind protects your survival by constantly monitoring your environment for safety. Apply for a job with a healthy salary attached and you will appreciate the skills and experience that are represented in your résumé. We need the healthy ego to create a foundation for further expansion of consciousness. However, there is more to the self than a good job and healthy body.

Discrimination Generates Witness Consciousness

How does consciousness expand beyond perceiving the world through the ego-mind, which experiences the moment dualistically, protects our autonomy, and operates out of the fear of losing its identity? Another dimension of the self, the *vijnana-maya-kosha*, arises when we make the discriminating observation that there is more to life than wanting, getting, and having. One ice cream cone is pleasurable. Two ice cream cones are even more pleasurable. But upon eating three or more ice cream cones, the original pleasure turns to pain. To the ego-mind, the moment of "now" appears to present a need for choosing between polar opposites, such as pleasure and pain. But from the perspective of the entire universal field of consciousness, all human experience is interconnected within the whole. What appear to the ego-mind as mutually exclusive choices, with mutually exclusive cause-effect outcomes, are in reality mirror images of a unified phenomenon—two sides of the same coin.

Discriminative wisdom begins to develop when we notice that the outcomes of our choices do not always yield the pleasurable or desirable effects that we once experienced from making that same choice. Examining our life experiences with such discrimination develops a mental "muscle" that begins to slow the reflex to act on every desire that surfaces in the moment. In slowing down to discern the possible outcomes of a given choice, we can suspend the reflex to fulfill that desire immediately. Placing this speed bump in the highway between stimulus and response allows the time and space to notice that there are deeper levels to our desires. I may notice that I don't really want the second or third ice cream cone and that what I really want is to sit down and get started on that project I've been avoiding. Applying discrimination in this way allows us to see ourselves more deeply and to make better informed choices in the future as to how to best care for, and nurture ourselves.

This muscle that we develop to see ourselves more expansively matures into witness consciousness. When the witness is present, we no longer judge ourselves for the choices we have made through the ego-mind. Witnessing allows us to compassionately accept the ego-mind and its actions by recognizing that it is performing a good job of doing exactly what it is designed to do: split the moment and make a decision for or against the seeming opposites. Compassion, forgiveness, and acceptance of ourselves are fundamental to releasing prana from its limited functioning through the ego-mind, opening the flow of prana toward discovering hidden potentials and expanding consciousness into greater dimensions of the self.

A physician once told me a story that illustrates the interrelationship between body, prana, ego-mind, and witness. An elderly gentleman came for an office consultation prior to scheduling surgery. The cantankerous old fellow was hard of hearing. His body was so stiff that he could not isolate the movements of his torso from his head, neck, and shoulders. Later, when the gentleman was under anesthesia, his body became so pliable that it took several husky orderlies to move him from the gurney to the operating table. After the operation, the doctor observed his patient coming out from under the anesthesia. At first he resembled a sleeping baby, his whole body moving in response to his breath. But as the fellow began to regain consciousness and to remember who he was, the doctor watched his body contort back into the shape of a stiff, old man. What the doctor noticed was that muscles and bones can return to their natural, flexible shapes and functional relationships when the ego-mind, the personality, is not present. But when the ego-mind resumes control over the body, the body shape-shifts to fulfill the identity.

How does the ego-mind lose contact with the intelligence of the body? Ordinarily the ego-mind is guiding prana to shape and direct the body to accomplish its tasks and goals. All thoughts, images, feelings, and experiences are related to the project of the moment, which is in service to maintaining the self-identity. For example, when you are sitting in front of your computer writing a letter, your attention is focused on the screen in front of you. You are thinking about the person to whom you are writing. You are thinking about what you want to say. You are thinking about doing a good job so the recipient regards you more highly. Everything that is important to your ego-mind is channeled into writing that letter. You forget to notice that your shoulders start to creep up toward your ears. You do not notice that you move your head closer and closer to the screen as you become more concentrated. Because you want to finish the letter today, you lose track of the time. You forget to take a break. You are so absorbed in that letter that it becomes the singular reality.

Suddenly the phone rings. You jump out of your seat. Reluctantly, you tear yourself away from the letter to answer the phone. When you reach for the phone, you notice that your shoulders are tight and your mouth is dry. You look at your watch. Where did those three hours go?

In this example, attention is directed toward particular thoughts about the letter, but you lose awareness of your body in the process. Witness consciousness allows you to remain involved in whatever project absorbs your attention at the moment while simultaneously maintaining awareness of the workings of prana in the body. Developing witness consciousness can be as simple as deliberately slowing down. Pausing briefly for stretch breaks, drinking water, and readjusting the height of your chair are little ways of checking in with your body to notice where tensions begin to accumulate. In listening to what the body is saying during these little pauses, you may notice other ideas or insights that can inform and enhance what you are communicating in your letter. In this way you attend to the task at hand while also creating the condition for prana to move toward fulfilling the evolutionary potential of the self in the same moment.

Robin Patino's book demonstrates of how the accumulations of a lifetime can lead to loss of body awareness and of the serious health consequences that can result when the ego-mind is left in tact as the primary operating faculty. It also shows in very real and human terms how it is possible to reverse the process, and to use yoga as a vital and relevant healing tool in the modern world.

The state of bliss, *ananda-maya-kosha*, emerges when we recognize that prana infuses every part of our experience, synchronizing all of the koshas within the whole of our being. The body will continue being the body. The ego-mind will continue doing its job of surviving and nurturing the emotional and physical needs of the organism. But the witness now has the capacity to redirect the flow of prana from its previously monopolized assignment of survival, instead beginning to use the ultimate creative powers of intuition and intentionality to evolve new circumstances that were not possible before. The body is more than simply a vehicle for the ego-mind to maintain; the body has the power to transform and evolve new capacities. Drawing from the bliss of having intuited and then realized the union of all aspects of the self within the whole, the witness now draws from the power of unlimited consciousness for manifesting new circumstances that support evolution of the self.

By following her own process of integrating all koshas, or layers of the self, Robin Patino demonstrates how we each have the power within ourselves to create a new life—and a new world—for ourselves and those we impact.

Introduction

Heal

I spent two and a half years on the journey of a lifetime.

One year was spent in the lush jungles of Costa Rica, on a fast track to healing my body, mind, and spirit in the paradise of Nosara, where I trained to become a yoga teacher. Four months in Spain nourished my soul: writing secluded in the Axarquia Mountains of Andalucia in the south, bursting with life in Barcelona, and walking out my past on El Camino de Santiago—a 400-mile pilgrimage across the country's north. The remainder of my journey was devoted to experiencing different pockets of the United States, seeing my country through clear eyes, and reinventing my life.

I made several conscious choices before embarking on my journey: I quit my job, gave up my home, and sold or gave away most of my belongings.

I also unplugged—I chose not to engage in media of any kind other than using social networks to keep in contact with family and friends. The last television program I chose to watch was President Obama's inauguration. I watched that event seated on the open-air balcony of my yoga teachers' tropical home in Nosara with forty-five other yoginis, sending a blast of positivity from Central America outward to a man who represented hope and change for the world.

Over the course of my travels, I tuned into media sporadically while visiting family or friends who lived with televisions or radios turned on. I didn't like what I heard.

Having worked quite successfully as a strategy professional and problem solver for the twenty years before my journey commenced, both in politics and the corporate world in Washington, D.C., Los Angeles, and New York City, I could interpret pretty quickly what was going on in the United States from the messages I caught, in passing, as well as from what I experienced firsthand during my travels.

Fear and uncertainty had taken over my nation. People had become blind to what was happening around them and their own power to change things. The U.S. was firmly divided—an "us against them" mentality prevailed and great energy was devoted to proving which side of any political issue was right with little or no regard to broader consequences of divisiveness. My country was in crisis, and no one seemed interested in solving problems, only in winning.

That dynamic was something I uniquely understood. It's the same inner state that led me to pursue my journey, leaving a secure job in the midst of a floundering economy. I had fallen asleep at the wheel of my own life. I was tired through my core from living an unsupported life of fear and separation. All my creative energy had been diverted to daily survival, and very little was left over for purpose and vision. Then I was fortunate to have several exceptional mentors drop into my life like gifts at crucial moments. This began my process of waking up before steering my personal car into the walls I had built in my own life with serious health consequences. I made a conscious choice to love myself by leaving a no-win situation, regardless of my fears.

So, off I went on a "year's" sabbatical. It turned into a two-plus-year voyage of contemplating the meaning of the universe and fundamentally changing my outlook and my life. It wasn't planned that way, but that was the beauty of it.

When I decided to leave behind a life that wasn't working to find one that would meet my needs, my goal was for healing and for change. In searching for my own way to happiness, a physical problem—a faulty hip joint—was the focal point that spurred me forward. Degenerative arthritis from a birth defect in my right hip had accelerated to the point that I was facing a joint replacement. My daily yoga practice had proven to be especially healing, so I took a leap of faith that the progress I had seen would continue exponentially the more time I devoted to it. That's why I decided to train as a yoga instructor in Costa Rica.

The results of letting go of an unworkable situation, and of deepening my yoga practice, were beyond my wildest expectations. Not only did I heal my hip, but I began living my life's dreams and bringing everything I needed into my life by following my own truth and believing in a greater good. I chose to stop talking about all of the reasons I wasn't ready or why it couldn't be done and just began to act.

To get there, I had to do some major healing on many levels. When I landed in Costa Rica, I knew only that I wanted a different, more fulfilling life. I had some ideas about the direction that my future might take, and trusted that I would find my path by getting to know myself better. I began my own healing journey through the *koshas,* or layers of the body, beginning with my physical form.

In the process I have learned that to achieve sustainable health and happiness, any healing process begins with the physical layer as a foundation, but does not stop there. Many people heal their physical bodies and wonder why they remain unhappy or cannot maintain their health, why no diet or exercise program seems to have lasting results. It is not enough to have a healthy body when so much of illness can reside on other levels of our being, such as the emotional, behavioral, energetic, and spiritual levels. These layers of our being— the *koshas*—influence how we think and how we act, and define us in the world. They influence our behavior, directly contributing to the health of our physical body.

When I left my life in New York behind, I did so not with physical transformation as my primary objective. I saw that I was deeply unhappy with where I had taken myself in life, and that the majority of my time not at work was focused on trying to achieve some balance just to survive. Like most of my friends at that time, I was like a hamster on the corporate "wheel," trying desperately to replenish myself while feeling continually depleted from putting my energy into something I didn't care about.

The course of my journey was not always easy. I faced and conquered many challenges. The financial and material security that I so valued in my life before were replaced by the security of knowing who I am, the faith that I am on the right path, and the trust that all that I need will be provided. As a reward, I saw many miraculous things happen in my life:

- My arthritic hip, once destined for replacement surgery, became strong. It remains relatively pain free through holistic and all-natural means to this day.
- Through daily yoga practice, walking, bike riding, conscious eating, and digestive cleansing, my forty-year-old body became strong, lean, fit, and sexy.
- I have become filled with an inner vitality and joy that make my physical age irrelevant.
- I conquered longstanding depression by learning and accepting my needs, setting clearer emotional boundaries in my personal relationships, and developing a lifestyle that supported me—breaking my reliance on pharmaceuticals.
- I began writing creatively again after struggling with a ten-year block.
- I regained faith in myself, in the intrinsic goodness of people, and in a greater power that supports me through whatever challenges I face.
- I healed a long-standing rift with my father through forgiveness and love, and thereby opened myself up to relationships with a series of amazing men who subsequently manifested in my life.
- Passion, purpose, intuition, and fun became the guiding forces in my life, replacing fear and my previous conformance to an external ideal.
- Most visibly, I shrank from a size 14 to my current size 6, and, at the time of this writing, I am proud that I have sustained my weight with little effort for over two years.
- I began to feel feminine, strong, and powerful most of the time, and remembered how to embrace whatever challenges lay ahead of me instead of letting them defeat me!

In life, I have found the most powerful teaching tool to be example—the marriage between words and actions. As children, we learn by observing our parents as role models, and then expand that group to include teachers, peers, bosses, and community leaders. Every day, each of us has a choice about what type of example we will be for others.

My challenge in writing this book has been to provide you the lessons I learned on my journey in a way that teaches, that creates a new understanding, and inspires and supports you in making good choices in your life, as well. My goal is to communicate a message that wakes you up to your own individual responsibility and brings consciousness to your own choices. By doing so, I hope to share the joy that I have found and believe is accessible to each and every one of us.

Our world has reached a place where it is imperative to wake up. Collectively we now have the very real power to destroy ourselves and our planet if we don't open our eyes, see where we are headed, and choose to do something different. We have the very real power within ourselves to make a change, to create a better world.

I hope that something here touches you and perhaps enables you to see your own life from a different perspective, and inspires you to question whether you have been allowing love or fear to govern your choices in life.

One of the very first and most important lessons I learned, not two weeks into my journey, was taught me by a beautiful twenty-year old woman at my first yoga teacher training.

The Turtle and the Vulture

A crescent moon hovered over the darkened landscape, only the vague outlines of trees could be seen as our subdued group followed our guide to the beach. Stepping carefully down the rutted path, we used the weak glow of the moon and the infrared lights of three guides to avoid stumbling in the dark.

The word had come the day before. The first of an *arribada,* or sea arrival, of turtles had been seen landing on Playa Ostional, marking the onset of an egg-laying period, and the trip had been quickly arranged.

Arriving on the beach, the sky turned a lighter shade of indigo, and the black sand, the sea, and the sky could be more easily differentiated. The shuffling of feet in the sand, waves shushing to shore, and hushed whispers were the only sounds in the predawn silence.

The group split into three branches, and each followed a different guide's red beam, stepping carefully on the dark beach.

A pale pink glow began to glaze the tops of palm trees and outline the mangrove bushes, painting the sky in rainbow from the palest baby blue into deep, lustrous lapis lazuli into cerulean and midnight. The crescent moon stood starkly in the heavens, reflected along with the trees and a few remaining stars in the still tidal pool.

The first turtle was spotted, glowing red against the black sand in one of the guide's light. The group crouched around as it hung suspended in a hole of its own digging. Paddle-like fins splayed on the sand, propping the turtle's head and shell above while the lower portions were buried. Deep in the hole, the turtle was laying eggs to incubate. The hatchlings would then follow their mother to the sea six weeks later.

Tracing the tracks engraved on the beach, the guide brought us next to a mother who had finished her task, and was making the slow crawl from her offspring back to the sea. Her pink and grey shell was curved like the helmet of a giant; the fat, meaty paddles of her legs swathed the sand like snow angels; black freckles outlined small eyes that stared stoically from her pointed face, as she moved imperceptibly towards her goal. Millimeter by millimeter, a study in patience, she crossed the black sand toward waves that would signal the end of her maternal duties.

Air and water brightened as the sun began its climb behind the jungle hills, while the sand remained dark and obscure. More lumps became recognizable as turtles. The group straggled into twos and threes as the red glow weakened with the dawn. Colors became more distinct and the black sand showed more variation.

The sea shimmered as shades of rose reflected the sky and the sun backlit the crests of the far hills. As if a switch had been turned on, life came into focus. Crowds of people materialized in all directions, walking quietly and searching out the turtles. Dark birds flocked the black beach, hovering in the mangroves and pecking in the sand.

Details popped in a contrast of earth tones: green mangroves, black birds, charcoal sand, pinkish-grey turtles, white and brown people. Strange striations of white appeared in the volcanic sand, which, upon closer examination, materialized into broken bits of egg shell and yolk.

A turtle nearby began rocking and rolling, gaining traction for a climb from the birthing hole back onto more stable sand. After several advances and retreats, she found solid ground and began the torturous journey of twenty yards to the water's edge. Without a backward glance, the mother left her eggs nestling in the hole, and the black birds came to life. A flock of vultures descended, pecking and clawing in the sand until they reached the pocket of warm turtle eggs. Cawing and flapping, the creatures grabbed, cracked, shredded, and sprayed eggs and yolks, a gluttonous feasting in the early morning quiet.

The violence of the activity shocked me out of the morning's meditative trance. Looking around, it was impossible to find a spot that wasn't marbled with broken shell and yolk. *So many destroyed after the mother's patient and stoic effort,* I thought with a dawning horror.

Poor creatures, I thought sadly, feeling protective sympathy for the unborn. "What evil there is in the world, what senseless destruction!" I remarked to the yogini next to me.

Ellen turned her tranquil and wise eyes on me, and offered a pearl of wisdom. "Who is to say whose purpose is more important: the turtle's or the vulture's? Both serve their own purpose, and keep the world in balance."

Feel

"Your body is a walking repository of every experience you have ever had in life. Many experiences occur so rapidly or under conditions of such stress that they are stored in the body's memory in undigested chunks."
—Don Stapleton

Physical Body *(Anna-maya-kosha)*

The physical form is the outermost layer of the body, the densest manifestation of who we are. What we take in and retain in this layer ultimately determines our health and our ability to live an active, vital and pain-free life. When experiences, poor food and nutrition, stress, stored emotions and so on begin to build up, these are the things that make the physical body age or manifest serious health conditions. When we consciously make choices about what we put into and take out of our body—through diet, yoga, exercise and cleansing—we have the power to live a life that feels good. By keeping "our human machine" in good operating condition, we enable the body's optimal performance and can move beyond our physical concerns to evolve to a higher awareness.

I.

Jumping Off the Cliff

"Look around and see where you've landed," my teacher said. I looked and laughed out loud.

That morning, I woke to the sound of monkeys howling. Only it was more like a deep-throated wildcat roaring. Sunlight was streaming down, and there was a color explosion in every direction. Red-tailed squirrels scurried up trees, silvery green iguanas clambered on the roof, a black armadillo waddled in the leafy ground cover, yellow geckos gracefully darted up the wall with tiny suctioned fingers, and orange, buttercup, and white butterflies swirled in the moving air.

I now sat in the thatched roofed rancho, surrounded by the verdant jungle and the forty-one women and four men I would be spending all of my waking hours with during the month-long yoga teacher training.

Civilization had fallen away progressively since I shut the door to my Manhattan apartment for the final time. After a last-minute frenzy to discard the remainder of my belongings, I arrived at the airport, boarded the plane, and landed in Central America. Squinting, I clanged down the stairs onto the shimmering black tarmac, holding my down jacket as far as possible from my suddenly sweat-covered body. Immigration was the first lectern I reached in the open-air hanger, and ten steps beyond was the one belt used to convey checked luggage to its owners. A driver met me about twenty feet farther, past customs, ferried my luggage into the tourist van, and took me off into the wilderness.

Toto, we're not in Kansas anymore. Eight years of New York City living melted away; snowy concrete jungle replaced by lush natural greenery.

Colorful buildings jumped out of dry fields, people sat under the trees at the edge of the road selling mangos, papayas, and watermelon, and the kilometers sped by. Passing through the large town of Nicoya, I observed my first Costa Rican city with its unique architecture of concrete and corrugated tin. About thirty kilometers out of town, we turned off the pavement onto the dirt road that would complete our journey in about an hour's time. The scenery became more mountainous, with tall, rolling hills topped with palm trees and pastures populated with grazing cows like the kind seen in India.

My first view of the sea peeked through the trees in a sweep of azul about fifteen kilometers down the coast from Nosara, according to the dust-covered sign. We bounced along the dirt road through a few more small villages until we passed the brief development of modern buildings that was Playa Guiones, continuing on to turn up a steep hill and heavily rutted dirt road to meet my landlord, Agnes, at her home to pick up the keys to my *casita* (one-room house).

Backtracking down the hill, with Agnes on her all-terrain vehicle (ATV) following me, we returned to Playa Guiones and turned immediately into the parking area for the Café de Paris, the cornerstone hotel and restaurant that marked the beginning of the town's main drag. We then followed a gravel path past several white and wood casitas and stopped at the steps to the yellow building that would be my home for the foreseeable future.

I sighed with relief; this ex-New Yorker would not be alone surrounded by jungle.

There began my very own hero's journey, leaving behind a life that had consisted of over-working and under-experiencing. I was hoping that the time away from the U.S. would change me, and help me to find the happiness that had mostly eluded me in my life. And it did transform me, in more ways than I had dreamed possible. The changes went much deeper than my physical transformation of dropping from a size 14 to a size 6, and had more to do with my overall health than any change in appearance.

I went to Costa Rica to become a yoga teacher because of the enormous impact that yoga had begun to have in my life as a healing force. My goal was to deepen my practice, understand more of the yogic philosophy underlying the physical postures I was mastering, and explore how I might be able to incorporate yoga into my future career. At the time, I thought it would manifest through opening up a health resort using my twenty years of business experience. I would soon see that very few things would turn out as expected.

What I found was a lifestyle shift that began cleansing me of the past from the moment I arrived in Costa Rica. By beginning to listen to what my body was telling me, I found I had a lot to release.

2.

Tres Amigos

All my life, my body has spoken to me in a quite emphatic way when I've been unhappy. I had just gotten very good at ignoring it. I had gotten very good at ignoring a lot of things in an effort to endure my life.

There had always been three primary ways that my physical body communicated its displeasure with the way I was living. The first communication was a slow and insidious one, easy to ignore since I was getting satisfaction and pleasure along the way. My body simply began to expand, to put on weight. Stress and unhappiness weighed heavily on me, and manifested in direct proportion to the size of my ass.

Now, my body didn't do this all on its own, it was responding to a change in my behavior—seeking gratification through food when other areas were not available. And the gratification food of choice was usually unhealthy, containing high volumes of grease, salt, and sugar.

My body gradually became bigger. I let notice of it slip for a long time, as I bought more clothes in larger and larger sizes. *I am still attractive,* I told myself, even as I began to hide parts of my body.

When it became apparent that size alone wasn't going to get my attention, my body turned to trusty signal number two. The evil monster psoriasis would begin to consume areas of my skin. This was a clear signal that life was out of balance. I'd spent more of my life struggling with it than I had without. Psoriasis began to at least get my attention, to make me notice that the situation was not a healthy one. Only it wasn't enough to spur definitive action. I was able to endure this situation for quite a while through the use of steroid creams and heavy sun/UV exposure.

Enough with the skirmishes, my body openly declared war when insomnia set in. Being an ever-so-creative and adaptable creature, I found ways to survive this new onslaught. But grave consequences could not be avoided at this point, and I knew that serious illness would manifest if changes were not made.

The first time I let things get so bad was during my relationship with Tom, the man I lived with in my late twenties and early thirties and for a long time thought I would marry. After a while my insomnia reached the point that he gave me a tiny book lamp so that I didn't disturb him when I woke up in the middle of the night. That way, I could read until my mind was quiet again, and the drowsy lull would eventually lead to sleep. The fact that I was remaining parked in an unhealthy relationship with the sleeping body next to me was not something I consciously recognized back then as a leading cause of my sleepless state.

Eventually, my body went into full and violent revolt at remaining where it was. It began bleeding profusely and painfully, my womb protesting at the ongoing and unrelenting stress of being intimately involved with the wrong man for me.

The onset of the bleeding led to months of playing run-around with my HMO at the time. Fed up with the health care system that thought constant and heavy dosages of antibiotics and steroids would cure anything, and the doctors who refused to authorize additional expensive tests for better diagnosis, I had to wait until the end of the year to change health plans through my job. With my new, much more expensive plan I was able to choose a highly recommended doctor who immediately authorized the necessary tests and I was quickly diagnosed with endometriosis. I underwent laparoscopic surgery to burn the growth off of several internal organs, including the outside of my uterus. When symptoms reoccurred just months after surgery, my doctor placed me on hormone therapy in an attempt to contain the disease.

"It shouldn't be this hard," I said to my sister, Annie, in the clear mountain air above Innsbruck, Austria. "My doctor said I need to think about having children very soon if I want them. The endometriosis keeps growing back. I can't wait for Tom any longer."

For years my family had watched me become unhappier in my relationship. Annie made sympathetic noises and said that no, she didn't think I should.

My sister had joined us for a week while I was visiting Tom on assignment in Southern Germany. We sisters toured the Alps during the day and met Tom for dinners in the evenings.

Returning home to Baltimore after the trip, I reactivated my admission to Thunderbird, a global MBA, international studies, and language program that I had put on hold when Tom and I moved in together. I had chosen to defer my dream of attending this top-ranked graduate school in favor of our relationship, and instead enrolled part time in American University's graduate program while I continued to work full time in Washington, D.C. My choice had meant a commitment to four years of working sixty-plus hours a week at my job in addition to carrying a heavy load of MBA courses and assignments, all while commuting three hours a day. Added on top of this load was the stress of waiting for Tom to resolve his continued ambiguity about our relationship. After four years, I was not willing to compromise further, especially if it meant that I might not be able to have children.

I sat Tom down and told him of my discussion with my doctor, laying out several options that would lessen the stress of my overextended and unbalanced life. These were:

One, I could finish my master's program at American University, but switch from part-time to full-time attendance, quitting my job so that we could begin planning a family in the next year.

Two, we could go to Arizona together, where I would complete my studies at Thunderbird full time so that we could begin planning a family.

Three, I could go to Arizona alone and move forward with my life without him.

When confronted with certain issues about our relationship, Tom resembled a scared rabbit, whiskers twitching and eyes darting around for escape. We'd had "the commitment conversation" many times prior; in fact, we had spent a year in couples counseling addressing the issue before Tom began several years of his own intensive therapy sessions. This time his reaction sealed off something in my heart. He began to reasonably discuss why no change was, in fact, needed. I left the ongoing conversation, the apartment, and, emotionally, the relationship.

The next day, Tom came home excited about a job opportunity he had found in Phoenix...

That was the way our relationship had traditionally gone throughout four long years. Just as I would reach the walkaway point, he would throw me a bone big enough to keep me satisfied for a little while longer. We flew out to Arizona, he for the interview, me to visit Thunderbird. Returning home, we went through a period of exceptional intimacy as we viewed the changing future. We discussed things we had previously kept hidden, allowed our fear and vulnerability to show, and even our sex life, the Superglue of our relationship, improved.

When the time came to move, we packed a U-Haul with my belongings and drove across country together. Unloading into my new apartment in Phoenix, it was still unclear whether or not he would be joining me, and whether we were getting engaged or separating. He received an offer on the job in Phoenix after returning back home to Baltimore, and tortured us both with indecision for several weeks. Finally, he called me on my birthday to say he wasn't coming.

Though I spent many an hour curled up weeping on the floor of my new walk-in closet, it was a relief to finally release the relationship and move forward again with my own life.

Interestingly enough, the regrowth of my endometriosis then slowed to a stop. In the ten-plus years since I took my power back and left my relationship with Tom I haven't been troubled by it again.

Graduate school at Thunderbird was an intense time of healing for me, a time of finding myself and my own path again after many years of denying my needs. After the schedule I had forced myself to keep with work, school, and relationship therapy, the demands of the tough academic program felt easy. I regained confidence in my talent, professional skills, and value. In addition, I felt as if I had finally found a community of like-minded people, who shared the same passions of travel and exploring cultural diversity. We were citizens of the world!

Upon graduation, I landed an enviable position in upper management at the Motion Picture Association, arguably the most powerful lobbyist organization in the country, and was transported to Los Angeles to work with the top minds in the entertainment industry.

Nothing had prepared me for the world I found in Los Angeles at the supposed pinnacle of global, national, and entertainment politics. My innate confidence in my ability to handle any professional situation was sorely put to the test. I entered an organization in disarray, hired to blow the dust off a department that provided essential industry information and build a world-class research group following a hostile takeover of the group and the subsequent enforced retirement of my long-term predecessor. In an industry founded on who you know and what information you control, I had to build my knowledge and contacts from scratch with a staff in place who had divided loyalties and no desire to see me succeed.

Always one for a challenge, and of the firm belief that "this too shall pass," once I proved myself, I naïvely put all of myself into my job. Working one-hundred-hour weeks, staying up nights before international press conferences and major public appearances by my boss, the infamous and lecherous Jack Valenti, my body began again to rebel. "What about balance and enjoyment of life?" it questioned. When it did not receive a satisfactory response, it began to make noise.

My three trusty friends, weight gain, psoriasis, and insomnia, resurfaced with a vengeance after that very pleasant hiatus during graduate school in Arizona. In California, the land of the so-called "beautiful people," I steadily put on enough weight to justify constantly updating my wardrobe. My psoriasis was so bad that I had to go for twice weekly ultra-violet light treatments at a dermatologist's office. And insomnia once again became my most frequent bed partner, particularly on those stress-filled nights fulfilling last-minute requests before any of Jack's government testimonies or diplomatic events.

Before my health took another blow, the world took a huge one. The collapse of the Twin Towers shook me out of my lethargy, and I made the move back to New York City soon afterwards. The violence of that terrorist act brought home the fact that life was too precious to waste in a place where I was not happy.

And so I tuned into my own internal guidance, and came to New York when many others were fleeing in the wake of September 11, 2001.

As the trio once again followed me to my latest location, I began to realize that maybe it was something in the way that I was living that was causing their reoccurrence. I was aware that each of the conditions that plagued me—weight gain, psoriasis, insomnia, and also the one-time appearance of endometriosis—was tied by numerous studies to stress.

I was more awake to what was happening in my body, but was unsure what to do or where to go next. While my move to New York had been inspired by the need for drastic change in my life, I wasn't clear on the direction I should take in order to do more meaningful work. As for many, 2002 was one of the most difficult and challenging years of my life. The economy collapsed and corporations stopped hiring, particularly for strategic positions that didn't directly bring in sales. The job opportunity I had moved for disappeared before it started, and despite all of my efforts, I could not find a job—for the first time in my successful career—during 2002.

The next year dawned with more economic optimism, and I quickly generated three job offers by the third week of January. I chose the position that provided a comparable salary and lifestyle to the one I had lived in Los Angeles, but was considerably less stressful and draining, and offered a good work-life balance. With less demands on my time, I was able to begin exploring some of the underlying reasons for my unhappiness and chronic health issues.

However, balance without a purpose or goal to pull me forward was not enough.

3.
Cuts like a Knife

"And this is where we will cut the bone."

I slid off the examining table and picked up the model. The hip joint was fairly simple and well contained, said the doctor. "See how the ball of the femur fits into the socket of the joint? These days we can go in with minimal invasion, without severing any of the muscles."

Stop. Where they will be cutting off the bone? My bone. And replacing it with metal, grafted to my leg bone and into my hip socket? "The hip bone's connected to the x bone," I sang to myself with a mild edge of hysteria.

"I recommend that you consider the replacement surgery within the next six months," the doctor said as casually as he then directed me to medical clerk for my insurance policy on the way out.

My mind flashed to the vision of my father lying in his hospital bed after having his knee replaced, my seventy-year old father. When they wheeled him away that morning, his hair had been the same charcoal hue as it had been during most of my adult life. Laying in recovery, I had wondered at the lack of demarcation between his hair and the bedsheet. His skin, post-op, had completed the monochrome vision.

"I'm sorry," I called after my doctor as he rushed to his next patient. "Six months? Why six months? What about physical therapy?"

Shaking off my umbrella and the cold of the gloomy February morning, I limped up the subway stairs and rode the elevator back to my office.

"Bad day, huh?" asked my friend Jennifer, commenting on my expression and my stride.

"Bad news, too. I need to make some calls," I replied, closing the door to my office.

On rainy days, my hip spoke to me. It told me that it was all hopeless, whispered that I would never get what I wanted, that I was defective and damaged. It spoke in a hollow baritone that ached from deep in my right groin down the bone of my thigh like a rotted tooth's throb. The gnashing, grinding soreness at times made me want to whimper. Too often I believed this voice, believed that I was lucky there wasn't something worse to contend with. But viscerally I rejected the cutting of my bone, the insertion of metal. There were other options, and I would find them.

I was born with a type of hip dysplasia similar to that prevalent in golden retrievers. My right joint was not formed properly, the ball positioned at the head of the socket instead of firmly within it. Thus I wore a brace from birth through the first four years of my life, one that forced my legs open in a V so that the joint would form properly as I grew. While an infant and toddler, I wore the brace twenty-four hours a day and first learned mobility by using my arms to propel and waddling the block of my abdomen and legs to accelerate movement. By age two, the brace was used only at night, and with a high guardrail on the bed to prevent me from falling and injuring myself.

When the doctor released me from the brace before I began school, he told my mother that I would likely be troubled by degenerative arthritis in my hips when I approached my forties.

Ding, ding. Right on schedule in my late thirties I began to have pain in my right hip. When I was no longer able to walk without a pronounced limp, and arthritis "medicine" (really just pain killers) was no longer able to manage the pain, I consulted a joint specialist and was given my dire prognosis.

Physically, emotionally, and mentally rejecting the idea of surgery, I began the search for a second opinion. It became an obsession, my primary topic of conversation. Friends, acquaintances, casual encounters—they all knew about my hip and were quizzed for resources. Armed with referrals, I got an appointment with a highly recommended, preeminent surgeon. Presented with my juicy package of imminent surgery, the doctor fit me into his schedule and ordered a full battery of the most sophisticated tests. In addition to x-rays, I had MRI tests to assess my hip and lower spine, an ink test to identify potential ligament damage, and a cortisone injection for temporary pain relief. Tens of thousands of dollars pumped into the medical system.

The resulting diagnosis was: "It's all a matter of pain management." How far could I walk? Whether they did it then, or did it in a year, how much pain could I tolerate?

"But what about other options?" I asked. I insisted on being given a prescription for physical therapy in addition to the battery of tests. "Yes," I was told, "that may help for a while, but ultimately a hip replacement will be required as your joint continues to deteriorate."

A funny thing happened on the way of physical therapy...my twice-daily home exercises were similar to yoga poses. *What would happen,* I wondered, *if I incorporated those into a daily yoga practice, heavy on the hip and hamstring openers?*

I did just that, with a little help from Cyndi Lee's book, *Om Yoga: A Guide to Daily Practice.* At least three nights a week and both days during the weekends, I spent several hours on my yoga mat at home breathing and stretching. I felt my way into my body, holding the poses for as long as necessary to feel release, which was usually signaled by a bout of tears or a burst of joy.

My yoga time soon became addictive. When I missed a session, I found I was less balanced and focused the next day.

Over the following two years, I developed my home practice into what I learned later was a system of Yin Yoga, a series of postures held for up to five minutes each that allow connective tissue and ligaments to slowly release and create more joint space. The process was intensely painful at times, but marijuana used medicinally enabled me to shift my relationship with the pain. I began to separate from the discomfort and see it as blocked energy that could be managed by sending my breath to it. Limited, focused use of the natural medicine provided more long-term healing than the prescription pharmaceuticals that masked the pain temporarily and all came with strong warnings about long-term damage possible to my liver with continued use.

With the pain in my hip joint lessened as a result of this daily regimen, I began to take longer walks with my dog, Lucy, in Riverside Park and Central Park. I participated in frequent weekend programs at The Kripalu Center, a yoga retreat two hours north of the city, and went on yoga vacations in addition to hiking trips, just like the ones I had previously taken before my hip became painful.

Hmmm. Stronger muscles and more open joints meant less pain, less bone-on-bone friction. It was time to go back to the doctor and see how my hip was faring before I considered leaving my job and health care coverage to go to Costa Rica. After being thoroughly scolded for not following his instructions, my surgeon took an updated set of x-rays and was amazed to see the deterioration of the joint had slowed to a stop. Two weeks later, I received a large package in the mail with my x-rays and file. I had been fired as a patient, as I was no longer a candidate for immediate surgery.

4.
A Yoga Journey

"A small task well done will give you the power to do a bigger one better."
—Yogi Pramananda

My first yoga class, October 1993: "Pushing the floor away with both feet, feel the strength rise from the earth up through your body," my yoga teacher instructed as he guided us into the pose Warrior One. "Center yourself in your breath, feel the strength flow through you." His class offered the only hours of peace during the painful few weeks of a temporary split with a long-term lover. I was new to the practice, and immediately found it to be an essential addition to my life.

Throughout the '90s and early '00s I practiced yoga on and off, depending on my work schedule and finding a teacher that I really liked. Yoga vacations and retreats kept my practice slowly advancing until several key events speeded up the momentum.

October 2006: These exercises are really just yoga poses, I thought as my physical therapist demonstrated what I needed to do every day to relieve some of the pain in my hip joint. I developed a daily home practice. The discipline took hold.

Yoga retreat, May 2007: "Feet rel-aaaaxxx," said Maria, my Mexican yoga teacher, as the warm Caribbean breezes flowed into the space and we settled into *Savasana,* or Corpse pose, after class. "Legs rel-aaaaxxx."

Wow, it's as simple as that—I can tell my body what to do, and it will obey! Sometimes it just takes the right time and place for the knowledge to finally click.

One week at the yoga resort, Maya Tulum, living in a round hut ten-feet from the lapping waves of the turquoise Caribbean, eating fresh local and organic food, doing yoga every morning, and just relaxing had provided enormous healing. An intense massage and energy treatment with a Mayan shaman had released years of emotional buildup in my body. "You have more light in your eyes now," he told me in the gathering twilight after our session.

August 2008: "Write your fears down on the paper, and then place the paper in the bowl on the altar," instructed my teacher Krishna Kaur. She was leading a three-day Kundalini yoga workshop on embracing joy and releasing fear at Kripalu.

Fear of failure, fear of being alone, fear of being defective, fear of expression, fear of judgment. I filled up the small slip of paper and placed it in community with others in front of the glowing candle. I was ready to release them all.

"Marketing, how great!" Krishna said, as we chatted during a break between sessions. I had come upon her while walking in meditation under the tall trees on the beautiful campus in the Berkshires. Sunlight dappled the lush green leaves high above into a pattern of such beauty I was mesmerized. She appeared on a bench under a tree when I finally brought my vision back to earth.

I was at a low point in my career, wondering what I was doing putting my energy into selling products that didn't do anything to make the world better, for a company lacking leadership. I had told her my profession with shame in my voice and in a second she recast the whole thing. "Don't think of it as getting people to buy something meaningless. Think of it has having the skills to reach people. We need more people like you to get the word out about yoga," she taught me.

Yes, that's exactly what I want! I thought excitedly.

"If you want permanent change following this workshop," Krishna explained in the last workshop session, "take back your paper from the altar and follow the meditation I have taught you for fifteen days. The change becomes permanent when you practice it consistently for that period. Then burn the paper and your fears."

I reclaimed the paper holding my fears, practiced the meditation Krishna had prescribed faithfully every morning before work for the allotted period. The final day of the meditation coincided with my departure on a planned vacation at a yoga retreat on the Spanish island of Menorca to celebrate my birthday.

September 2008: "What, you think you will break?" was an interesting question posed by Francisco, my yoga teacher at the workshop on Menorca. I had been complaining about the stiffness in my legs as he guided me into a position. "Breathe through it and it will loosen," he instructed. "Do not give up at the first sign of discomfort."

Over the last few years, that had become my first response when faced with challenges: complaining and feeling hopeless, lacking the energy required to face them down. Something big needed to change in my life. I felt like I had nothing pulling me forward, nothing nurturing and supporting me. I didn't like who I was when I looked in the mirror, or who I was when at work, or who I was with my family. I didn't like my job. I didn't like what was happening in my country. I didn't like much of anything.

Now, I wasn't entirely sitting still in my cloud of negative emotions and powerlessness. In addition to my daily yoga practice, I had been doing some pretty heavy transformational work over the last several years to climb out of my depression. In fact, for the past year, I had been participating in an intensive Transformational Coaching and Leadership Training (TCLT) program with the goal of transitioning my energy and talents from the corporate world into a career that felt more meaningful. My goal was to use my strategy and leadership skills in service of others by coaching clients through the areas that were blocking them from what they wanted in life. As part of TCLT, I was also squarely facing and clearing a lot of the issues that were standing between me and my purpose.

I had come to this yoga workshop on Menorca following a series of signs relating to my long-held dreams of moving to Spain and opening a retreat center. The first of these signs had occurred a few months earlier when, one Saturday afternoon, something prompted me to plug the old search term "yoga Menorca" into Google. All the previous times I had done so over the past few years had yielded nothing. This time it came up with something. I clicked through on the link.

A bolt of energy such as I'd never felt went through me. I sat paralyzed for a moment or two, staring at the exact picture of what I had always dreamed of creating when I would eventually leave the corporate world. My excitement grew as I clicked through the photo album on a yoga retreat website. In that moment, I knew that I would do whatever it took to go there and begin the process of making my own, comparable dream center a reality.

I had a lot of reality to wade through before I could begin manifesting my dream of leaving the corporate world. The smallest challenge had been getting myself to the yoga workshop that the site advertised. Back in real life, my boss and mentor in my workplace had just announced her resignation. She had brought a blast of leadership, vision, and energy into a rather lifeless and leaderless company. I had spent several years building the business intelligence and market research department after joining the company in 2003. Recognizing my problem-solving skills and market knowledge, she had promoted me to oversee and infuse strategy based on market intelligence into the creative and communications area of marketing. For nearly two years we had worked as a team, with her mentoring as a resource for the technical skills that were not my strongpoint.

Riding on a wave of personal power and charisma, we had implemented exciting new changes and infused energy into a company based mainly on operational efficiency. My boss saw the writing on the wall as the economy started to tumble and the division's leadership took to infighting and base politics in their struggle for limited resources and who would ascend to power when the current CEO announced his intention to retire. Before leaving, she clearly communicated the desperate nature of the situation in explaining her choice to quit, and then left me to deal with the mess. It was one challenge I had no energy or desire to conquer.

I had spent the weeks before I left for the yoga retreat on Menorca reviewing and trimming the budget in preparation for a review with top management. Presenting my budget, I endured the endless bickering of the executive team as one questioned why one business unit got this and they didn't, why they didn't want to pay for this, why they couldn't just divide up the corporate budget and use it for their product marketing. I patiently answered questions, demonstrated the return-on-investment of each initiative, and explained that if the corporate goal was to truly compete against the two largest players in the industry they needed a strong, cohesive corporate brand. Were we a band of conflicting warlords or were we a cohesive nation? I asked.

The executives, known more for their towering individual egos than for clear strategic thinking, paused briefly before their infighting resumed. My words had no impact.

Coming home from the meeting, I had turned on the news and watched in disgust as the day's national politics mirrored the divisiveness I had just experienced in the boardroom.

My work situation, as well as my conversations with Krishna at the Kripalu retreat a few weeks earlier, were very much on my mind as I participated in Francisco's workshop.

After several days on Menorca, I was exploring the possibility of quitting my job to study yoga full time. My goal had always been to do a yoga teacher training after my life coaching certification course wrapped up, but I had originally planned to do it on a part-time basis while working. After going deeper into yoga philosophy on this retreat, I found that I wanted to immerse myself in it rather than cram it into my spare time. Francisco truly inspired me. He was spending half of his time studying with teachers based in India and the remainder of his time leading classes and running workshops in Barcelona and on the Spanish islands.

One afternoon on Menorca, I opened up my laptop computer and, much as I had when I found the Spanish workshop, Googled. This time my phrase was "yoga teacher training Costa Rica." Up popped the Nosara Yoga Institute. *Hmmm.*

It seemed to me that studying in Costa Rica would provide two benefits that India did not. First, I could bring my dog with me. Second, I could pursue my dream to open a healing center there sooner than I could in Spain, because costs were significantly lower. I had found in my research done during this trip that Menorca wasn't a viable place for me to begin a business due to seasonality, high costs, and the current market conditions. Building a successful brand and business in a lower-cost market, and perhaps then opening a second location in Spain later on would enable me to have a better chance of success at fulfilling my dream. This was something I would have to take up again when I got home.

I flew directly from Menorca to San Francisco for the final weekend of my life coaching training. In the evenings, I continued my research. Costa Rica was calling me. The night before the closing session of the program, I went to my computer and clicked again into the website for the Nosara Yoga Institute in Costa Rica.

"The privilege of a lifetime is being who you are." A quote by late mythologist Joseph Campbell was the first thing that I saw.

Well, okay, that's exactly what I want. I was desperately tired of distorting myself to fit into situations that didn't fit me.

Let me see what else "they" are about. Ahhh, creativity, growth, freedom, connectivity.

The teachers, Don Stapleton and Amba Stapleton, had solid credentials and were closely affiliated with Kripalu, the yoga center in Southern Massachusetts that was helping to keep me sane in my life.

It just felt right. *I'm going to do it,* I decided immediately.

The next afternoon, during our wrap-up exercise, I declared to my coaching community that I was quitting my job and moving to Costa Rica to pursue my dream. I also hired my teacher to coach me through the process of closing down my life in New York and maximizing my savings over the remaining three months of the year for what was likely to be an extended sabbatical.

When I gave my notice at work in early December, my department and colleagues cheered me on as a hero and an inspiration for following my dream and leaving a no-win situation.

Packing up my apartment in New York over the next few weeks, I gave away or sold all of my belongings except for my books and my bed. Whatever came after my sabbatical, I didn't want to be weighed down by the past.

Then I took a running leap, and jumped off the cliff.

5.
What, You Think You Will Break?

Something crashed through the undergrowth. I jumped and cast the beam of my flashlight into the darkness bordering the dirt path. *What the hell was that?*

The darkness shifted perceptibly from ink to charcoal to a hazy smoke grey as I walked on cautiously, and I began to make out distinct shapes of tree trunks, branches, swaying leaves, and hanging vines. A monkey howled overhead, startling me again as I made my way down the jungle path to the first morning practice of the teacher training program in Costa Rica.

Walking endlessly in the predawn forest, I finally came to the wooden planks over the dry ravine that I was looking for and climbed up the hill to the dirt road that would take me to the Institute grounds. The sound of gravel crunching and the bouncing beams of flashlights signaled other students with the same destination.

Two hours later, I lay in *Savasana,* not sure whether or not I'd ever move again. *Well, that practice kicked my ass. How many more hours of yoga today?*

My body took a beating as I settled into my daily routine. A two-hour fast vinyasa yoga flow, followed by four hours of detailed asana training for alignment and teaching cues, followed by three hours of self-inquiry movements or other techniques were all combined with hours of sitting on a hardwood floor. Add in the long walk required to get anywhere, and it was no wonder I woke in the night with back cramps. Thank God I had a microwave in my basic little casita, so I could heat damp towels to apply to my back and hips for some relief.

While I had a daily practice in New York, it had definitely been more yin (feminine/passive) than yang (masculine/active). The fast flow was certainly kicking me into shape, and moving energy around, but it was also seriously confronting my hip. Or rather, my hip was confronting me. Certain poses, like Pigeon, made me spontaneously weep. In fact, I was spending quite a bit of time on my mat crying.

It's all good, I sniffled. *I'm releasing.*

During the first month in Costa Rica, I learned to conserve energy where I could. My limp had resurfaced with a vengeance as my body struggled to adjust to the physical activity. The fifteen-minute walk to the beach was torture more often than not. I made the walk in the morning so that my dog, Lucy, would get her exercise, but rarely made it twice in one day. The famous Nosara sunsets remained a thing of legend to me.

Through necessity, then, I began to change the way that I ate. Fresh fruits and vegetables were abundant, brought by the fruit truck every Monday and Thursday to a location a mere two-minute walk away. By comparison, the closest food market was a good twenty-minute walk each way in the blazing heat, as I had found out on my first day in town. I borrowed a bike when I absolutely needed staples, like rice and beans, but for the most part lived on fruit smoothies, vegetables, and healthy meals at one of the few local restaurants.

A funny thing happened along the way: I broke a lifelong addiction to processed foods. My body began to crave the fresh local produce I was eating and to feel bad when I ate something processed.

The first indication that I was dropping weight came in my sports bras. While yoga clothes are naturally clinging, I was feeling a definite lack of support during my movement. I had been blessed with a generous endowment, particularly when I gained weight, and it was the first area to go as I lost weight. Bras became the first logistical challenge of my weight loss, as I was living in a very small tourist town that catered mostly to surfers.

On the positive side, by the fourth week of the training program I was feeling younger and firmer than I had since my twenties. My body had adjusted to the activity, and the weight loss helped enormously with my hip pain since the joint was carrying less of a burden with stronger muscle support.

I had begun to truly listen to my body and heed what it was telling me. Even my walk changed to a slower, more natural flow, releasing the need to dodge and pass people in the fast pace of city living. *Pura vida!* as the locals, called Ticos, said for every occasion from a simple greeting to thank you to "no worries."

Pure life, indeed. I was now on Tico time.

6.

Cleansing, Colemas, and Conscious Eating

I eyed the stall apprehensively. "You want me to insert what *where?*"

Menhla calmly continued her demonstration of the colema process, showing how to fill up the five-gallon tank that would flush my intestines with a solution, how to position myself on the apparatus, and how to clean up the area when I was finished. *Yuk.*

When I had originally signed up for the week-long "cleanse" at Hacienda del Sol I'd been excited about the prospect of detoxifying my body from a lifetime's buildup of chemicals and food remnants. I hadn't been aware that the process would include several hours a day of bathing my innards and releasing their contents into a modified toilet bowl—all this occurring in an open-air stall with two other people inches away through a wood partition doing the same thing, insects buzzing around my bare legs attracted by the intoxicating aroma.

I was in deep jungle at the cleanse retreat, living in an open-air cabina with only screens between me and all of the critters in nature. Thankfully, my hut was located close to the communal bathrooms and the main *ranchos* (thatch roof pavilions) where the participants met for yoga, meditation, and the scheduled juice and fiber drinks that made up my diet that week.

The days began with drinking a shot of fresh lemon juice mixed with cayenne to raise our body temperature and alkalize our stomachs before an hour of morning yoga. After practice, we received a green drink of spirulina, followed by a sharing circle of the group of women who made up the participants of this particular retreat, then off to give ourselves our first colema of the day. The twice-daily fiber drinks were the nastiest on the menu, since they had to be drunk with Olympic speed to prevent the mixture from coagulating into a thick gel. A lunch drink was served at noon, then we endured another colema followed by another fiber drink, then we had a mid-afternoon drink, and, finally, we took a short car ride to the beautiful local Venus Beach for sunset. The evening's excitement consisted of unlimited potassium broth and then the day closed out with meditation and journaling.

By the second day, I knew by heart the drink schedule and made sure to be lined up at the counter when the elixirs were presented.

Barely walking upright, I staggered up the stepped incline to my cabina after my colema. It was day five of surviving on juice alone. Warning lights flashing, the energy tank was running on empty. That night they would introduce the liver cleanse, rumored a trying ordeal for many.

I collapsed against the door of my cabina, panting, and used my body weight to move the barrier open. *Oh no!* The jolt of alarm made my vision black out temporarily. An entire section of screen had fallen, laying open my cabina to all the insects of the jungle.

I wobbled around the retreat complex in search of the handyman, mumbling to those I encountered of my dilemma. When I finally found him, I collapsed into a weeping mass and stuttered incoherently of my problem. I couldn't possibly face the liver cleanse with a multitude of jungle-sized insects feasting on me. "Please help immediately," I pleaded.

Several hours later, a makeshift screen of flowered sheet stapled in place, and two glasses of Epsom salts downed, I prepared for bed. Stacks of pillows were lined up to keep me on my side so that my liver could marinate, and then I chugged the bottle of olive oil mixed with orange juice I'd been given.

That wasn't so bad, I thought, before a burp brought up a nauseating aftertaste of the oil. *I will not throw up, I will not throw up,* became the mantra of the night.

Saturday morning, I woke up early, like a child on Christmas. We would break our fast today! After a torturously long yoga class, the women headed down to the dining area. The table was beautifully set with splashes of magenta flowers, green fronds, and bright orange platters of papaya bordered by the blood limes local to Costa Rica. We were advised to eat slowly and mindfully.

I had never tasted anything so delicious in my life. Papaya, never a favorite, was added to my list of luscious delicacies. A raw food preparation lesson and then raw pizza feast completed the day's food orgy.

Driving back to Playa Guiones, the town where I was studying to become a yoga instructor, I marveled at how crisp and bright and beautiful everything appeared. My senses were pure, as if experiencing every sight, scent, and taste for the first time.

I felt like a clear, still pond.

That cleanse was pivotal to my healing process in Costa Rica, so much so that I did a second one just three months after the first. Not only did it cleanse my intestines of forty years of buildup of toxins and regulate my digestive process, it provided me with key lessons in how to eat to support my body's energy and health.

The liver cleanse portion had required staged timing of drinks to properly wring the organ of toxins. Two glasses of Epsom salts had to be choked down at two-hour intervals, with an equal time before consumption of the cleansing solution of olive oil and orange juice. During the final queasy interval, I distracted myself from nausea by watching the DVD *Food Matters*. This eighty-minute documentary by James Colquhoun and Larentine ten Bosch completely shifted my way of thinking about food and nutrition, showing how nature provides exactly the fuel that the body needs to heal illness and promote health if you are conscious of what you are consuming.

The film also explained the benefits of naturally occurring "superfoods," a class of foods known for their very high antioxidant and nutrient-rich content. Used through the centuries by indigenous peoples, superfoods can help fight aging and illness because they have high amounts of flavonoids, nutrients, and immune system boosters, while being low in calories. A few examples of superfoods are cacao, apple cider vinegar, kombucha tea, spirulina, bee pollen, coconut oil, coconut water, chia seeds, and maca powder. They can be easily incorporated into fruit juices or smoothies, as well as substitute for other, more processed ingredients, such as cooking oil.

With a clear body as a base, I began to add superfoods into my daily diet and to slowly re-introduce other food groups to test them for allergies. I made a discovery about my body's reaction to wheat products that had a profound effect on managing the pain in my hip. The first time I reintroduced wheat into my diet, the pain in my hip joint flared, so I experimented with it for a while. Yup: Eat bread, hip pain. No bread, no pain.

I did some research to better understand the phenomena. Apparently, for many people with sensitivities to gluten (the elastic rubbery protein found in wheat products), it has an inflammatory effect on joints, particularly those with arthritis. By eliminating wheat from my diet, I was getting rid of a known irritant and greatly reducing my pain by natural means. This was much better for my body, I found, than taking the anti-inflammatory pharmaceuticals whose manufacturers all cautioned against the liver damage caused by their long-term usage.

Hmmm...There are several other benefits from going gluten-free. The substance is also linked by many studies to my dear old friend, psoriasis. And, with my ever-shrinking figure, I found that by eliminating wheat products from my diet, I was forced to make more conscious healthy choices about what I was eating.

All this may sound like it was an easy choice not to eat wheat. Intellectually, it was. But we're talking about a bread addict here... put me in a bakery, and I was like an alcoholic at an open bar. Chocolate croissants, cookies, brownies, cake, bagels and grainy, nutty breads...Crunchy, crusty white bread dipped in fragrant olive oil or slathered with creamy butter...Crispy pizza crusts covered with bubbling cheese and crusty pepperoni...The list of my favorite glutonous glutens goes on and on, and sometimes still haunts my dreams. What gives me the will power to continue to push it all away these days? The visceral memory of the deep, rotted toothache sensation I used to have in my hip joint, which I rarely ever feel, keeps me clean.

Another pivotal event in the healing of my hip occurred while at the cleanse retreat at Hacienda del Sol. With my body opened up from several months of focused yoga practice, weight loss, and the deliberate release of toxins, I had an intense bodywork session with Menhla. She practices Osho's technology of Power Rebalancing, which is deeply targeted massage aimed at correcting imbalances in the body's muscular system. She spent ninety minutes focused on releasing the muscles surrounding my right hip, and when our session was done, I stood, walked, and sat differently. For the first time in my life, I could sit in meditation in the traditional, easy, crossedlegged position (Indian-style) without pain.

7.

Balancing in the Sun

With all the changes in my life—yoga, diet, cleansing—I was finding that balance was essential to my health. The times when I had suffered the most illness were times when my life was seriously out of balance. All work and no play not only make Jack a dull boy, they also make Robin an unhappy person. Too much of any one thing can be harmful, no matter how good it is for you in moderation.

In addition to my yoga and my spiritual studies, I was staying balanced by listening to what else my body needed. I rounded out my physical routine of daily yoga with lots of walking and bike riding. Granted, these things were essential to living, as I was in Costa Rica without a car, but they also provided great opportunities for me to have fun.

My morning bike rides on the beach with Lucy, my dog, running after me, not only made everyone on the beach smile, they also brought me joy. I took long swims and luxuriated in the feeling of the water and the sun on my skin, the sensation of floating on the waves, and on the sight of Lucy nervously pacing the shore before determinedly swimming out to me and riding the waves in.

My sunset walks were a means of connecting with the rest of the townspeople, who all came out to see nature's show at day's end, and also the beginning of a cherished meditation practice. I would walk towards the setting sun, tossing sticks for Lucy, absorbed in the spectrum of orange, rose, red, and yellow light dappling the sky and the waves, and walk back home as the first star rose in the sky. Nightly walks on the beach to and from neighboring Playa Pelada were intense experiences in the beauty of moonlight on the water under the vault of stars and next to the ocean's show of phosphorescence. With no light pollution, particularly under a new moon, you could see the nebulous cloud of the Milky Way and feel the immensity and raw energy of space.

And so my time went in Costa Rica, until eight months passed before I knew it. Like my own body, mind, and spirit, the seasons had also changed. The dusty dry season I had flown into had been replaced by the green season, with lush growth sprouting visibly and blooming flowers everywhere. Dark purple crabs with bright red-orange legs that had sprung up from the ground with the first rains migrated everywhere, and filling the jungle with new sounds of scuttling and smells as they died in unseen places. Puddles formed and changed the landscape of paths and the dirt roads, and also brought new and ever-changing populations of insects. First the spiders came, of all sizes and shapes, and then the flying creatures, mosquitos biting and huge junebugs buzzing and bombarding. And finally, dampness brought on mold growing in the soles of shoes and between layers of clothing, as the climate prepared to change again to the full-on rainy season.

Sneezing, itchy, and perpetually damp, I began to look forward to my return to the United States with something more than apprehension. I had changed so much. How would my country appear to me now?

8.

Culture Shock and Cross Country Driving

"Help me, Daddy, I can't get out of this hole."

I gasped as I woke from the latest nightmare, sirens blaring and traffic noises bouncing up the concrete jungle and seeping into my new bedroom on the sixteenth floor of my Upper East Side Manhattan apartment.

In this dream, I'd been in my father's garage while he was working under a car. I walked around the vehicle and fell into a deep, water-filled hole and was stuck floundering there.

The night before, I had dreamed I was back in Nosara riding my bike when a small, black snake had leapt from the road to attach its fangs to the soft juncture between my thumb and forefinger. I could still feel the panic and the sharp point of its teeth as it clung to me and wouldn't let go.

I've got to get out of this city, I thought desperately.

Visiting my parent's home in Pennsylvania for a few weeks, I spent as much time as possible in the local state park under the tall, peaceful trees with my dog.

"I'm making baked potatoes with the chicken. Can you eat those?" my mother asked.

"Yes, Mom, it's just wheat products I don't eat," I said for the tenth time.

"Have you seen today's paper?" my father asked, standing directly over me.

I looked up from Child's Pose, midway through my meditative yoga practice and sighed. "No, I'm still not reading the news," I replied.

In Pennsylvania, I planned out an upcoming drive across country, and looked forward to my move to Taos, New Mexico, which was where I had decided to relocate.

Three weeks home from Costa Rica and I was clinging to my yogic calm by my fingernails. My recently married cousin had graciously offered me her vacant furnished studio on the Upper East Side while it was on the market. But I knew I wasn't going to stay there long.

The first thing I did once I was back in the city was to visit my old neighborhood just south of Columbia University on the Upper West Side, walking around in a surreal daze. I strolled through Riverside Park, taking the path along the old stone wall that I used to walk daily with Lucy, until I came to the large granite outcropping under the trees near 116th Street. I climbed up the rocks, sat down, and cried for the home that felt like mine, but wasn't. Lyrics of an old Neil Diamond song were running through my head: *New York's home, but it ain't mine no more...*

Before leaving for Costa Rica a year prior, I had lived in the same apartment in Manhattan for seven years, and loved it, along with my neighborhood and my community of dog owners in the park along the river. My home had been my sanctuary and creative expression. With colorfully painted walls, each room paid tribute to a part of the world I had explored and loved. Large, quiet, and sun-filled, it was a peaceful oasis from the frenetic activity of New York City and had felt like my first permanent adult home. Giving up my nest had been the hardest part of my journey, and it hurt me deeply to feel homeless in my beloved city. Where was my home now?

At the time that I left New York, the only place in the world other than Manhattan that I could even consider calling home was Barcelona, the beautiful Mediteranean city of Catalon art, food, and energy. I had an ongoing love affair with Spain, the country of my ancestors, and my goal was to one day have a home there. A few years earlier, I had collected all of the necessary paperwork on my paternal grandfather, who was born and raised in Spain, to become a citizen of the country myself. My connection with the place went much deeper than a curiosity about my roots and about my grandfather, however.

Something deep in me came alive whenever I landed in the country, and I felt plugged in and powerful in a way that I couldn't quite articulate. My senses drank in the energy, the culture and the earth. I felt most alive when in Spain.

All the old friends in New York that I reconnected with had the same story: They felt overworked, underpayed, stressed out, and unhappy, like hamsters on a wheel. I could feel myself getting sucked back in to their dramas, tendrils of fear creeping over my heart. "Wow," they all said, "I can't believe how great you look!" And inevitably they asked, "So, what will you do now?"

Thankfully, I had a plan, and several months left on my intentional year-long sabbatical. I would be driving cross country to Taos, a conscious community of writers and artists in New Mexico. My plans were to write there, while living with friends from my yoga training.

Another Nosara friend, Lisa, was also back in New York for a family visit, after five years of living in Costa Rica's capital city San Jose. She was nursing a tender heart from a very recent breakup with a Costa Rican man. We clung to each other like lost children in a dark wood. She was also searching for her next steps, and decided to accompany me on my drive across country.

Now road trips are notoriously fattening experiences. Think about spending the majority of each day sitting still in a car with no physical exercise, stopping frequently for food breaks at the plethora of unhealthy eating establishments along the U.S. interstate highway system. Just the thought of fast food was enough to make my intestinal tract feel remarkably similar to the way it felt after my first few colemas.

Oh no, this trip is not going to derail my svelte and healthy new body, I determined. I pulled out my trusty raw foods cookbook from the cleanse retreat, and made a cooler full of raw treats to eat along the way. You can keep your McDonalds and KFCs; I had mixed greens, baby carrots, and raw falafel followed by dark chocolate bliss balls made with almond and cashew flour and raw cacao. All raw, all natural, all delicious, and healthy. In addition, I planned the route so that each day we would be passing a state or national park that would allow the two of us and my furry little companion, Lucy, to get out and move our bodies. And, of course, there was our morning yoga practice.

"Excuse me, Miss, are you alright?"

I opened my eyes as I came out of a prolonged side twist, and looked up into the alarmed eyes of the pool technician who cautiously crept towards me. Apparently, I'd been too still for too long. After assuring him that I was not in distress, that I was practicing something called y-o-g-a, he left me with a puzzled shake of his head.

At each motel, the reaction was slightly different.

Across Ohio and Illinois, we found out that the small workout rooms were best avoided. Shortly after we two women in our yoga clothes walked past the breakfast bar and into the gym, the door would open again to admit other guests. A middle-aged man or two, clothed in jeans or business attire, would enter, sit on an exercise bike, and avidly watch us assume Downward Dog.

In Wisconsin and Minnesota, we moved to the indoor pool rooms where there was generally some privacy to be had in the mornings. That is, until the first harried father would come in with his children. The youngsters would gawk with jaws hanging open, and whisper loudly, "What are they doing, Daddy?"

By South Dakota and Wyoming, I began to feel like a yoga evangelist spreading the good news to fellow travelers on the road. "It's called yoga," I'd begin, "and it's more than just a series of flexible postures..."

Oh, the joy, I thought, opening my eyes and taking in the ceiling painted with fluffy white clouds. My first actual yoga class after eight days on the road was taught by a highly experienced teacher who ran an Anusara studio in Jackson Hole, Wyoming. To be led through a challenging class, brought deeper into my body by the Anusara languaging, and sharing the energy of a packed classroom full of yoginis, was bliss.

It doesn't get much better than this, I thought, until I walked out the door and got an eyeful of the Grand Tetons looming over the town.

Setting out on October 1 with the changing leaves, Lisa, Lucy, and I sped across the interstates in the Midwest. Our goal was to spend most of our time in the Western national parks, experiencing the physical beauty so breathtakingly portrayed in the PBS special *The National Parks: America's Best Idea* that my parents were watching during my planning process. Pushing ourselves, and my poor dog, to our limits, we made it to Madison, Wisconsin, late the second night on the road. Eating our raw falafel and mixed greens on a table in the motel reception area, we learned of two exciting events in town. One was a regional dairy convention showcasing cheese of all kinds and livestock, and the other was the weekly organic market in the center of town the following morning. Though a tough choice, we opted for the fresh-air market.

Walking around the market and the town center, I was struck by the possibility of bringing the best of Nosara living back to the States. It was possible to live in balance with nature with like-minded people right here in my own country, if that's what I wanted. Something to store away for consideration once my year off was over and I was looking for a home.

Over the course of our two weeks on the road, we saw many beautiful sights and spoke with an interesting array of characters. In the hills of Eastern Iowa overlooking the mighty Mississippi River, we hiked the Effigy Mounds National Monument in the yellow and orange fall leaves. Native Americans had built prehistoric burial mounds that took the shape of bears, birds, snakes, and other creatures when seen from an aerial view.

Driving through the dark night and an early snowstorm on the deserted plains of Western Minnesota, we pulled off the lonely highway to a cozy motel, where Betty welcomed us as if we were family and tucked us into homey accommodations. Shaking off the wintry road, we nested in our warm room, crunching on carrots, rice crackers, and hummus.

After visiting the famous Wall Drug Store in South Dakota, advertised for hundreds of miles, we were treated to a serenade from our neighbor who was playing guitar and trilling cowboy songs in an off-key warble. The gusting wind creaking the motel sign outside our window and whistling through the ventilation system completed the acoustics and properly set the mood for the next morning's visit to the desolate Badlands National Park. Coming out of the park, we drove through the Black Hills, hoping to see Mount Rushmore and the Crazy Horse monument, but both were covered in mist from the recent snow. We consoled ourselves in Deadwood at the Gem Saloon, where we broke our raw foods diet with big, fat, juicy steaks. While in Rome, or in this case, cattle-country...

In the tiny town of Ten Sleep, population 304, we stopped for lunch at a picnic table outside its one gas station and convenience store. Black beans, corn tortillas, and mixed greens fed our bodies, while our eyes drank in the surprising number of hunky cowboys who passed in and out of the store. Wyoming jumped onto the list of possible homes, based on the per capita ratio of manly men we were observing.

In Cody, Wyoming, we took a much-needed, early break from the road before entering Yellowstone National Park and treated ourselves to a night on the town. Arriving at the local watering hole, The Silver Dollar, we parked ourselves under a sign that broadcast "No hippies allowed." Did that include a couple of yoginis? Justin, who was flipping burgers on an open grill, and eventually onto a plate in front of us (*sans* bun for me), shared his story of reform. Though he looked as he if were barely shaving, he had spent the last few years in prison for aggravated assault and passed the time there reading the classics and developing an evolved viewpoint well out of range of his years and experience. His only time spent outside of Wyoming had come during a spring break trip to Panama City, which we eventually figured out was the one in Florida not in Costa Rica's southern neighbor.

Enough of supporting the local cattle industry. We got back to our healthy eating as we drove through Yellowstone and down the Rockies through the Grand Tetons and eventually to Boulder, Colorado. We pulled into Taos in late afternoon, the glowing yellow aspens and cottonwoods lighting the town to celebrate our arrival.

My time in Taos was a brief but pivotal time in ensuring that my newly acquired healthy practices became ingrained in my lifestyle.

I had the great luck of sharing a house with an original hippy and a second generation one, who both lived and breathed environmentally friendly practices and organic eating. I soaked up their example, and lived quite deliciously. And I found a way to convert my morning walks along the beach in Guiones to morning hikes in the mountain, each foot placed consciously as a walking meditation.

As my year off drew nearer to a close, I found myself yearning to go back to the place it had all started for me: the country of my soul, Spain. I did a little research and found a writing retreat in the southern mountains of Spain that boasted an impressive literary library and close proximity to a yoga studio. I was sold!

9.
España, Mi Amor

"Do you know where you are?" asked a masculine voice flavored with an accent of Northern England.

"Yes, I'm on my morning walk," I smiled back into the open car window. I had met Joe a few days earlier with my yoga teacher at a gathering of British expats. We were currently on a remote dirt road climbing up Masamullar, a local landmark and one of the many signed walks in the mountains near where I was staying.

"Very impressive, and so early on a Sunday...," he waved and drove on up the mountain and around the bend.

This time, I was deep in *el campo* (remote country), according to the Scottish handyman who looked after the writer's retreat where I was staying. Like all the other places I had chosen to live that year, the area was connected mainly by dirt roads. I was enjoying getting closer to the earth.

Scrubby brown and green rolling hills dotted with white stone houses made up the view in all directions, and the dirt roads in question were mostly tracks carved out of the side of these tall mounds and peaks. Olive and almond trees and prickly pear cactus covered the red dusty dirt of the terrain, and through a break in the mountains to the south I could see the gleam of the Mediterranean Sea.

Each time I stepped outside I breathed in deeply and could feel the energy of the place filling me up from the soles of my feet to the soul of my spirit. God, I loved this place.

And nothing to do but write.

Mornings, I took a long walk along the dirt roads up to Masamullar, where I sat in an olive grove and meditated on a rock overlooking the rolling vista. Walking back, I organized my thoughts for the day into a handheld digital recorder and worked out my ass and heart on the steep inclines. An occasional twinge in my hip reminded me of how far I had come.

During the day, I wrote, made pots of tea, and then wrote some more. For food, I climbed about 1,000 feet in elevation to the white village of Comares and a small supermarket, or walked down to the neighboring village where my yoga teacher had a small organic market with fresh produce of the region.

In the evenings, I made a fire in the lounge to chase off the early December chill and did my yoga practice before the cheery flames.

David, my housemate from the Lake District, had lived in the retreat for nearly six months while working on his novel. He kept me updated on his daily word count, and provided me with motivation to write religiously each day. Also gluten-free for health reasons, he had chosen a different route than mine and consumed massive amounts of substitute products. He became quite nervous when his stash of gluten-free white bread or gluten-free tea biscuits ran low, and marveled at the lack of garbage I generated with my fresh foods.

Once a week, Sarah, a burgeoning yogini and friend from Nottingham, and I rode the daily bus down to Malaga for supplies, a bit of Spanish culture (versus expat British culture), and some fun. On my first trip, I succumbed to my cravings and had pastry with my *café con leche* and ate a crusty roll dipped lovingly in olive oil and sprinkled with salt. The next morning, I woke up with a skin rash and a rusty ache in my hip.

Okay, it was really more like three rolls, I admitted guiltily. *Back on the wagon...*

10.

What's Next?

I arrived back in the States just in time for the holidays and to debut the new me for my entire family at our annual celebration. I withstood the doubletakes as well as the Christmas cookies, and enjoyed being with my loved ones from an open-hearted and grateful place. When the drinks started flowing a little too freely among the adults for coherent conversation, I joined in with the kids and had fun playing on the floor.

What would the New Year hold for me? I didn't know, but trusted it would continue to bring me closer to what I wanted in life. My task now was to define what that was.

Perhaps one year off was not enough...

To even put myself in a position to begin that task, I had to become aware of what my body was telling me. And then, by listening to my body and its cues—some call it *intuition*—I could begin to make the necessary changes in other areas of my life to achieve meaning and purpose.

My time in the jungle and all of my physical changes do not seem hard in retrospect; perhaps the process was similar to the process of giving birth: Once over, the specific pains do not stick in memory as much as the outcome of the effort.

I had been very fortunate in my journey to be supported along the way by the structure of yoga programs, an amazing community of loving souls, and by my own intentionality and commitment to change. I realized that the hard work would come in keeping my health in the long term, and trusted that the discipline of yoga and the other healthy practices I had developed would support me as I went forward.

There were four ingredients that I identified from my experiences as essential in managing and maximizing my own physical health:

1.   Incorporating sufficient and varied exercise was necessary to keep my body functioning at high performance. By periodically bringing my body to physical exhaustion, followed by regular periods of complete relaxation, I was able to release the backlog of stress stored in my body and keep it clear going forward. The practice of yoga provided a perfect model, with its ninety minutes of focused physical exertion followed by a period of *Savasana,* the Corpse pose, to integrate and rest the body.

2.   Creating space, both in my joints and in my lifestyle, allowed smooth functioning of my body while experiencing life in the moment and enabling me to release stress as it occurred. Meditative practices, such as Yin Yoga, walking in conscious alignment, and sitting cross-legged with my spine straight ensured that the appropriate amount of space was maintained in my mind, body, and spirit.

3.   Feeding my body with the proper fuels to enhance my performance, well-being, and enjoyment was also a necessity.

4.   Optimizing my weight and the load carried by my joints was essential for remaining pain free.

Living in the jungle where entertainment options were limited, as well as more simply than I formerly did in Spain and the United States, had transformed food preparation and cooking from a necessary chore into an activity of creativity and enjoyment. Consciousness of the impact of different types of food on my body had shifted my ability to consume anything that I knew to be harmful, so that processed and unhealthy foods no longer appealed. In contrast, I began to crave healthy foods not only for their taste, but also for the energy they gave me.

Being more in tune with my body, its reaction to specific foods, and its level of physical well-being also enabled me to closely monitor slight changes and reverse any weight gain before it became permanent. I simply refused to let one new pound grow into two new pounds, and found maintaining my weight a simple process by adjusting food intake and exercise immediately.

Flow

"Our feminine consciousness exerts its power through attraction rather than activity, like a magnet will attract the iron shavings."
—Marianne Williamson

Energy Body *(Prana-maya-kosha)*

The energy or prana body represents our life force, the underlying vitality that animates our physical body. It determines our ability to create the things we desire in life—whether they relate to life's work, to relationships, to artistic endeavors or anything else productive. When we fail to regulate our energy, unhealthy conditions manifest such as depression, stress related physical conditions, lack of focus or purpose, and interpersonal and sexual problems. Our ability to attract what we want into our life is seriously impacted. Once we begin to manage and focus our energy using tools such as yoga, meditation and martial arts, we are able to eliminate the blocks in the flow of our vital life force. We develop skill in concentrating our energy in a productive way and increase our ability to manifest what we want in life.

II.

Nosara, Year One

The wind through leaves of all shapes and sizes was constant music. At times, it sounded like rain falling. For the first week or two in Costa Rica, I thought it was rain, a comforting sound, but not a remote possibility planted firmly in the dusty dry season as we were. Even with the gale force storm howling outside, which knocked out electricity and water, and downed trees, not one drop of rain fell.

Sleep was again elusive, restless like the crazy wind. My energy was on high, and had been since I arrived in Nosara in early January. Leading to this state, and fueling an almost euphoric sense of goodwill and well-being, were several factors.

I was finding it impossible to be unhappy or concerned for very long with the sun shining and while living in complete freedom. Add to that base the mystical enclave of Nosara, populated by golden, green goddesses and sexy surfers of all colors and forms, and an electric current amped from fifteen years of yoga awakenings like the one I just had experienced. Positivity. Wrap it all up with the overwhelming raw natural power of this particular piece of jungle and ocean: a Central American island of Atlantis.

The place had already started working its wonders on my physical body, which was stronger and fitter than ever in my life.

With the help of Zac and Tatiana, Playa Guiones' acupuncturists and holistic health care practitioners, I was kicking my pharmaceutical problem, weaning off anti-depressants after a ten-year habit. What had started as a temporary bridge to boost me out of my postbreakup rut when Tom and I split had turned into a chemical dependency over the years. Since releasing my body's chemistry to its natural state in Nosara, my ability to fully feel the world around me was returning, and my atrophied energy receptors were healing rapidly.

Yoga is a proven natural alternative for treating depression, increasing serotonin levels by means of the body's own intelligence. With it, and without artificially altering my natural body chemistry, I was happier than I could remember being in my life. And while yoga is best known as an excellent means for releasing tight muscles, it also balances the body's energy flow through breathwork, or *pranayama*. By bringing focus to parts of the body through the breath, blocks in the flow of energy in specific channels can be healed and released.

Each day, I was finding just how much blocked energy I had stored in my body. I had some releasing to do.

"Maps have come to us by wisdom traditions from ancient times," said my teacher Don Stapleton as he taught us about the chakras.

Yoga philosophy is by no means the only wisdom tradition that symbolizes or characterizes the transformational journey through a path. Christianity, for instance, utilizes the Stations of the Cross, Judaism provides the Kaballah, and Native American spirituality has the Hopi Sundance around the Medicine Wheel. Chakras are the way that yogis tell the story of transformation: how we are born and, through the way we live, are able to interact with our life circumstances in a way that doesn't leave us stuck by them. The chakras are domains of experience that begin to open as we take the inner journey, and tell the story of all the lessons we learn as we go through life.

Modern psychology also utilizes similar concepts of development through stages or dimensions. Abraham Maslow spells out similar domains in his hierarchy of needs. Erik Erikson details defined stages of development. Sigmund Freud, Alfred Adler, and Carl Jung all focused their work on areas pertaining to specific chakras, though they did not intentionally do so.

It is possible to use the chakras as a practical tool, a way to map your own inner journey by exploring the question "Where is my power to interact with this experience?" By taking that deeper look, you can begin to redirect your life force from a direction that is not positive to where you want to go, into a direction that is positive.

Chakras engage different intelligences in the learning process. Physically and energetically, they are centers rising in a column from the sacrum through the crown of the head, and are tied to the functioning of different glands and parts of the body. The movements, sounds, colors, visualizations, and other little things we bring into the chakras are a way of anchoring mental awareness on the internal domains of experience. They introduce a multi-dimensional and multi-sensory way of engaging the body at all levels: physical, emotional, mental, and spiritual.

After he concluded his background talk about the chakras, Don then led us in a meditation incorporating the specific sounds associated with opening each center, called the beej mantras.

A laminated white and orange poster detached itself from the wall above me, floated gracefully through the air and landed on my head.

Very interesting, I thought, as I disentangled from the sign and noted the second chakra description and key issues it detailed.

According to the sign, the second chakra is the focal point of our creativity, emotions, and sexuality, and it symbolizes our sense of self-worth and how we relate to others. It concerns emotional flow—feelings, fluidity, and openness—and, when it is open, represents grace and acceptance in dealing with life's changes. When blocked, it can manifest in problems with the hips (hence my birth defect, arthritis), our reproduction organs (my endometriosis), creativity (my ten-year writer's block), and emotional repression (my depression).

Signs are all around us, whether we choose to see them or not. This was one sign I could not ignore.

I decided to engage Don's teachings and use the second chakra as a practical tool to explore healing in those key areas of my life.

Painful as it was, our morning asana practice was heavy on the hip openers, stretches and movements designed to work this area of the body. I began noticing the thoughts that arose when engaged in those postures, and focused on releasing more than just the tight muscles. *You can't have it, you can't do it right, it's hopeless,* a little voice whispered to me as I brought my right ankle to my left wrist and settled into Pigeon pose. Despair washed over me and I flooded my mat with tears. "Breathe in, breathe out, hip relax, hip release," I chanted to myself as I held the pose.

"You were the madam of a bordello in the Wild West," Andy informed me towards the end of our energy healing session.

While clearing my chakras of blocks and drawing in vibrant color for each, she had glimpsed one of my past lives. Once again, I had been a strong woman making myself hard to survive in a rough man's world. "There was a man who held your heart," she told me, "and you saved your true self for him, only fully living during his visits despite knowing that he had many like you in other towns."

Very interesting. The story she told, whether I believed it or not, represented many of the patterns I was beginning to recognize in this current lifetime. Second chakra. It also fit the little voice of despair that whispered to me during Pigeon and other poses.

Swinging in my hammock the next day, doing the homework assignment Andy had given me of drawing with bright colors, something clicked. The *why* didn't matter: I could spend all of my life and energy focused on figuring out why things were the way they were, or I could move forward by accepting what was and choosing a different way for myself in the future. Whether from this life or a past one, I could accept responsibility that my issues were explained by my own choices and stop worrying about where to place the blame for them.

I made the decision to use my energy in a more productive and creative way.

"And you think that wouldn't be welcome?" I asked, smiling.

Bam, I was slammed with an electric current so strong I lost track of where I was. Markus smashed and swallowed me in an intensely connected kiss. Vaguely, I became aware of background voices as a crowd gathered around us in the small square. Shaking myself and then shaking him, we broke the kiss and ended that portion of the evening's entertainment for the neighborhood.

We had come outside the coffeehouse for air, walking out into the square in the cool Amsterdam evening. I shivered with cold and fear, as the feeling of being really stoned and out of control settled over me. Instead of attempting to hide it, I told him how afraid I felt. He hugged me close for comfort and warmth before abruptly jerking away, mumbling under his breath.

"I'm disgusting," he said to himself, "I can't comfort without getting hard."

I put my hand on his arm, looked into his eyes and asked my question.

Unable to sleep with the restless wind, I had pulled out my laptop and opened the last short story I had written several years before about getting lost in the flow of the moment. This particular story also illustrated my pattern with men over the past decade, of staying safe by only getting intimate with unavailable men conveniently located at long distances away from me.

I decided at that moment, I would write the book that I had been talking about for twenty years.

Jack was a brilliant and charming man who had risen to power by sheer force of intellect and will. His faded blue eyes rarely missed a thing: not a detail of your clothing or figure, a nervous gesture, an inflection of voice or an opportunity to exploit.

When he came into my life, he was in his decline and had held sway over legions of the world's most powerful men since he was scooped up after John F. Kennedy's assassination to serve in the Johnson White House. He could stun me into confusion with the same force as a cobra preparing to strike. His Texas drawl unnerved with ease, and his power emanated from a place much larger than his silver coiffed 5'4" frame.

While he was charming, ruthless, calculating, and almost always whittled his way to what he wanted, he possessed the single most brilliant mind I've ever encountered. Working with him was damaging personally, but also presented a life-changing opportunity to learn about strategy.

He also offered me a valuable lesson in the importance of using power wisely.

I jumped as I felt the bony, old hand dig into the soft crease of my upper left thigh.

The president of the international cinema chain, seated to my right at the annual ShoWest dinner, paused in our conversation, dropped his eyes to the tabletop, and then looked back up smirking slightly.

What do I do? What do I do? I wondered frantically. *Jump up in outrage? Rip Jack's hand off my leg and fling it away in front of my conversational partner?*

He knows, he already knows what Jack is doing, I thought, as shame blackened my soul.

I dropped my hand to block further assault and then excused myself abruptly. In the ladies room, I stood in a locked stall, face in hands, breathing loudly through my fingers until I could bottle up the frantic distress. Memories rose of earlier that evening in the suite, when Jack had grabbed and held my head while he planted one on my mouth with his wrinkled and wet lips. I gagged up some of the gourmet dinner. I had more than just distress to suppress.

Returning through the opulent restaurant, housed on the top floor of the pseudo Eiffel Tower that overlooked the Vegas Strip, I passed many of the film industry's elite as I returned to my own select table of CEOs and lobbyists. I moved my chair far out from the table so no additional attempts could be secretly made. After dinner, I politely declined repeated invitations to join the fun-loving group at the high stakes craps table. "No, I really must go prepare for the morning's international press conference and speech."

And I had thought the grilling on my year's work by the fifty largest entertainment media would be the most stressful part of the business trip.

The memory torpedoed to the surface during morning meditation on the third day of my Tai Chi course.

That morning, my parents had emailed me a link to an article about Jack Valenti as a joke, detailing rumors of how he was under investigation for his sexual conduct during his White House years. These rumors suggested it was conduct with his same sex as well as the opposite. My parents had always been so proud that I had worked for a celebrity and historical figure, and I had always made a joke of his advances towards me.

Not long into the meditation, the waterworks began as the memory torpedo exploded in living color. It was time for a big release of suppressed emotion.

Flood gates opened and not showing imminent signs of water subsiding, I left the Tai Chi course to nurture myself with a private yoga practice. Once home, I hung my banner of chakra-colored sarongs around my patio and emotionally vomited up the suppressed wad of Jack Valenti on my yoga mat.

I used to joke that it was just part of doing the job, of surviving the pressure at the pinnacle of international and entertainment politics in Hollywood. It didn't bother me; Jack did it to every attractive female. *I am a strong woman, see how I can laugh about it.*

Now that I was in the business of living, not just surviving, I found that it had bothered me. Quite a bit.

A car alarm blasted in the distance, the first to be heard since my arrival six weeks earlier. My city reflexes registered, then ignored the sound, until a mosquito bite reminded me that I was swinging in my hammock in Costa Rica.

New York. Hard to imagine now how I had survived the sheer cacophony of sound bouncing up the concrete canyons, fed by the masses of humanity and machinery. At one level, the energy of the city had fed and stimulated me for years, but it also had offered little peace, just a deadening of senses to survive. My time there seemed like a hazy dream as I thawed out and steamed up in the vibrant jungle, splashes of color and life and movement everywhere...

Like that life and movement over there, in the form of a very attractive, bare-chested Tico coming towards me with a wheelbarrow and smoldering eyes. Paradise was spending hot, golden and green afternoons swinging in my hammock, listening to the wind and the birds and just watching each moment unfold. My mind spun into a fantasy involving wheelbarrows, until it was displaced by the image of a shirtless and sweaty Troy coming up the steps to my casita.

Troy was teaching my one week Tai Chi course, better known as "Troy Chi" among the yoginis who'd had the pleasure of his assistance during our teacher training the month before. Forty-one women in my class had watched him with hungry eyes as our energy started awakening and accelerating during the four-week intensive program. He was now teaching us how to move that energy according to another ancient Eastern tradition.

"Hi," he said from across the patio, hairy chest gleaming and blue eyes piercing. "I'm staying next door for the week."

Mercy. I needed to release some energy.

"AAAAAAHHHHHH! I RELEASE YOU AND OPEN SPACE FOR SOMEONE NEW!" we shrieked to the Milky Way on the dark beach, howling from our guts until the energy felt spent. The sound of waves crashing was our only response.

After a week of hanging out on the patio being assaulted by his shirtless and sweaty hotness, the word came out that Troy was involved with a beautiful and dear woman from my yoga training. Nichole, another good friend who was also suffering from a crush and a repressed libido, had joined me in the ritual of release as we walked the night beach to a bar at the far side of Playa Guiones.

I flew up the broad trunks of the ancient twin oaks and up to the star field high above, into a million points of golden light. I saw how we were all connected, and felt an overwhelming sense of peace before crashing back down into my body and seeing how alone I had made myself in my life.

Never felt anything like *that* before.

I opened my eyes and saw Asil and Jon resting on their heels at my head and feet. They had just completed a joint energy session for me. Asil was trained in Reiki and Jon in Native American shamanism. We were in a meditation grove at the retreat center hosting the Arete Experience, a transformational workshop we had done together in the past and were assisting this weekend.

Something needs to change in my life, I thought to myself as I thanked the men for the healing.

My introduction to energy work had come back in New York at the hands of Asil, my first Reiki healer and a fellow participant in Arete a few years before. He had taught me how to open up to another's powerful energy, and also the distinction between universal healing love and sexual, romantic love at a time in my life when I was starved for any kind. This dear friend and brother was my first visitor in Costa Rica, and the first person from home to witness the dramatic changes taking place in my body and spirit.

The Arete Experience had been a powerful opening for me. It was the first time I had been able to release some of the enormous buildup of energy stored in my body during an intense guided exercise. Just one week after the workshop, I had taken my first trip to Costa Rica feeling wide open and fearless, and eagerly absorbing the raw energy of the country and the people.

Asil's visit here in Nosara now coincided with my own first training in giving body and energy work, as I began a two-week course in Pranassage, which is a one-on-one yoga experience. With similarities to Thai massage, this therapeutic treatment guides recipients into deep relaxation in the present moment by connecting with their own *prana* (life force) by means of the breath, touch, gravity, and yoga postures.

The night Asil and his friend arrived, I took them to the beach and we lay in the sand absorbed in the Milky Way high above, feeling the stars pulse with life like the grid I had seen in my vision.

It had been an interesting week, dipping back into the intense training schedule with a different cast of characters all while entertaining two hot male guests. Two hours of fast vinyasa flow yoga started each day at sunrise, and then energy was exchanged with two different partners, both giving and receiving body work during the day and evening sessions.

My creativity exploded. I wrote more in those two weeks than I had for fifteen years.

I also cried enough to nourish the dusty landscape around me, flowers sprouting and splashing color on the pages I drew every moment I was not in training or writing. One day, my hip screaming, I decided to sit out a session at the back of the room, drawing a tropical downpour of tears into my course materials.

Stored energy and repressed emotions were being wrung from my body like water from the wet cloths I used to heat at night for my aching back and hip.

⟡

"Let's walk El Camino de Santiago," I suggested to Dana after we completed our morning practice together surrounded by the jungle in an open-air pavilion on the yoga institute grounds. It had been in the back of my mind since my first trip to Spain with a lover nearly fifteen years before.

"Yes!" she exclaimed, electrified. Pranassage had just completed, and we were discussing next steps for growth in our life. "When?" she asked.

We agreed on September that year, after I had returned to the States from Costa Rica and she had some more yoga teaching time under her belt.

While yoga was opening and strengthening my body, my legs were still vibrating with energy and felt as if they had decades stored in them needing to be walked out. With my hip feeling so much better, I had begun walking miles along the beach each morning and each evening, trying to burn off their restlessness. A pilgrimage, particularly one through the land of my ancestors, resonated deeply. I was determined to make it happen before I completed my sabbatical and rejoined the mainstream.

Dana was a beautiful creature of light that I had met during Pranassage, glowing from the tips of her golden hair to the pure soul that shone from her clear eyes. She had come into the program nursing a broken heart, and had made a commitment to herself to use her time and energy here in Costa Rica for healing and abstain from new romantic relationships for the period. From her example, I first began to consider using my sabbatical in a similar way. With all of the energy that was exploding inside of me, I knew it could be a powerful force for creating a new life for myself.

What would happen if I consciously chose to direct my sexual energy and focus it on my own healing, instead of releasing it through the sex that I so craved with my awakening senses?

"Something to consider," my spirit said.

"Absolutely not!" my man-starved senses screamed.

I lay completely still, Manuel's nose hovering just two inches from my right hip bone.

In his hands, the tattoo drill buzzed as he pressed it into my skin. First, the black outline of the second chakra symbol with Sanskrit lettering in the center. The drilling was not so bad, just manageable pinching bursts of pain. This hip had definitely felt much worse. Next came the colors: bright orange filling in the circle, and red and yellow highlighting the lotus petals that flaired on the outside of the circle. More pinches of pain, a bit sharper this time, as the skin became raw. Not a problem, though.

Two hours with an attractive man focusing all his attention on imprinting the second chakra on my hip was causing me sexual "pain," however. The needle drill sent vibrations through my abdomen to the energy center in my womb. His breath tickled my skin.

His other arm wrapped around me and clasped my lower back, rough hand holding the hip still. Yes, getting this tattoo was extremely uncomfortable in my present over-energized state.

Primal forces can be released when you set and mark an intention. With this tattoo, I was making a permanent commitment to blow through any blocks to being the powerful woman I was, to live my life being heard and seen.

Am I ready? I wondered.

Time for that question had passed, as I admired my new tattoo. *Yes, I am ready for anything.*

My old friend, insomnia, came back with a vengeance, along with the crazy wind.

It feels a bit like my emotions, howling and swirling. I'm totally confronted by everything I want and the lack of it in my life right now. How much work can I do on myself? How much do I need to? What I want is not so unreasonable.

Was it the hunger from the juice fast? The swirling mass of emotions that were being released through the cleansing process were wreaking chaos in my body, trapped inside with the energy built up over the last two months. I needed a good raging scream, a soul deep bout of weeping, a hot session of very physical sex.

Laying in my cabina at Hacienda del Sol, I wondered at my energy after three days without solid food. My mind came back and back to sex. *Do I harness all of the energy inside of me for healing and creativity or do I need some mind-blowing sex to burst that last block?*

I want that release, I crave it, I keep coming back to the need for it. What do I choose?

Two more days without food, half a dozen more colemas and a liver cleanse helped the built-up energy to subside. Walking up the hill to the main pavilion for my juice drinks took all that I had.

I would make my decision on how to manage my energy when I returned to Nosara, senses pure and clear from the cleanse.

12.

Don Juan de Costa Rica

"And in comes the two to the three and one..." Thievery Corporation pulsed into the jungle air.

Suddenly, I could see what all of the fuss was about. Carlos was dancing alone under the trees, soft beams from lanterns uplighting the leaves and outlining his body as he kicked out the rhythm in the steamy night. Longish black hair flying, brown skin gleaming, he was raw energy surging to the music. Up until now, he had been a background character, the guy from El Salvador that my friend Lena had a fling with during the teacher training. He had just jumped into focus.

Carlos was the chef at La Luna, an oasis of food, drink, and music nestled among tall trees on a slight rise above the beach at Playa Pelada. The restaurant was housed in a funky old villa, vivid colors painted on walls and splashing up columns supporting the graceful veranda that overlooked the ocean. Random seating arrangements were scattered around the lawn, accented by pavilions swathed in white fabric over foam mattresses for comfortable lounging.

As on many nights, La Luna was graced with yoginis draped in flowing dresses, tonight a group of us celebrating our graduation from Pranassage training. My energy was higher than ever after two weeks of intense body and breath work. And it had just found a new focal point.

Arriving back from my first cleanse at Hacienda del Sol two weeks later, feeling like a clear, still pond, I made my first visit to Gonça's shop of goddess wear in the Harmony Hotel.

I had resisted the store earlier in the training season as friends purchased flowing sexy dresses suitable for wandering the marble temples of Atlantis or ancient Greece. I had not felt ready to join their ranks as my body shape-shifted with my physical transformation. The intense cleansing process had washed that feeling out of me, along with a lifetime's worth of other toxins. For the first time, I felt like a goddess.

"Wow!" Dana exclaimed as I met her before sunset for a long beach walk to La Luna, draped in vibrant purple silk. We were meeting her visiting friends for a birthday dinner.

Carlos joined us as we sat around a low table, finishing the meal he had prepared and watching the last of the sunset shed its orange, red, and gold into the dark ocean. As the night descended, Dana and her friends reminisced about shared experiences during a training program the previous year. My attention wandered away from the group and out into the blackness, yearning to be on the beach under the stars to celebrate the new moon and set my intentions for the coming month.

I felt Carlos' eyes on me as my senses strained toward the night sky. "Do you think it's safe to walk back alone on the beach?" I asked him, coming back into my body and to our group. "I need to be out under the stars."

"I will walk with you," he said, "if you can wait until the kitchen closes."

"Thank you, but I want to go now," I replied, "I want to walk alone."

"Try to walk without your flashlight then," he advised. "No one will be able to see you."

The lights of La Luna at my back, I paused to sink my bare feet in the sand and let my eyes adjust to the darkness. I breathed in the powerful energy that seemed concentrated in that particular cove, body vibrating slightly.

Shimmering stars guided me to the path up and through the mangroves and across the point separating Playa Pelada from its neighbor, Guiones. The jungle rustled and creaked with life in the moonless dark.

Crossing the rocky outcropping and out into the triangular cove on the other side, the wind picked up. I walked the wide beach under the Milky Way absorbed in the stars. A silver glow caressed me like my silk dress, as it rippled against my skin in the gusting air. Lost in space and time, I declared my intention to the new moon.

I would put all of my energy into loving myself, so that in the future I could better serve. I felt the power rise in me, a rebirth, another awakening. A goddess was born.

Self-love is the key to any other kind of love. My energy for the coming year would be devoted to my own healing. I would be celibate.

"Where have you been?" Carlos exclaimed the next afternoon as I entered Zen Café. "I have been waiting here all day, worried that you did not make it home safely."

I dragged my bike up the short steep path to La Luna, left it leaning against a tree as I crossed the lawn to join Carlos on the porch. After exchanging greetings, we sat silently watching the midday sun glare on the ocean and listened to the waves crash as he finished his lunch.

A foursome of tourists in crisply pressed shorts entered the lawn and wandered around until they spotted us sitting in the shade. The two men disengaged from their female counterparts and came up to us. "Do you work here?" one of them asked Carlos. "We'd like to make reservations for this evening."

I slipped into the role of observer, noting the condescending tone of voice that I hadn't heard since New York when a corporate colleague addressed a Latino busboy during a business lunch. "You will mark it down, the name is J-O-N-E-S? We want reservations for 8:00," the man insisted as he noted no pen, only a fork, in Carlos' hand. "Do I need to speak to the manager to have it confirmed?"

Ouch, so uptight and unpleasant. Laughter bubbled up in me at the stark contrast between the life I now lived, and the one I had left where that behavior was common. I felt as if I were in a cartoon.

Carlos gracefully replied that he was the manager, and assured the man that no reservation was needed but that he would ensure a table was ready for them at 8:00. Grumbling self-importantly, the man rejoined his party and the people made their way back to their car.

"Are you okay, Carlos?" I asked as we approached his car a little later. "Your energy feels really bad." I had decided to ask him what was going on by telling him what I felt. In the past, I would have made his bad energy mean something about me, that he didn't want to spend the afternoon with me. This time, I just observed and questioned what was without assigning meaning to it.

He stopped and looked at me, dark eyes serious and intense. "It's been a long time since anyone asked me how I was doing," he replied. "Thank you."

"If it's a bad time, we don't have to do this now," I said. Carlos had offered to drive me around to help find larger and less expensive housing for the upcoming rainy season.

"No," he replied with the first genuine smile of the day lighting his face and changing his energy. "I'm glad to spend this time with you."

As we bounced around the dusty dirt roads in the bright afternoon sunshine, the car provided an intimate container while we chatted about beliefs and desires and dreams. Green trees, brown earth, golden sunlight, and brilliant blue sky provided the backdrop for the colorful houses of purple and yellow and pink and orange that we passed on our magical mystery tour of Playa Pelada.

Lucy and I walked along the beach early on a Sunday morning. A pack of dogs approached and surrounded Lucy, led by an aggressive boxer. She dropped to her back and immediately exposed her white belly in submission. The boxer was not impressed and growled menacingly as he advanced, teeth bared.

"Hey!" I roared, slamming him with ferocious energy as I jumped between him and my sweet dog without conscious thought. "Back off!"

As the boxer slunk away with the others following, I thought to myself, *Perhaps that wasn't the smartest thing to do in a pack of aggressive dogs.*

Legs shaking from adrenaline, I continued my walk down the beach doing my morning chakra meditation. I focused my energy in my core, rolling my hips in the natural gate that released and opened the tight muscles.

"Hey!" I looked over my shoulder at the greeting to see Carlos speeding to catch up with me as I reached a deserted part of the beach. Lucy ran up to him, sniffed his hand, and allowed him to fondle her ears.

"I saw you back there with the dogs," he said. "That boxer is dangerous; he attacked my dog, Andy, last week."

Picking up our conversation where we left off a few days before, we walked for miles down the beach and back, Lucy a white shadow trailing us and frolicking at the water's edge. Parting ways after breakfast, Carlos invited me out to visit him at La Luna. "I will drive you home at the end of the night," he said, "so you don't have to walk alone in the dark."

Shyness kept me away until there was an occasion for the visit. Brian, my friend from several yoga trainings and one of the deejays at La Luna, was spinning his last night before returning to the States.

Lucy and I walked the water's edge again as the sun sank closer to the ocean, climbing the path through the jungle and then down to the edge of the cove that sheltered La Luna at its center. The tide was high, water swirling around my calves and up to Lucy's belly as we hugged the mangroves bordering the beach.

Crossing the lawn, I joined Brian at his makeshift deejay station under the trees, sitting next to him to watch the sun complete the day's journey. Nikolas, a French artist and co-deejay with Brian, sat down next to me and we enjoyed the colorful show in the sky and the sound of the waves combined with the music. Carlos drifted out of the kitchen and joined us in our corner under the trees.

Soon, only the light from Brian's laptop pulsing in time with the music and a few scattered candles illuminated the dark night in front of us, the glow from the bar behind us barely perceptible.

"Have you noticed the changes coming?" Nikolas asked. "You can tell the rainy season will be here soon because the insects have started to change and the spiders are coming out." The changes I had felt were more in the population of humans, as faces from the yoga community began to disappear and the town's population thinned out. I wondered how I would feel when Brian left in a few days, and when Dana left the following week.

Nikolas spoke of his own changes, having moved to Nosara with his wife two years earlier and expecting their first child here in a few months. Carlos pulled out a picture of his own daughter back in the States, and passed it around. "She is seven now," he said, "I can't believe I've missed so much of her life."

I mentioned my brother and his birthday coming later that week. "I haven't spoken with him since I arrived nearly three months ago," I said. "He disapproved of my decision to quit my job and come here, and his emails were so critical that I had decided to cut contact with him and his negativity."

"He was just worried about you!" both Nikolas and Carlos exclaimed, as they assumed a brotherly demeanor and lectured me on the concerns that men have about their sisters. I smiled and allowed myself to be cared for. Perhaps I was ready to speak to my brother again.

At the end of the evening, Brian brought his bicycle around to walk home with me while Carlos stood with his car keys. Like the wild dogs on the beach, the two men faced off briefly before Carlos gracefully bowed out saying he would see me at Zen Café the next morning.

Following our farewell walk along the starlit beach, Brian and I hugged goodbye when he deposited me at the foot of the steps leading to my casita. He mounted his bike and rode off toward the jungle path, disappearing into the darkness. I climbed the stairs and approached my door.

A black shape scurried across the patio and crouched against the bottom of my door.

A giant tarantula. Even in my horror and revulsion, some part of my brain could appreciate its velvety black beauty.

Spiders were a childhood terror from as far back as I could remember, so bad that each night my father had to check the bed and closet for them before I could rest. The fear had just begun subsiding toward adolescence when a *Brady Bunch* rerun set in Hawaii renewed the terror after watching Peter Brady wake up to a tarantula crawling across his bed and up his arm.

The jungle night was dark and quiet. Not another living soul around, just me and the spider staring at each other, the creature standing firmly between me and my bed.

Well, I have to get in there, I thought as I stood frozen.

Looking around, I noted the woven cotton mat at the edge of the patio. Grabbing it, I tossed it on top of the giant tarantula and flung it off the porch with the leg of a plastic chair. I shuddered in revulsion.

Oh no! The monster had not been flung far enough, and had darted back to its position crouched against the bottom edge of the door.

More focused placement this time of the cotton mat, two legs of the plastic chair rooting down on it, and a more powerful fling sent the giant creature, mat and chair flying into the foliage halfway down the hill. I raced to the door, fumbled my keys into the lock, slammed it shut behind me, and stuffed towels into the crack between the wood and the tile floor. Even with these precautions, I had a hard time falling asleep, lights illuminating every corner of my casita.

Yes, I definitely got the message that change was coming. I was proud of the way I had faced down my fear and whisked it out of my path.

Each day, the world around me changed perceptibly.

The beach community thinned to long-term residents, as my dear friends from the yoga training programs cycled out of town and returned to their homes. Replacing the humans were the crabs, thousands rising from the ground and scuttling through the mangroves on their bright orange-red legs and marching inland to the town.

Shortly after my episode with the tarantula, I had a close encounter with a crab in my shower. A scuttling sound and flurry of movement caught my attention as I rinsed my hair, and I leapt out of the stall spraying water everywhere before locating the source of the activity in the corner. His beady eyes assessed me, pinchers flashing, before he scurried past me fleeing the stall as well and hiding under a kitchen cabinet out of my reach.

It seemed I had a new roommate whether I wanted one or not. Good thing I was moving in a few days.

I had found a new casita on the other side of the jungle path, closer to the yoga institute but further from the town center. It offered me a separate bedroom, a full kitchen, a distinct dining and living area, and a larger, more sheltered porch. All important features as the skies began to cloud over, precursing the rain that would keep me inside a good portion of each day. Life, which had been lived outdoors since I arrived four months before, would move within four walls while the skies saturated the earth over the coming months.

Every day, dark clouds consumed the sky for longer and longer periods, and the humidity between heaven and earth grew. Still, the first rain did not come. Jungle trees dropped green vines toward the earth, strange buds opening to suck moisture from the heavy air. Distant rumbles of thunder occasionally shook the pregnant atmosphere, and the town and its inhabitants operated in slow motion.

Walking the beach before nightfall, sunset once again hidden behind the dark clouds, the sky rumbled before finally opening its floodgates. Laughing with joy at nature's dramatic release and the ocean roiling response, I walked the last mile towards home with water pounding me and tearing at my soaked clothes.

The earth's energy had shifted. It had also disrupted manmade energy, pulling down power lines and plunging my new casita and the surrounding community into darkness for the night.

I sat on my covered porch in the pitch black, listening to the sound of water pounding the roof and watching it stream into the ground. A small tea light flickered on the table. My laptop had long since run out of juice.

I was completely alone with my thoughts in the dark jungle.

"You need some supplies," Carlos informed me, noting my wild-eyed look after a third night on the dark porch. "You have to be able to get around in the rain, or you'll go crazy there alone."

"You think?" I cackled with mild hysteria.

"Let's go to Montezuma for the organic market this weekend," he suggested. "I'll help you find what you need on the way."

I decided that kissing his feet would be a bit much, and settled for thanking him profusely and reserving a four-wheel drive rental car to negotiate the dirt roads.

Carlos and I had become close since the town had emptied out, and he was an important source of support. What had begun as an attraction had developed into a deep friendship, as I focused my energy on healing and creativity and he focused his on the many other women in town not so occupied internally. He was a man who loved women. And he knew how to use his considerable magnetism to draw as many as he wanted to him romantically in his continual search for the perfect one who would hold his attention. He was an interesting choice of friend for a woman with trust issues. Friendship enabled me to get close to the man without the attachment that can come from a sexual relationship, and he proved a true friend.

Carlos took the wheel as we set out early that Saturday morning, after a powerful cleansing experience at my first sweat lodge the night before. We drove the long dirt road out of Nosara, connecting with pavement near Nicoya where I took over driving before turning south. Montezuma was an old hippy settlement on the bottom tip of the Guanacaste Peninsula, and we would spend several hours road-tripping to reach our destination.

"Pull over!" Carlos commanded as I turned inland. He jumped out and began collecting fallen mangos on the side of the road, juggling four or five as he returned to the car. The fruit trees were in full bloom and dropping their ripe bounty for those passing by.

A wicked looking knife appeared in his hand as I pulled onto the road once again. He expertly sliced the top half off around the giant pit and handed the juicy fruit to me.

"Eat it down to the skin," he instructed. "There is a rich cream in the outer layer."

One hand on the wheel, one clasping the oval fruit in my palm, I sunk my teeth into the orange flesh. Flavor exploded in my mouth as juice washed down my chin. This had to be the most delicious thing I had ever tasted. Was it possible to have an orgasm from food?

"Can I have another, please?" I asked him with a satisfied smile and dreamy eyes.

Minus the cigarettes, we chatted in post-mango bliss, enclosed in our bubble of car intimacy. He spoke of growing up in war-torn El Salvador, dodging violence and explosions, and being the man of the family from a young age when his American father returned to the States. He learned to cook in his mother's restaurant, and had been raised among the women of his family. At age fourteen, he had contacted his father for help in coming to the U.S., knowing that if he was to survive he had to leave before the war destroyed him. Entering high school in Miami with very little English, he had honed his skills with the girls as a way to fit in when the boys harassed and bullied him.

Turning onto a dirt road an hour later, I kept up my speed, bouncing and jarring the rental and tossing us around in our seats.

"Do you drive like you live," Carlos questioned me, "plowing full speed ahead to get to your goal without seeing what is right in front of you?"

Um, yes, I thought sheepishly.

"You must adjust to the road," he advised, "adapt to what is before you right now. It will make for a much smoother and more enjoyable ride."

Wise words to keep in mind. I slowed my pace, focusing on steering the car around the immediate ruts and bumps. *It is much more comfortable,* I thought until I was distracted again by conversation and my foot crept down on the accelerator. A particularly large ridge caught the wheel and slammed the car towards the side of the road, both of us flying sideways in our seats.

"Stop. Let me drive, so we make it safely," Carlos commanded. I meekly complied.

"Do you know what you want in a man?" Carlos asked me quietly in the dark.

The stars were pinpoints of light in the inky expanse above us, shedding a soft glow through the dusty cloud of the Milky Way and onto the silent beach around us. Lucy and Andy wandered ahead, white dog prancing, brown lab plodding, as Carlos and I followed on our nightly walk.

I had trouble articulating my answer. What did I want, other than a strong, kind, and attractive man?

"How can you manifest what you want if you don't know what that is? You must have a list and be as specific as possible," he said, and then went on to describe what he was looking for in a woman.

A List. A very interesting concept, one that had relevance in all areas in life. A list of requirements to guide and focus my choices, similar to so many that I had created and used in my professional life.

A light bulb flashed on above my head. I needed to develop my own personal BATNA for my right man.

I had first learned of the BATNA years ago in a pivotal negotiation, diplomacy, and bargaining class in graduate school, and the concept had always served me well when I used it. Literally translated, it means your "Best Alternative to a Negotiated Agreement." Figuratively, it was a boundary, the walkaway point at which a situation, person, or event crosses from meeting your needs and begins to detract from you.

Without articulating your BATNA or boundary, you cannot fulfill your needs, because you have no real clarity or awareness of what they are. Your energy is not focused on a goal, rather is it diffused, sprayed around by attempting to read all external cues and questioning everything in a constant search for something undefined. Without it, you are likely to accept less than what you need because you don't know any better, and you are likely to give your power away to others.

By defining your needs, your energy can be focused on being open to situations that meet them and eliminating situations that do not. You create the ability to manifest what you want because your power is focused on listening to your intuition and needs.

Wasn't I fortunate that I had this time now, this year of freedom, to define what I wanted in my right man and also in other areas of my life?

No better time to begin than now, I thought. Walking with Carlos in the starlight, I began to develop my list and saw right away many things that I did want.

My Right Man BATNA:

- A conscious, smart, sexy, strong man of integrity following a spiritual path and continually growing and stretching
- A partner who gets me and is an open and clear communicator

Carlos seemed to have those qualities. In many ways, he was my best friend in Costa Rica and I could talk to him openly about what I felt and thought without feeling judged in any way. I couldn't remember another man that I felt so open with, but I also realized that was heavily influenced by the fact that I was a different person now than I had ever been.

Okay, so what else was important? Sexual attraction and a powerful energetic connection were vital. Next item on the list:

• We share a powerful and sustainable bond of attraction

Hmmm, not so much. Whether it was a factor of trust, or where I was in my healing process, or the whole myriad of things going on inside of him, Carlos and I generated barely a blip of heat between us. My sexual energy was tied up in my own growth, and his was spread out over the surrounding beach communities searching for a goddess who would devote most of hers to focusing his.

However, the fact that he had lost his job as chef at La Luna in the slow season and was living with me part time, clouded the issue of sex as I began to develop my BATNA after our discussion. One dark and rainy night, we strayed across the boundary line and it was not an experience either of us cared to repeat. The fact that we were able to address it through open communication and clear it out of our path just cemented our friendship.

"How is it possible that we have found each other?" Carlos exclaimed on another dark night as we walked the dogs miles along the moonlit beach.

Yes, the universe was certainly presenting ample opportunities for learning, as Carlos continued to fulfill everything that I wanted in a man except for the sexual energy. *How healthy is this relationship for me?* I wondered, as I began to question how truly important the heat was compared to the companionship. He tutored me in cooking organically, mentored me in living in communion with nature, shared deeply personal experiences and desires, and even took over training my dog when Lucy's terrorized panic during the daily thunderstorms made me fear I would have to put her down.

Be grateful for his help and support and friendship, a resolute voice inside of me insisted. *Remember your BATNA. You don't want to do without the spark, focus your energy on healing yourself and your right man will come. You've seen what the wrong relationship can do to you.*

❧

I made an unexpected plunge back into the States after five months in the jungle.

A supply trip was required when my computer started failing and I could no longer make due dressing my shrinking body in the surfer chic clothes that were my only option in Nosara. Reconnecting with friends and an easier life in Houston and San Francisco nurtured and stabilized me at a time when so much was changing within and around me. One week was spent with my dearest girlfriends in Texas, and then another with family and life coaching friends in the Bay area.

I was feeling the hardships of jungle life intensely as I adjusted back to Nosara. Before my trip, the hills looming beyond my casita had brought such peace as I swung in my hammock, imagining more hills and jungle rolling beyond, just nature and space. That same image now brought on claustrophobia, a desperate feeling of being stuck with no transportation, conveniences, or friends, and no resources to get them. What was I doing there?

About a week or so after I returned from my trip, Grace came back from two months in London. She was a beautiful woman with an open and loving heart, a quick wit, and an infectious sense of humor who had made her own change from a busy life in London to the jungles of Costa Rica the year before me. Her honey-colored curly hair was usually pulled back tightly in a small ponytail, framing a face dominated by sparkling sherry eyes, dimples, and a ready warm smile.

Grace was in a similar state of transition when she returned, and we forged a tight bond of support immediately. It was wonderful to have a female friend again on a similar path and wavelength.

Walking back along the jungle path to her casita in the dark, because she was afraid to go alone, I explained to Grace how I had used the jungle path as a parable to teach myself not to fear. As I walked alone in the dark, listening to the jungle rustle with life, I would practice trusting that I could see all that I needed in the glow of the moonlight or the short beam of my flashlight. I saw that life was like the jungle path: You have to trust that you have all you need right in this moment, that all will be revealed as you need it. I would picture myself held safe within a glow of light, or picture myself passing by invisibly. And so on the dark nights alone, I breathed and practiced affirmations, and soon it became natural not to be afraid.

"I have seen you," Carlos pronounced with focused energy, a grave face, and a significant look when I introduced my two friends several days after Grace's return. Walking on, Grace and I had laughed about his intensity in light of his reputation and what I had shared about my evolving friendship with him.

Don Juan had found a new focal point.

Carlos' situation had become increasingly difficult as the rainy season progressed. After a month of sleeping on my couch and the sofa at Zen Café, he had moved back into a house in Playa Pelada that he had leased months before and sublet. There was another woman and a whole story about that one, as I had found there usually was with him. His options for another full-time job as a chef were limited in the small community and he had a lead on a job in Northern California. He set a date for return and, as with all his newest passions, he was enthralled with the move and increasingly negative about his current situation. He also became a bit desperate for resources, and so, as many do in such circumstances, he fell out of integrity with his word. He began to see himself as a victim of external forces and crossed a line into using people to accomplish his means.

On the day of his departure, I thanked him for the role he played in my life, and breathed a sigh of relief that he and his dark cloud were gone.

Walking towards the jungle path the next day, I glanced up at Grace's casita and was surprised to see Carlos camped out on her porch with a pile of his belongings scattered about.

"They took my car away at the border," he called down from the porch, launching into his tale of woe at the injustices heaped upon him. "I'm going to see if Grace will let me camp on her porch for a few days."

Right, I thought, seeing how it would unfold. Grace, with her big heart, would be unable to resist his story and invite him to stay though she was going to be assisting fifty new students through an intense training and would need personal space in her limited downtime. In his current desperate state, he would suck her dry like a starving vampire, as I had seen with his other conquests that spring.

"Why don't you stay with other friends who are not doing the training?" I asked Carlos. "There are plenty who will help, and Grace will be under a lot of stress for the next month."

"No, I will just camp on her porch for a week or so," he replied. "Maybe this was fate, so that Grace and I would have time to be together."

It's not about me, I told myself. *Their actions have nothing to do with me.* My two best friends had found each other and there was no room for me while they explored the powerful attraction between them. That didn't stop it from hurting, though, or help with the feeling that I'd just been dumped by both of them.

The rainy season in Nosara had been hard, and friends were scarce as electric lights scattered in the dark jungle at night. When had I ever been so alone and isolated in my life? I had grown up in suburbia and then lived my adult life mostly in big cities with a large network of family and friends around. Sure, I'd spent a fair share of time alone, but people had always been easily accessible. Now they were few and far between.

And so, I was alone. Grace was absorbed into her busy training schedule and disappeared along with Carlos into their tumultuous love affair. And I felt lonely and dumped, two pillars of support knocked out in one fell swoop. And, to be honest, a bit jealous and hurt that I no longer mattered.

When offered the opportunity to teach yoga for a week at Hacienda del Sol in exchange for another cleanse, I jumped on it. I recruited Mónica, a Thunderbird friend who lived two hours north, to join me, and we set out for San Juanillo on a sunny Saturday.

This second cleanse went much deeper than the first, and I was plagued by migraines, fear dreams, and night sweats for the first few days. The deep jungle had changed with the rainy season, as well, and the spider and insect population had exploded. Mosquitos attacked all exposed areas when mounted on the colema equipment, stinging where no bug should ever touch. The nights were torture as I lay in my damp sheets under the mosquito netting, trying not to touch it, and the multitude of critters it housed watching me through the white weave. I could not get comfortable and I could not sleep.

As with the first time, my energy gradually dissipated as the week progressed until by the end I had released an enormous amount of toxins as well as fear.

The familiar sense of clarity and peace had returned. As Mónica and I drove the coastline back to Playa Guiones, I felt more peace than I had since returning from the States. The still pond was back.

Entering town, I glanced out the window at a crowd on the corner by the Café de Paris waiting for the bus. My eyes caught Carlos' and held as the car slowly rumbled by on the dirt road, bringing me back into town as the bus took him away. I wished him well on his journey.

13.
Animals, Intuition, and Expression

Golden trees like a celebratory parade lined the streets as we drove into town. Mountains, deserts, forests, and creeks combined with a creative and conscious community to make Taos feel as if it was going to be the perfect place to write.

And it might have been, if not for a number of things. It taught me a valuable lesson about recognizing when a situation is not working, and making a change when intuition prompted rather than staying stuck.

When my friend Andy, whose energy work had been instrumental in bursting my ten-year writer's block, offered me a room in a group house of yogi-artists in Taos, I jumped on it. It gave me a sense of direction for life after Costa Rica, and an opportunity to continue learning about conscious living in the U.S. And so Lucy and I jumped in the car, with the last-minute addition of my friend Lisa, and set off on our cross-country adventure.

From day one, the energy in the house was unstable, and that continued to grow in intensity until hostility became the norm. I found it impossible to write a word.

When we arrived in Taos, Lisa had decided she wanted to stay, and that added a fourth woman to a house with three bedrooms and an art studio. Competition was introduced as to who would actually stay in the house, and who would leave. Also building up tension was that fact that Andy was in the midst of a painful and bitter separation from her husband, a successful businessman with a similar mindset and way of thinking to me. I became the focal point for the grief and anger of a powerful energy worker going through an emotionally unstable phase, and was confronted again and again with my triggers of not being seen for me and of being judged.

Using what I had learned in the past, I spent as much time in nature and did as much yoga as I could. I took long hikes in the mountains with Lucy under the golden aspens and pine trees, did yoga on the sunny back patio, and walked the dirt roads in the neighborhood absorbed in the looming mountains and riffs of cloud marching across the sky for miles. I also began going for regular horseback rides with Jerry, an old friend of Andy, who had several horses needing exercise.

Jerry and I began riding a few days a week, taking the horses out for fifteen-mile treks through the desert arroyos and up into mountains that looked the same as they did in the days of the Wild West. We were a contained community of man, woman, horses, and a pack of dogs schooling Lucy in manners and mountain living. I was happy for a new friend and mentor, who taught me much about the energy of animals and how it relates to broader areas of life.

Jerry, however, had other ideas about our relationship.

I first became conscious of what was happening when Andy began making caustic comments about it, and the fact that I needed to address it if I wasn't interested. Point taken. I was quite good at not noticing things that I wanted to avoid dealing with, particularly with men. I used to laugh about the strategy in the business world and during my time in LA when I found it was best to pretend I didn't understand the comments and insinuations of Jack and other powerful men I dealt with. By not allowing their comments to penetrate me, I felt that I negated their power to impact me. I didn't realize that I also squandered the opportunity to set clear boundaries around what behavior was acceptable to me and therefore created a situation that kept repeatedly occurring.

This same lesson had come up during my very first week of yoga training, when speaking with a new friend about how important it was to remember how powerful we are even when we aren't choosing to be powerful. Not making a decision is making a decision, as is avoiding. Not focusing your power toward a positive goal doesn't mean your power isn't there, it just means that it is being used unconsciously. You become powerful in negativity versus positivity.

The next time we went out riding, I began to notice things. The comments that I had brushed off before stood out more clearly. Perhaps the fact that Jerry always gave me his stallion to ride and had begun making analogies between the horse and parts of his anatomy was communicating a message in addition to being a joke.

Crossing a dirt road into the desert with the horses and dogs, we ran into a friend of Jerry's, who climbed out of his pickup truck to speak with us. He referred to me several times as Jerry's girlfriend. Jerry didn't correct him. As the friend left, I decided the time was perfect to address it.

"Your friend called me your girlfriend several times," I began. "I want to make sure that you understand that I'm only looking for a friend right now. My focus is on writing, and I'm not looking for a romantic relationship."

Whew. That wasn't so hard.

"I am interested in more," Jerry said, "but I'm also happy just to be your friend. Friendship is what lasts."

I thanked him for understanding and we continued on the ride feeling closer as friends. Cleaning up at the end of the day, however, Jerry commented that while I said *now* that I only wanted friendship, he wasn't going to give up hope on more. He was confident that I'd come around.

Okay, I thought, *I'm going to have to work at this one.* Clear, continued, consistent communication was required. And still, Chaco the stallion and I continued to bond on our rides, and Jerry kept up his comments. I persevered in speaking my truth, and let him have his own response. And I began to see how his persistence was a strategy that could pay off for him, as our friendship deepened and my appreciation for his wisdom and insights increased.

Consider your BATNA, I cautioned myself, *and do not accept less than you want because one aspect is good.*

My head swiveled around the room. *Who is THAT?*

I was at a Thunderbird party in a shiny suite high above the Las Vegas Strip, and had spent the earlier part of the evening debuting my new svelte and sexy self with friends I hadn't seen in years—and dodging the attentions of one over-zealous acquaintance.

Seriously, who was that man by the door? I hadn't seen him earlier, and did not recognize him from Thunderbird. A bit older than the crowd, he looked comfortable in a worn blazer and faded jeans. Shaggy blondish-brown hair framed the handsome face of the Marlboro Man, and an aura of relaxed confidence enveloped him. The only thing missing was the cowboy hat. *Yum.*

I had just driven twelve hours across the deserts of New Mexico and Arizona, crossing the Hoover Dam before arriving at the madness of Planet Hollywood in the alternate universe of Las Vegas. My day had begun clearing snow off the car in the predawn dark of Taos, cautiously driving down the canyon towards Sante Fe and warmer temperatures. Past Albuquerque, the expanse had opened up rosy orange desert vistas empty of man's presence, which had eased me into deep meditation for most of the drive. My channels were clear and open.

Matthew was his name I learned when a friend introduced us. He was an ex-pat friend from Costa Rica, a surfer who dabbled in real estate and produced most of his food from a sustainable garden on his land.

The electric connection was intensified by the following day at the Hard Rock pool and some very direct conversation. "Am I acceptable to you?" he asked, as we sat on the pool edge, thighs touching and feet soaking in the water, cowboy hat perched on his head.

"Oh yes, indeed, you are."

Luckily for my commitment to celibacy for the year, two days of hard partying caught up with him and he crashed early, missing the evening's events. The weekend wrapped up with an invitation to stay with him when I returned to Costa Rica in January.

"I'll make you breakfast with eggs from my own chickens," he offered. Mercy.

Driving back to Taos, I felt my mood getting heavier and heavier the closer I came. Being around fellow Thunderbirds had always energized and focused me on my life's passions. Conversation kept turning again and again during the weekend to Spain. Mónica was planning a trip to visit her cousin in Madrid, another friend had recently returned, and I had renewed conversations with close friends about a business idea in the country. My familiar longing to be in Spain had reemerged along with other passions. What if I considered ending my year's sabbatical where the idea originated?

My first day back in Taos, Lisa and I decided to rent a movie and *Vicky Christina Barcelona* toppled off the shelf at my feet. Very interesting.

Watching the movie, I felt my longing intensify and decided to listen to my intuition. The next morning, I did an Internet search and immediately found two viable and economical writer's retreats in Southern Spain. An hour or so later, I heard back that there was space in one starting in a week. The retreat boasted a proprietor who was a yogi, an extensive library of both literary and yoga books, and access to a yoga studio and an organic market just a ten-minute walk down the mountain road. A quick check of airfare found me a highly discounted ticket to Malaga. I packed up my things, loaded the car, and Lucy and I sped back to the East Coast for an early Thanksgiving celebration with family before departing for Spain.

Interestingly enough, on my farewell ride with Jerry he gave me his cranky old mare to ride. When a man no longer lets you ride his stallion, you know he's gotten the friend message.

14.
Sabbatical or Life Change?

I learned a lot during my year's sabbatical. One of the key lessons was that one year was not enough.

As I prepared to return home from my writer's retreat in Spain, I found a position posted on my grad school job board that looked as if it was meant for me. Using the writing skills I had spent the last month honing, I drafted a clear and persuasive cover letter and sent in my résumé. When I woke up the next morning, there was an email from the organization looking to schedule an immediate interview. I explained that I was travelling and we scheduled a phone interview for after I returned.

The job was for a well-known environmental lobbyist organization, spearheading the marketing for a high-profile new program working with organizations on socially responsible and sustainable initiatives. There were big-name celebrities attached to the project, as well as a number of leading corporations. Everything in my background indicated that this position would be the logical next step for me.

Early on in the interview, warning signals began flaring up in me. The political and corporate speak that I heard coming through the earpiece about competencies and deliverables and job grading and lines of reporting physically assaulted me. The ego and the lack of clear vision from the man who would be my boss raised more flags. My instincts screamed that I did not want to go back to speaking that language, that my energy was better spent on a different path where I was engaged with the concerns of real people rather than on corporate jockeying and positioning.

Following the call, I reviewed my finances and decided that I would continue my time off and devote it to completing the writing

I had started. What I was doing was no longer a sabbatical; it was a full-out radical life change. A new beginning.

So what had I learned about myself and what nurtured and supported me? I spent January tucked into my family's cozy beach cottage integrating my experiences and practicing gratitude for all of the beautiful people who crossed my path.

Necessities of life after one year on the jungle path:

- A yoga mat and time to practice
- An uncluttered space
- A deep, hot soaking tub
- A romantic relationship with the right man
- A morning walk in nature
- A home that feels comfortable
- A goal to work towards
- The belief that I am exactly where I need to be
- Peace and privacy, as well as ready access to a like-minded community
- An abundant income

Not so much really, I thought, amazed at the simplicity. It takes concentrated energy to determine what you want. Once expended, however, you can relax, place yourself in circumstances likely to contain what you want, and observe what life presents you until the right situation manifests. Your energy can be focused productively on other areas.

15.
Costa Rica, Year Two

Looking out the airplane window framing the jungle trees and the blue ocean far below, I set my intentions for this second journey to Costa Rica. This trip would be all about having fun, being open, exploring, and surrendering. It was time to start some new practices.

By the time the wheels hit the tarmac, I was ready for whatever would present itself, particularly the sexy man I had arranged to meet that evening in Playa Flamingo. I would have some play time before I returned to the transformational cauldron of Nosara.

Walking around his broken-down, half-finished home littered with garbage, I wondered if perhaps I'd been a little hasty in my enthusiasm about Matthew. It does pay to get to know someone better before jumping in. You never know if attraction is going to go deeper than appearance, and I was someone who needed more, even for a casual relationship.

Choosing to go a year without sex is hard in any circumstance. Going a year without sex when all of your senses are awakening and you are in the midst of a creative explosion is torture. Matthew was the first powerful connection I'd felt in a long time, and I got carried away in the pure promise of it.

I was going to be open-minded, see what developed without expectation, and just go with the flow. Despite the rather disgusting interior of the house, the outside was as well cared for as a garden with a groundskeeper. Vegetables, herbs, fruit trees, and more were healthy and productive. And we still had great energy, bumping, nuzzling, and kissing as we hung out, relaxed, and enjoyed talking and cooking.

However, there was another thing that I hadn't known about him. Matthew was an alcoholic. He had decided to go sober about fourteen days before I arrived. Perhaps I served as a healing force for him, a new incentive to regain some ground in his life. Who knows? Earlier in my life, I may have gotten sucked into that drama, but I had done enough work by now to know that I wanted a whole healthy man. I did not want to be my man's healer; that was a different kind of bond. I also needed a serious infusion of male energy, and his was taken up completely in his own healing process. It became quickly apparent that this was not going to be the release I needed from my year's celibacy.

I left for Nosara, grateful for the lessons and looking forward to going to the place that had been my most recent home.

Back in Guiones. Yesterday, upon arrival, it felt just like home, like the day before I had walked down the dirt roads a part of the community. Today I felt outside, an intruder at someone else's party. So much time had passed in the five months that I had been gone—Costa Rican time, where every moment is lived and experienced. People around me seemed focused and directed, moving forward, while I was stuck floundering for solid ground.

Emotions go up and down and all around here, I thought, *jarring like the wooden roller coaster on Coney Island. I'd forgotten about that, how the powerful energy of this place takes hold as the heart begins to open.*

I felt so lost. I had started this journey the year before with so much hope, believing that the future was wide open ahead of me and that the courage and power of my leap would take me where I needed to go. I felt like I'd lost that. I needed a purpose for being there.

What was my new practice? Oh yes, surrender.

The dislocated feeling continued even after several days back in Guiones. It felt soothing and natural for a while, an overwhelming sense that this was where I needed to be. The next moment, all I wanted was to be out of its container and the supercharged energy. It was too limited and did not have enough outlets for fun and flirting. I had energy to release, goddammit, and it wasn't going to happen here!

I called my friend Mónica, feeling claustrophobic. "Let's do a roadtrip, see other parts of the country." We agreed to go in two weeks and, with an outlet in sight, I could relax and enjoy the remainder of my time with my friends in Nosara.

I lay on the chiropractic table, listening to the volley of rapid-fire questions. No answers were needed from me verbally, they were all being given by my muscular reactions as Dr. Sheel tested resistance in my arms and legs.

Dr. Sheel Tangri came highly recommended by my yoga teachers and various healers living in Nosara. While trained as a chiropractor and kinesiologist, his practice was a combination of those areas and acupuncture, craniosacral therapy, reflexology, and neuro-linguistic programming. His specialty was called neural organization technique, and his therapy was to clear traumas to the nervous system. Mine, apparently, had frozen in a fight-or-flight state, which was impeding my ability to receive and act on the guidance I was given.

My problem, according to Dr. Sheel, was that I was disconnected from spirit because I had never really bought into being here in this lifetime. I was allowing myself to be powerless for fear of causing harm to others, based on experiences in previous lives. It was time for me to break the cycle. I needed to stop fearing judgment and forgive myself so that I could fulfill my life purpose and balance my karma.

"Stay in the present and stop trying to figure out the future. Trust that you know everything you need to know at every moment. Open yourself to receive."

All familiar messages, coming at me from just about everywhere I turned these days.

My time with Matthew had left me feeling restless and over-energized. To say I was sexually frustrated would be a gross under-statement. I was vibrating with energy, shaktified, and needing an outlet for release. For the first time in my life, my mojo felt like a tractor beam.

On the night of the new moon, my housemate Stacy and I went to the beach to set and release our intentions for the month into the ocean. The tide was exceptionally low and the sand stretched out for a mile to the water's edge, little pools in mini-dunes reflecting the star grid above. The wind rippled my hair and clothing as well as the paper containing my intentions, as water gradually covered my feet. The thought that we were alone in the universe seemed impossible when presented with the enormity of space above.

I chose to declare two intentions for February. The first was to manifest my life partner according to my updated Right Man BATNA, which had gone through significant revisions and additions since spending time with Matthew. The second intention was to help with the more immediate problem. For that one, I would manifest a mind-blowing, earth-shattering, playful, delicious, and satisfying re-lease of my sexual energy within two weeks.

With that in mind, Stacy and I went dancing at a local bar for reggae night two nights later. As the music began to pulse, my energy channels opened and took over. Walking through the crowded bar to the dance floor, I felt the power in me focus into my second chakra and then expand out over the area. I could palpably feel the energy from every man around me and drew it in as if I were a supercharged magnet. As Stacy and I began to dance, I released my body to the mu-sic and observed the activity as men jostled around us, several joining to dance in our circle. I was vibrating at a frequency I had never felt before.

Walking back through the bar to get some air a few songs later, the dynamic continued. I passed a hot Tico surfer that I had noticed earlier in the week, sent a blast of energy at him, and saw him visibly move toward me.

It felt good to be a woman.

Every morning I was up with the sun, walking the beach by 7 a.m. as the first crew of surfers hit the waves. Focusing on alignment, I moved from my core so that my hips flowed loosely and freely, tight muscles letting go of their constriction. I placed each foot consciously, and hummed the melody that came naturally as I attuned to the beach and the waves. As the beach became more deserted, I started my chakra meditation, going into my breath and chanting each of the beej mantras while picturing the energy centers that are the chakras flaring with bright colors: red, orange, yellow, green, blue, purple, and brilliant white. It was several miles down to the rivermouth, where a giant boulder marked my turning point for the walk back.

Returning to the stretch of beach near the Harmony Hotel, I dropped my things on the sand, stripped off my red polka dot fedora and shook out my hair. The water called me and I walked into the ocean asking for her healing and grace, one goddess to another. And then I frolicked joyfully, much like Lucy had done the year before. I dove under giants waves, smiling broadly as I came up and floated on my back, laughing as waves crashed on me and filled my mouth and nose with water.

Flowing out of the water and up the wide beach, I shook out my hair and sat in meditation for a few moments before surrendering to the sand. When it felt like time, I gathered my things and walked back to my casita to begin the day.

"You and Grace are the hottest things on the beach," my friend informed me, according to the buzz from her surfer boyfriend.

Huh? I'd never been the hottest anything anywhere before, and I was just being myself natural and free. *Amazing what focusing on my own energy can do,* I thought, feeling more confident than ever in my life.

I lay on yet another massage table, and focused on my breath. My teacher Jane was giving me an energy healing and chakra balancing session.

"There is something still stuck here," she said, as her hands hovered a few inches over the approximate location of my second chakra. "Tell me."

"When I was fourteen, I was molested. I got into a black van with strangers and my friend Maureen, and then smoked a lot of pot. All I remember of what ensued were blunt fingers, a sweaty body, and a feeling of violation. It was my first sexual experience."

Wow. Where did that come from? I'd never spoken it aloud to anyone ever before, and had buried it so deep for most of my life that I barely remembered it.

"Yup, that's it," Jane said, as she went about clearing the stale energy out and replacing it with healing orange. "Things should flow much more freely now."

Part of my disconnection with Nosara and the community came from seeing a whole new crop of yogis going through all the trainings. They were immersed in the power of their own awakenings and experiences, of which I felt I was not a part.

Some quality time was needed with my teachers, I felt instinctively: another program to accelerate growth after almost a year of integrating the past year's teachings. I changed my flights and extended my stay in Costa Rica to be able to participate in an upcoming training that focused less on the asanas, or postures, and more on being an educator, a yogic life coach.

I chose to listen to my intuition, rather than the little voice of fear that cautioned about money and extending my homeless state at a time when I was beginning to crave security. Perhaps I had more to learn about living in uncertainty.

What had Dr. Sheel told me? Stay in the present and stop trying to figure out the future.

Direction, focus, perseverance, belief.

The airplane has flown and I was not on it, I thought. *Here I am, out of my comfort zone once again, floating free with a slight but sharp edge of fear. Feeling the need to be attached to something, anything, and breathing through it alone. Trusting that all will be well, that I know what I need to know now. Sitting with my discomfort, allowing it, but not attaching to it. Opening to receive what life offers me.*

My choices have been made for now. There is no point in revisiting them, worrying whether they were correct. I am on the path that I have chosen and there is no turning back. Put my energy into right now, living and experiencing my life as it happens.

Pep talk completed, I settled into Grace's home. I was grateful for her generosity while traveling, and to have my own space to be alone and free from other people's energy for a while.

The absolute peace of the jungle on a hot, still afternoon. Leaves rustling in the wind. The bird sounds, low and twittering, until a lonely, mournful whoop-trill breaks in and accentuates the tranquility. The wind picks up and crackles the growth before settling again into a softer sound. Heavy trucks occasionally grind their gears and thunder down the dirt road on the outskirts of town.

The previous year had been about being a lone wolf, cutting out all of the noise and getting quiet enough to actually hear myself. The transformations came fast and furious as I caught hold of a faint whisper and started trusting it.

I am afraid to rejoin society again, to lose the peace that I have found. The whisper, now a clear voice, suggested that perhaps a way to start was there in Nosara, with the support of my yoga family.

There was a single room available in Casa Rebecca, an ashram of yogis organized by the yoga institute. I would move in and begin to assimilate back into community living.

A sleepless night in the cell block. I will give it a few days to see how I adapt. I loved the community space of the ashram, the shared kitchen, the energy, and the conversations.

My room, however, was straight out of my nightmares. It was built on the jungle dirt, encased by foot-thick stone walls painted white, and crawling with insects. The door had no handle on the inside. To exit, I had to jam the key into the lock for leverage then pry the wood out of position with my fingernails.

Two more nights of horrible dreams, overwhelming claustrophobia, and the sense of being crushed alive while buried in the earth prompted the decision to move elsewhere. My instincts toward community were right, but the situation was not. I would move to my friend's casita next door to Grace for the remainder of my time in Costa Rica.

"You aren't seeing me," I kept saying. "You are so caught up in your own experience that you are not hearing what I'm saying."

I felt caught up myself in an ancient dynamic, triggers flaring the way they did through most of my adolescence with my mother. I would not give in to them now, as I had learned not to with my mother when she was triggered. The situation could not escalate if one party was conscious and responsible enough not to allow it.

"Grace, I empathize with your situation and the pain you are feeling. I was merely trying to share something important that happened to me, one friend to another. My words are not a reflection of you, or a veiled attack. I am trying to share with a friend about the incredible experience I have had, how empowered and healthy I am feeling. My words are not about you. I wanted to celebrate my joy with a dear friend."

"Please stop making my actions be about you. It leaves me with no room to be me."

She followed me as I left her porch and returned to mine. "I can't believe you would start something like this right before we go into a program," she accused.

"Stop playing the victim," I finally snapped. "You are much stronger than this. You are giving your strength away, for what?"

Something reached her. The tension drained from her face. "I'm sorry," she said. "It's been a difficult few months and I'm not quite myself."

"I know, honey," I said. "Remember last year, when you and Carlos got together? I totally made it about me, how you both had deserted me and turned myself into really pitiful victim until I got away and the cleanse helped me get some insight. We all have a tendency to do it when we are in pain. The trick is becoming conscious to when it is happening and making a different choice."

"Unfortunately, it happens frequently between women when we forget that we are all sisters and become jealous of what one has that we lack."

"Let's choose to support each other in growth and in pain," we mutually decided, bringing our relationship to a deeper level and cementing our friendship.

16.
Manifestation

Mónica was my teacher in the womanly ways of the Latina. She is a beautiful and sexy Mexican *bruja* with a warm, loving heart, and a fellow citizen of the world from Thunderbird. A decade of martial arts training, certification as a Thai massage therapist and a reiki healer, a burgeoning yoga practice, a conscious outlook, and an irrepressible sense of fun made her an ideal choice.

My transformational journey thus far had brought me to a place where I needed a mentor to develop my energy skills. My adventures had provided training on how to manage my own energy for optimal health, but I needed practical experience in the more interactive areas of dancing, flirting, and attraction.

All my life, I had been blessed with a natural prettiness and sparkle that attracted the men I wanted, but I had no idea how to use energy proactively. Other cultures instill the womanly wiles from birth, but my Irish-American Catholic upbringing from my mother's family did not impart such wisdom. Twelve years of Catholic school and a strict discipline based on punishing offenses versus rewarding initiative taught me to avoid notice. Mixed messages about what it meant to be a woman abounded, and several life experiences, including the first violating one that happened in the van, taught me that it wasn't safe to be attractive.

What I did learn was that being smart was the way to getting ahead, and I was programmed to succeed. The softer skills were not as important as intelligence and wit. That left me at about half power, as my feminine side suffered in favor of more masculine qualities. I needed balance to access my full potential.

I had reconnected with Mónica during my first trip to Costa Rica several years before, when she and her husband hosted a group of Tbirds for a Mardi Gras celebration. I had come on the trip after a powerful transformational workshop that had opened me up to life and the importance of releasing energy.

Checking that the harness was securely fastened, the guide hooked me to the cable and I jumped into space. The zipline hung high above the rainforest and stretched half a mile to a distant unseen platform on the next rise.

I howled from deep in my belly, releasing the fear inside me, as I flew down the cable and was eventually caught in the strong arms of a man. He quickly unhooked and then reattached me to another line, hurling me into space again before I had a chance to catch my breath.

The second time, my roar held less panic. By the third, I began to look around at the verdant jungle below, the beautiful lake glinting in the sun, the majestic volcano across the water. I began to laugh.

On the fourth platform, I was unhooked and made to wait for a few moments before continuing. My whole body was vibrating with adrenaline. Come on, come on, come on, I want more.

I screamed with laughter and joy during the remaining five ziplines, and wanted to begin all over again when it was finished.

The memory of that first trip to Costa Rica, and its significance in releasing fear and embracing courage, strongly influenced my decision to study yoga in the country.

Throughout my first year in Nosara, Mónica and I had numerous fun adventures and growth experiences. She and her husband lived in Playa Flamingo, about two hours north up the coast in a community mostly known for real estate development and partying. They were friends with Matthew and had hosted the Las Vegas party where he and I had met.

During a quick overnight layover in New York on her way back from the holidays in Madrid, Mónica and I had agreed to work together on a writing project. I was at a point where I needed a sounding board and some outside energy to fuel my efforts, and she was looking for a project to pull her through a difficult period. Her own energy needed a boost out of depression.

We had an agreement that our time spent working would be both productive and unconventional. Our work environment would be as fun as it was creative.

A road trip provided just such an opportunity, and I departed the mystical enclave of Nosara to meet Mónica for a last adventure before my next teacher training.

Before setting off with Mónica, I had accepted Matthew's invitation for another visit. Something didn't feel quite finished with him, and he had remained on my mind while in Nosara. I was going to listen to my intuition and see what I learned.

"You want to leave me here alone?" I asked him in disbelief.

I eyed the deserted beach, looking like Corona beer ad with a row of palm trees offering shade from hot sun, white sand, and blue ocean. Not much else in sight.

I had no money, no water, no phone, and no idea where I was. A beach somewhere near Playa Grande on the Guanacaste Peninsula of Costa Rica was as specific as I got.

He shoved the equivalent of five dollars at me, "I'll be back in two hours. Don't worry."

Already knowing from experience that he was not reliable about time, and feeling slightly worried about possible liability with my rental car, I expressed my concern. "I am not getting out of the car."

"What's the big deal? You wanted to go to the beach. Here is the beach, I'll be back in two hours."

"I wanted to go to the beach with you, the person who invited me to visit and spend time together."

The circle went round several times.

"Matthew, I need you to promise you will only be two hours. Do you give your word?" It had crossed my mind that perhaps this was an opportunity to work on my practice of trust.

After several commitments that he would indeed keep his word, I got out of the car and started walking away. I made the mistake of looking back and before I knew it was opening the car door again, asking for another reassurance. He looked at me like I was truly crazy.

"I'm not going to let this issue follow me through another life-time," I declared passionately to his bewildered face before slamming the door and walking resolutely away.

During the next two hours, I meditated in the shade, focused on my breath when I felt anxious, went to float on the big waves when I felt the need to move, and stayed in the present moment. At some point during my third or fourth trip to the ocean, I looked up saw Matthew coming towards me across the sand. He swam out to meet me near the breakers and we generated some pretty hot energy.

I had advanced in my practice of trust.

Shortly after we returned to his house, the relationship disinte-grated as if it had served its purpose and was no longer necessary. His mood turned dark and he acted as if he wanted to be alone. My ener-gy fed on his and we ended up fighting. I called Mónica and asked if I could crash with her before our scheduled road trip. Matthew apolo-gized as I packed up to leave, but it was clearly done for me when the energy shifted. My boundary had been crossed and I recognized it instinctively. Though I saw him again several more times during my stay in Costa Rica, I had no interest in rekindling despite his efforts.

Matthew taught me many lessons about what I did want, the tragedy of living with addiction, and how too much time spent alone can make you lose touch with other people's needs.

My Right Man BATNA, newly revised, after my visit with Mat-thew read:

- A man who teaches me to be a better person with his love
- A conscious, smart, sexy, strong man of integrity follow-ing a spiritual path and continually growing and stretch-ing
- A confident, committed, passionate, and focused lover and best friend who adores me and the abundant life we create together
- A proactive partner who is an open and clear communi-cator who helps me along my own path as I help him on his
- We share a powerful and sustainable bond of attraction; he is a good lover

- A natural embodied leader who is clear on his purpose and committed to it as well as to me

Mónica and I set off on a bright morning, driving south and ready for adventure. Colors and images, we decided, would be the theme for our writing project. Immediately these images began manifesting. Twenty-five grey crocodiles napping under a bridge, green groves of palms stretching from mountain to sea, gleaming golden sunbeams streaming through clouds, bikers in black heading south in packs.

We were on our way to visit her old friend from Mexico who lived in one of the most beautiful spots in Southern Costa Rica.

What do I want to manifest on this road trip? I thought. *A steady stream of quality, hot, focused male attention and loving.* I had energy to release, and a new moon intention to manifest.

He looked me up and down slowly, yoga sandals to red polka dots on my fedora, and then came back for a second look, and then a third after Mónica introduced us. His eyes focused.

Antonio was a joyous soul encased in smooth chocolate-milk skin, silky shaggy jet hair, comfortable in his athletic body and beautiful manly face.

Yes, I think you look pretty hot, too, I thought.

Later that night, Antonio tutored me in the particular type of poker he played with his friends, sitting close at the game table. I crashed out early, but stayed on next to him observing his hand and betting patterns for entertainment.

"You look like Sigourney Weaver in *Alien*," he commented during a break in the betting.

Later that night, Mónica and I settled into his apartment as Antonio ran some last errands. I showered quickly and came out in my little cotton nighty, surprised to see him and Mónica viewing pictures on his Mac. He shifted the laptop to show me as well, and I leaned across the back of the couch to look over his shoulder.

A drop from my wet hair rolled down his muscled brown arm as I leaned forward. We both watched it for a beat, before refocusing on the rest of the photos.

We all woke early the next morning to go whitewater rafting. Antonio appeared concerned about our level of experience in the category 5 rapids, but we were up for the challenge. Every time I looked up during the upper course of rapids, he was watching us in the white water.

"Time for swimming," he informed us as he paddled up in the slow water and jumped in himself. Suddenly, I felt my life jacket jerk as he pulled me into the river next to him. I came up laughing, as I had through every rapid so far.

Later on the beach, I drifted into my Nosara ritual of chakra meditation, sun salutations, and floating on the waves before joining Antonio's friends on the sand. He came up a few moments later, carrying his surf board and shaking out his wet hair.

After hearing the itinerary with his other guests, Mónica and I decided to take the time to see another friend of ours before meeting again in the evening.

Antonio met our car as we pulled up to the disco, coming to open the driver's door, and doing a doubletake at my transformation from beach bum to sexy dress. Dropping his hand to rest on my waist, he murmured that he'd be back as soon as he got his friends settled, blasting some delicious male heat on me as he trapped me between the open car door and his body.

"Are you confused?" he asked later as we tumbled out of the disco and onto the dirt road. Off balance, I leaned into him. It had been a long day of physical exertion followed by hours of dancing, and I had no energy for another club.

"What does Robin want?" he asked with smoky energy.

I looked away caught by the gleaming disk high above. "I want the moon," I answered, yearning towards it.

"And I want what Robin wants," he said, looking up, too, and pressing in.

He climbed into his beat-up Landrover, while Mónica and I dropped down into the small rental. We both made U-turns and ended up facing opposite directions.

He laughed, "Turn again and follow me."

Shoes off, door open, lights on, and into the apartment. Our host went to the kitchen, I sat on the couch, and Mónica went into the bathroom.

Antonio glided silently in.

"Well, you are going to get more confused now," he murmured as he straddled my knees, grasped my neck, and kissed me. As he leaned back smiling, his hand began a focused slide of dress up my leg.

A laugh burst out as I sucked in air and grabbed his wrist. "What are you doing?"

Looking into my eyes, he broke my grasp. "I'm making you more confused."

I am going to come right here right now, I thought, and found him watching me waiting.

Mónica clanked the bathroom door loudly before yanking it open.

I *was* confused with the way the late night was speeding along. I had felt it building all weekend, but knew that Antonio was not available. Yet, it was impossible not to appreciate what a beautiful man he was.

What was my intention here? The energy between us was very strong, and lord knew I needed the release. Be open, explore, have fun, and surrender indeed.

I leaned against the balcony rail in the silver bath of the full moon as I considered my situation. The radiant light gleamed on the tin roofs below, colorful houses shaded in grey, the Pacific glinting under the bright night sky.

Finally, I pushed away and went in to shower, fantasy firing and flaring. This was my short-term intention manifesting.

When I opened the bathroom door again I could hear voices in the kitchen. I quietly slipped into the guest room, shut the door lightly, and sat on the bed, wet hair streaming down my back.

Before the mattress settled, the door was yanked open and I was flat on my back.

"Where's Mónica?" I asked. He continued his assault.

"Where's Mónica?" I asked again. He hesitated for a second, got up and checked the living room, and closed the door.

His hands grasped the towel and stripped it off as he pressed me down again. His own clothes had disappeared. No time for thought. Immediately, he sought entry. I backed away preventing access. Again and again and again. With his arms, he banded me against him and thrust us both toward the headboard. A second wave. The new positioning made delay more difficult, as did the massage of his hard penis. Sound released deep in my throat as he pressed home...

"...tell me the most you've had before," Antonio demanded as I came down from my most recent orgasm.

"You've matched it," I managed to say, gasping for breath and wilting into the mattress after my fifth.

Twice more, just to be sure the record was properly shattered. Still he wanted another. "Please come with me," I pleaded, thinking I would soon expire.

The next morning was casual. I had slept like the dead, and apparently missed two shifts of activity. The other group of visitors had already been picked up and ferried to the airport. Antonio and Mónica had breakfasted and completely caught up on each other's lives.

"You really slept through all that?" they asked in wonder.

"I told you I was tired."

Later, Mónica and I negotiated the road out of town before turning to each other to grin. It had definitely been worth the long wait.

Manifestation.

I was primed and ready for my next yoga awakening.

My Right Man BATNA, with subsequent revisions read:

- A man who teaches me to be a better person with his love and through our partnership something greater is created
- A conscious, smart, sexy, strong man of integrity following a spiritual path and continually growing and stretching
- A confident, committed, passionate, and focused lover and best friend who adores me and the abundant life we create together
- A proactive partner who is an open and clear communicator who helps me along my own path as I help him on his
- We share a powerful and sustainable bond of attraction; he is a good lover and we have frequent mind-blowing, earth-shattering, playful, delicious, satisfying sex
- A natural embodied leader who is clear on his purpose and committed to it as well as to me
- Available on all levels, free and clear from all other romantic attachments and looking for a life partner
- A man who steps forward and claims me

17.

The Inner Quest

My mojo meter crashed from about one million volts per second to about one. One step inside the rancho for the Inner Quest of the Yoga Educator, and my blazing energy converted from external to internal focus in the time it took to place my foot. It was time for again for some radical healing.

Coinciding with the energy shift was a corresponding jolt in my right hip, which popped out of alignment painfully. Very interesting.

"Your experience is the teacher," said Don Stapleton, as he described the learning environment he and his wife, Amba, would be leading during the two-week training.

"When the deeper experiences and understanding of yoga emerge from practice, it becomes obvious that everything we need to know is already inside of us. If your yoga practice is to take root beyond the formal classroom setting, then you, as a learner, need to take responsibility for the experiences that unfold from inside your own world."

Learning yoga requires that you slow down and enter the present moment, the eternal now. The ordinary sense of "I" recedes into the background as mental awareness becomes absorbed in the sensations of present experience.

However, while your physical body lives in the present moment, your mind is free to go anywhere into the past or future. To capture the attention of the mind and to draw it back to the sensations in your body, you need to provide something interesting and worthwhile for the mind to observe. Your mind needs a job to do. So you give it the job of watching the sensations in your body. It begins to slow down and anchor on the bodily sensations, and that awareness becomes a bridge to join your mind and body.

"As a yoga educator," Don taught, "the goal is to take our students on a multi-dimensional journey that engages each layer of the body in the experience. There are many tools we can use to do so, including movement, breath, color, sound, visualization, and intention.

"It all begins," he said, "with building trust—a sacred space—within your class, your community."

Trust.

Very interesting. The quality named on the slip of paper I drew walking into the rancho that morning, which would determine who would be my yoga guide for the day's deep exercise. It was also a core issue in my life.

Sho wandered by, carrying his matching slip of trust.

He was tall and handsome, with a thick head of salt and pepper, and a showman's big personality, which had originally put me off. In fact, the only thing bigger than his personality was his enormous loving heart, which I was about to see for the first of many times. The universe had very deliberately placed us in each other's paths, starting years before we actually met with the strange coincidence of living just one block away from each other in Manhattan. How we never ran into each other in our fairly contained neighborhood was a mystery.

We sat together on the floor and prepared for the exercise, each of us struggling to build the trust required to go deep.

"Your eyes are so dark, I can't see the pupils," he said. "Can I trust you?"

I breathed slowly, calmly, and smiled into his eyes. "Yes, you absolutely can."

Going into his experience first, I allowed intuition to guide me, using words and energy to facilitate. His heart creaked open a bit, receiving being an uncomfortable activity for him as well.

When my turn came, I relaxed into the bond we had formed through his openness and went deep quickly. Without conscious thought, I shared my most intimate fears about being unlovable based on experiences of broken trust with my father and with Tom. His beautiful voice murmured directly into my ear, soothing and guiding me.

Half an hour or so later, I gradually became aware of other sounds, as Don guided the group toward completion and into the closing circle. Still speaking softly in my ear, Sho brought me back to the room. I opened my eyes, which were caught first by Don's light filled ones and then by the smiling love coming from each of the men in the program. Sho helped me to my feet and we joined the circle.

Throughout the closing ceremony, bubbles of laughter tickled up and out my mouth in uncontrollable bursts. The world had never looked brighter.

Courage.

To complete the course, we would celebrate three days of yoga creativity, with teams of four working together to teach a two-hour class providing a multi-dimensional guided yoga experience.

My group had drawn the theme of courage, as well as the very last class slot. That position in itself was guaranteed to grow the quality in me, as I strongly preferred leaping first into exercises to get my portion over with. Expectations were lower if there was nothing else to be judged against, and I had lived a lifetime trying to measure up to expectations.

Sitting with discomfort seemed to be a theme for this second year in Costa Rica. I surrendered to the class order.

I decided to take a new approach along with the novel position of being last. I thoroughly enjoyed and absorbed the creativity and beauty of the other classes. Working with my group in developing our own class, I restrained my tendency to strongly lead group discussions in favor of a more feminine approach. I consciously softened the expression of my opinions and allowed others the freedom to contribute in the way they wished, while focusing on my own portion. My leadership centered on making the class a cohesive whole, keeping the transitions smooth, and the overall impact and theme of each section combined.

Trusting my own process, I allowed my portion to evolve through intuition. An angel card drawing suggested that my focus be on music, so I developed a Yin Yoga class to clear the chakras by engaging all of the koshas. As ideas came to me, I wrote them down and eventually they took shape into a multi-dimensional experience incorporating colors, words, images, music, and vibration. Specific songs with lyrics representing the issues of each chakra were used as the *drishti,* or focal point, for meditation, and gratitude toward members of the community was used as the healing agent.

My section began our group's class, and I introduced the theme of courage speaking from my heart before channeling my class. I don't remember much of the experience beyond the peaceful energy in the room.

"Your words are like scripture to me," my guru, Don, told me privately after the class was completed. His words were a treasured gift to me, as I felt my open heart fill with the confidence to teach and write.

Home.

"Close your eyes and focus on your breath. Connect with your prana body and ask it to take you on a journey," instructed my teacher Amba. "Picture yourself in your home, clearing out all of the furniture and things. See it as an empty space. Now begin to fill it with the things you want in your life, redecorate the space to suit who you are now."

I lay on the floor, feeling every ridge in the wood, every insect in the jungle landing on me. I could not connect with my energy body. I could not picture home.

A tight band of frustration squeezed my heart. I have no home. *I don't know where I'm going when I fly home to the States in three days. I can't do this.*

Surrender. Stop trying to force it. If you can't see anything, then just focus on your breath. Three counts to fill up the belly, three counts to fill up the ribs, three counts to fill up the chest. Reverse the process with your exhale. I slowly calmed. An image arose in my consciousness.

Suddenly I was lying in a bed with my nose pressed into the crinkly chest hair of the man I loved. We had just made love and were glued together, connected and close. I could feel the dampness of our skin where it clung together, and heard the steady pounding of his heart. White walls were all I could see of the room around me.

Home was to be found in intimate connection with the right man. I saw that I could be happy living anywhere and adapt to most circumstances that met my core needs. I didn't need to be specific about anything else. I created my vision of home.

"Waking in my own body's time next to the man I love, his hairy chest tickling my nose. Making love feeling connected and close in a room streaming with light and colors of flowers and nature outside and all around. Gently dressing and going outside for a walk in nature surrounded by trees and views of the sea. Coming back refreshed and sitting at my desk and creating the day working on my projects, both written and otherwise."

The future would sort itself out as long as I was clear on what I wanted to manifest, focused my attention on it, and just started walking.

"I see so much of myself in you," Don beamed at me as we said goodbye at the end of the course. The approval I saw in his eyes reminded me of what I had stopped seeing in my own father's eyes, and healed something deep inside of me.

⚘

A last walk at sunset provided two final gifts before I closed the chapter of my second year in Costa Rica. Brenton, a beautiful man from the training, paddling out on the orange and gold water with his little daughter tucked in front on his surfboard, burned a vision of fatherly love into my memory. It vividly brought the image of my own father walking me at a similar age around home on the tops of his shoes, dancing and laughing.

It was becoming clear that my relationship with my father needed to be healed, and that I could make that happen through the power of love.

Smiling, I continued my walk thinking about my father, Spain, and my ongoing desire to walk El Camino de Santiago. Was I ready to commit to it? It felt like an important part of my healing. It also meant prolonging my journey and keeping a more grounded home on the back burner throughout the remainder of the year.

As I walked along, lost in my thoughts, I glanced down. A giant red scallop shell, the enduring symbol of pilgrims walking El Camino, lay at my feet looking prehistoric and out of place on the Costa Rican beach.

Signs are everywhere, and I had experienced such joy in following them over the past year and a half.

I would follow this one, too.

Believe

"Sometimes I feel the fear of uncertainty stinging clear and I can't help but ask myself how much I let the fear take the wheel and steer/ It's driven me before and it seems to have a vague haunting mass appeal/ But lately I'm beginning to find that I should be the one behind the wheel"
—Drive/Incubus

Personality Body (*Mana-maya-kosha*)

The personality body is the control system that directs our thoughts and emotions, built over the course of our life based on the meaning we assign to the events that we experience. This layer of the self is also called the ego, which has as its main concern our individual survival. When overly identified with it, we manifest illness and unhappiness by becoming rigidly attached to the way we think things are instead of seeing there are many perspectives. When operating from this "me-focus", we lose sight of the impact we are having on other people. Achieving happiness and well-being relies on our ability to see that there is something deeper than that control system that is our internal essence or spirit. Awareness that we are not our thoughts and emotions—that we actually create them—enables us to actively create the life we want. This allows us to be powerful, instead of powerless, in the face of what life presents.

18.

Free Your Mind and the Rest Will Follow

I opened the door and slipped out into the early morning quiet, not even a dog barking at this hour. Sunrise came late in this part of Spain and the full moon still hung low over the mountains. I climbed the slight hill of the driveway and caught my breath as I always did at the view from the road. In the moonlit dark, the hills rolled away with stars of light I knew to be small white houses, but which appeared as a reflection of the night sky above.

The road ran over a narrow mountain ridge, and I followed it in the dark, sensing my way as I had learned to do on the dirt roads of Costa Rica. Breathing in the quiet stillness of the heavens, I gave thanks again for my year of discovery and experience since leaving my corporate life in Manhattan.

The crunch of my boots on the cracked pavement was the only sound as I walked towards Orion's Belt hanging high above Masamullar. Round the first bend, and then the next, I encountered not a soul until the flashing of lights up the mountain indicated that a car would soon pass. Bright beams flickering as it made the hairpin turns down from Comares, the car reached me as I turned onto the final stretch to Los Ventorros where the street lights began.

The white houses in the village were dark and quiet. I stopped by the wrought-iron table outside La Duende, where we sat in a circle for tea after each yoga class, and waited quietly for Sarah and the bus.

Sarah stayed in a series of rooms above my yoga teacher's shop and studio, and ran her German translation business from there for now. Originally from West London, she was a fellow traveler searching for her place in the world. Tall with dark hair framing a face that could have been my mother's in her youth, she was a marathoner who had also found yoga in recent years as a balance and a ballast. She was a veteran of Comares, and was showing me the ropes.

With the edges of three euros creasing my palms, I saw the arc of lights high up in Comares signaling that the bus had begun its journey just a moment before the muted engine roar broke the morning stillness. A gate door clanked quietly as Sarah joined me on the street, and we watched the long descent as the bus disappeared and reappeared before eventually rumbling to a stop in front of us.

It was a huge diesel machine with large mirrors like grasshopper antennas sprouting from both sides, a modern anomaly on the narrow road of the old village. The hydraulics hissed as the door slowly swung open, and I clambered up the steps after Sarah, releasing the coins from my palm to the driver's in exchange for a paper receipt.

Sarah claimed seats in the fifth row, behind a scattering of villagers tucked compactly into their regular spots.

"They invested a lot into putting in the string of street lights through the village," she said. "I don't know why they haven't put any money into actually fixing the road or building guard rails. The road is quite bad for the first twenty minutes."

With that warning in mind, we passed out of the light and made our way from the relatively flat ground of Los Ventorros into the mountains. Curiously, I watched the road unfold in the short beams from the bus. It looked about five-feet wide and was heavily pocked and patched. The giant bus wheels bounced as it accelerated slightly and then swung out wide, lights disappearing into a deep void of darkness before lurching back to face the sheer mountain wall. Struggling to regain my stomach from the first vertical drop, the second and third were upon us. Twenty minutes, I reminded my now wide-awake senses.

Accelerate, swing, hover in space, lurch back.

The rhythm also brought the regulars to life, who flashed an ongoing volley of rapid-fire Spanish with Pablo, the bus driver.

Shouldn't Pablo be paying strict attention to the road? Isn't he driving a bit fast for the road conditions? Isn't this huge modern bus too big for these old roads? Why didn't they make better roads? How many more turns are there? It couldn't possibly be like this the whole hour drive, could it? Why are the regulars talking so loudly? DOESN'T ANYONE NOTICE WE ARE IN A PRECARIOUS SITUATION?

Stop, I told myself. *Remember the calm quiet of the morning so far. You really have no control over this situation, so stop trying to assert any. The only thing that you can control is your reaction. Now look, the sky over the Mediterranean is turning a stunning color of red. Isn't that beautiful?*

You can choose to notice the beautiful or you can attempt to control the uncontrollable.

The fact that Pablo had been driving this route for many years, and was still alive and unmaimed, and actually laughed very frequently, gave support to the argument. The villagers, who put their faith in Pablo's driving on a regular basis, were not at all concerned with the speed or the spins out to the void and back. From the Spanish I could understand, they were more concerned with whether their baker in Malaga would have the Christmas tart.

Seems kind of silly to waste my time being upset when I'm only in Spain for a month, I thought, and relaxed into the ride. The scarlet sunrise really was magnificent.

I made a choice that day. I chose not to fear. I chose to love myself by having a pleasant experience.

Recognizing that I had that choice, that *I* was in charge *not* my fear, was an awareness that had taken me many years to learn. At a certain point in my life, I asked a crucial question: What would happen if I simply faced my fear instead of running from it?

To do that, I needed to have faith that I was supported, that I was loved. And then it would be a simple choice: to believe in fear or to believe in love.

That bears repeating, one hundred times a day, for every decision: Do I choose love or do I choose fear?

Now to feel comfortable making that choice, I needed to have a pretty clear understanding of who I was and what love meant to me. I'm talking real love, the beautiful, accepting, clear kind. Love without ego.

I also had to know and recognize my fears, without judging myself for having them. Herein lay the conundrum. Could I separate the fear instinct from the trigger, the specific action/word/feeling that raised it? To do that I had to develop the skill of discrimination through detachment, observation, recording, and learning. There are many practices that help to develop that skill. I found yoga and meditation worked best for me.

And how could I know my mind, unless I was separate from it, in charge of it? My yoga training gave me the perfect analogy: Think of it as if a little electric light bulb (your mind) would declare "I am the electric current" and then proceed to describe electricity as a pear-shaped glass object containing filaments of wire. We have the same type of distinct current, our essence or spirit, which illuminates and directs our mind and emotions. Tapping into that source enables us to make clearer choices by consciously creating our thoughts.

Once I made that distinction, the game was on. All I needed to do was strengthen it through regular practice.

I am not my mind. I am not my emotions. I have a choice about what I will think and what I will feel.

Power.

The minute I let go of indecision, I had it. I could create my world.

19.

Sweet Child of Mine

"Daddy, were you like the Fonz?" I asked him, sprawled on the floor in my footie pajamas and picking through the box of old photographs. I held out my favorite picture and one of the few from his youth. My dad sat on a motorcycle, scowling, with dark hair slicked into a pompadour looking like a Spanish version of the coolest character from my favorite TV show, *Happy Days*. He was so handsome with his fierce dark eyes and his white tee-shirt, jeans, and leather jacket. "Did you take Mommy for rides?"

"No, honey, that's when I was a teenager," my father replied, "before I met your mother." He had grown up on the rough streets of 1950's Newark, New Jersey, lightyears away from my mother in her private all-girls Catholic school in wealthy Summit, just a few towns over. Driven to find a better life than those streets offered, he had worked his way through college to graduate as a chemical engineer, despite a deep love for nature and an early desire to work for the national parks. He put aside his personal preferences to build a successful career and family.

"Was this the wedding where you and Mommy met?" I asked, pulling out my second- and third-favorite photos. One was an awkward shot of a groomsmen and bridesmaids in fancy clothes, all strangers except for a young version of my father and mother at opposite ends of the picture. The third was of my parents at their own wedding, looking joyful and in love and ready for the top of a cake. "Did you really both have other dates when you met? When did you know you would get married?"

Swinging me up off the floor and walking me to bed standing on his shoes, he repeated the answers he had given many times before. "Time for you to sleep, young lady."

"Will you check the closet first for spiders, Daddy?" After a thorough check revealed a safe and empty closet, he kissed my forehead, turned on the nightlight and left the room. "Sweet dreams, honey."

Raised in the traditional way, with two parents whose love for each other and for their family was never in doubt, I grew up in a cocoon.

When my hip defect was discovered shortly after birth, I was fitted for a brace and our home was configured to minimize accidents or injury. I found a way to maneuver around so effectively that I never realized the extent of my injury until much later in life.

Summers were spent packed into a beach house on the Jersey Shore split by four of my mother's five siblings, cousins tumbling over each other like puppies and my sister and I leading the pack by virtue of age. Our neighborhood gang roamed the swamp behind our new development, commandeered the street for kickball in the afternoons, caught lightning bugs and played flashlight tag in the warm evenings. Twelve years in Catholic school ensured that we were brought up with a strong sense of morality, a clear definition of what was right and what was wrong.

In sum, I was born an average American into a family of the children of immigrants, steeped in the Ellis Island/Irish Catholic tradition. I had a fairly charmed life with none of the tragedies that many less fortunate children face. There was no addiction, no desertion, no physical or sexual abuse, no poverty to cause trauma as a child.

Despite all of that, I grew up afraid.

My first memories of fear were transmitted from mother to daughter, a trill of alarm blasting from her that drilled into my heart. The alarm came in all kinds of situations. The common pattern among them was that they involved something new, something unknown, or a choice point: a situation out of my mom's control or comfort zone.

As an empathetic child, unconscious of choice, I started choosing fear. I learned to fear the unknown, to control what I could and feel alarm when confronted with an unknown situation.

The fear first manifested itself in a major way when it was time for me to venture from the family sanctuary and join the society of my peers in kindergarden. I was terrified of being alone in the unknown place and of being separated from my mother.

Picture a small girl, big brown eyes and dark wispy braids brushing each shoulder, released only the year before from a hip brace she had worn since infancy. I was as comfortable waddling on the floor like a tadpole as I was with walking. Time for my first day of school, and I was very frightened of leaving home—and adamant that I would not go.

A promise is made to comfort me, to get me on the bus. Jeannie, my best friend, will be in my class, my parents assure me. "No need to fear, you will not be alone."

The school officials had other plans. Upon arrival, I went off into one section, Jeannie to the other. I began to cry, and cry I did every day as if my heart was broken. Crying in a way that disrupted class, I was made to stand in a corner by the front blackboard until I was better behaved, in control of myself. Every day for weeks, I stood and cried while the other children watched and the teacher scolded.

I am alone. I am different. I cannot trust my parent's word. Expressing emotion is shameful. All this I decided without rational thought and began to live it as my truth.

Even with the best of intentions, promising a child something that you cannot deliver can have a profound effect on their world and who they become as a person.

Around the same time that this happened, my grandfather died and my grandmother moved in with us, lost her eyesight to diabetes and her mind to dementia. I had nightmares about going blind myself, being trapped in darkness, cut off from the world, and losing touch with reality.

Later, as an adolescent, two key events shaped my outlook. Sitting in the bathroom stall my first month of high school, I overheard several of the older girls laughing about me and some others in my class. "What goody-goodies!" they scoffed. Residue from my shameful and alienating first introduction into the school system prompted my decision to radically alter who I was in order to fit in. If being smart and good was not cool or popular, then I would be neither. I assumed a tough persona, a hard shell to protect my soft core, and began to smoke cigarettes, drink alcohol with my friends, smoke pot, and let my grades drop.

When I was fourteen, I was molested in the black van. As a rebellious teenager, I had made another stupid decision. I had decided to get into that black van with strangers and my friend Maureen and then to smoke a lot of pot. From that day forward, the event's soundtrack, Pink Floyd's album *Dark Side of the Moon,* never failed to induce a feeling of darkness and despair in me.

I learned two key lessons that particular day that have been difficult to unlearn. The first was that I needed to maintain control over my environment so something like that never happened again. The second was that the world was not safe.

"Daddy, please come get me. I'm scared and I don't know what's happening," I cried into the phone toward the end of my first semester at university.

One November evening, I found myself hovering above my body on the dorm room bed in the midst of a massive panic attack. Suddenly faced with a million decisions, looming adulthood, and the loss of an established community, my fears had spiraled out of control. What had begun as dizzy spells in lectures and claustrophobia in confined places had blossomed into a generalized fear of being out of control.

Life had been very simple for me up to this point, and my day-to-day decisions had been fairly limited. Breaking out of the cocoon was a confusing and frightening process, without the safe borders that had previously marked my territory.

When I hung up the phone with my father that November evening, I realized that life was going to change. I had always buried my fear deep inside, and understood now that I couldn't keep doing so. It had broken free of its cage.

My father drove six hours to get me at the university the next morning. Once home, I was diagnosed with agoraphobia, an anxiety disorder about being in places or situations that I could not control or from which escape may be difficult. I returned to my parent's house for treatment, choosing not to go on drugs to mask the anxiety, but rather to address the fear at its source through therapy and desensitization techniques.

I thrust my foot out, blocking the elevator doors from closing.

"I'm not ready," I said to my therapist. "Can't we just stand here with the doors open?" Somehow the thought of being enclosed in the metal box filled me with terror. What if there was a malfunction and the doors didn't open again? I would be trapped!

"Breathe," my therapist instructed, "and continue breathing through your discomfort as the doors close. We will only ride one floor at a time until you are comfortable with the fact that the doors will again open. What's the worst that could happen if they didn't open?"

Good question. It could get hot, we would have to stand or sit on the floor for an undefined period. I would not be trapped forever, someone would eventually rescue us. It wouldn't physically harm or kill me, it would only inconvenience me. My own thoughts about it were the biggest threat.

It was a question of surrender and trust. I let the doors close.

Thanks to the support of family and friends, I was able to resume my study at university only one semester behind.

"You make us proud," my father said gruffly, as I prepared to go back to school. "You're the smartest of the bunch. Go do well."

I also grew up refusing to let anything stop me.

Born with the ball of my right hip joint perched at the top of the socket instead of firmly within it, I came into this world with a challenge to conquer. I was fitted with a V-shaped metal brace that forced the joint into proper position by spreading my legs wide open. I wore it from infancy through my second year, when it was relegated to a nighttime-only confinement until age four when we moved to England.

No brace could stop me, my mother used to laugh, as she'd hear me clunk out of my bed, waddle across the floor. Coming running she would find me at the top of the stairs as I turned to shimmy down clanking the V of my legs from side to side and dragging my torso with my arms. A beautiful darkhaired, bright-eyed, little tadpole, she described how I would draw people in with the joy of my smile glowing against the metal of my brace.

"We'll never have to worry about Robin getting what she wants out of life," my parents had joked as I grew, partly in exasperation partly with admiration. I had a fierce way of demanding what I wanted and didn't take kindly to being denied or not being able to do something well. The stereotypical middle child, I demanded attention and autonomy even though my family position qualified me as neither the first born nor the only son.

Combined with my strong will was a deeply ingrained sense of justice and a need to understand. If it didn't make sense to me, I wasn't going to do it. If the explanation provided didn't intuitively feel right, well someone was going to hear about it.

My upbringing, however, was designed to mold me into what my parents thought I should be: a good Catholic, an obedient daughter. I fought to be seen, I fought to be separate, I fought to have a right to have my own thoughts and opinions.

"I grew up with it," snarled my father, "I will not have it in my home!" His grip bruising the back of my neck, he dragged me away from my mother and our latest fight and hurled me into the garage. A good portion of my teens were spent in virulent disagreement with my mother, who was sensitive, defensive, and easily triggered by my defiant rebellion. While the labels of "fresh" and "insolent" that I had acquired were fairly accurate descriptors, my mother's tendency to hear anything I said through the filter of her own insecurities magnified our arguments, as did my own fears.

"That's not what I'm saying, you're not hearing me," I yelled in a manner that closely mimicked my father's own angry behavior. "You leave no room for me to be me," I declared dramatically.

I remember clearly the moment when I realized that I could take the power in the fights with my mother. It dawned on me that it took two to engage in these things. If I, as a sixteen-year-old, could come to that awareness, could step away as my mother pushed my buttons, then no fight could happen. A conflict needs two or more parties. The corresponding anger that came from my mother when I stopped reacting to her words fed my sense of power. By withholding, I could be powerful and build space for me.

When my own fear did knock me down a notch or two, I learned more valuable lessons about my own strength and the first practice of two activities that would serve me well in life. The first was the very beginnings of a meditation practice, used as a lifeboat to calm my anxiety instead of drugs and enable me to desensitize myself to fearful situations. Music and guided meditation became source of centering for me when encountering difficult and stressful situations in my life.

After returning home from my first semester at university, I reconnected with a friend from high school who was also rumored to be housebound suffering from agoraphobia. While I underwent treatment, I speeded up my own progress by mentoring her, being strong myself so that I could help another. I learned first hand how service to another heals you.

Arriving at the Berlin train station in the wee hours of the morning, Wendy and I propped our backpacks against the wall as pillows and stretched out on the floor in a low-traffic area. The youth hostel did not open for another several hours, and we were beat from spending eight hours on a hot and crowded train crammed with ten others into a compartment made for six.

It had been an interesting ride, starting with a tattooed hand offering a wicked-looking switchblade to open the bottle of wine we had brought to make the ride more palatable. Bouncing out of Amsterdam and across West Germany, we had arrived at the East German border without the proper paperwork and had to bribe the border official to sell us documents on the train. Though the Berlin Wall had just fallen, its remnants were still felt everywhere.

Now here we were in the middle of a strange new city, behind the disintegrating Iron Curtain, with no place to go.

Amazing how much I've grown, I thought, as I reflected back on my agoraphobia and the desperate need to have access to a safe and secure zone. *I will never again let fear stop me from experiencing life fully,* I promised myself, feeling powerful and brave.

The opportunity to go backpacking with my college roommate had come up suddenly after struggling through the painful breakup with my first real love. Though I had boyfriends throughout high school and college, I didn't give my heart or my virginity to anyone until my early twenties. I was still reeling from the aftermath of my first sexual relationship and the decisions I had made based on it.

I was ready to explore the world and get a fresh outlook on life, drinking in new experiences and absorbing the beautiful surroundings, different cultures, and interesting people we met.

I had found my new passion in travelling.

I rested my chin on my crossed arms, and gazed through the open train window at the turquoise sweep of the Mediterranean ambling by. Warm wind caressed my face and the scent of the sea combined with the cinder and metal smell of the railroad. I breathed in the view, completely in the present moment.

My mind wandered over the course of my tumultuous relationship with Dave, the discovery and exploration and ultimately the painful separation and feeling of rejection. For months, I had dreaded waking each morning, knowing that when I opened my eyes I would be confronted with his absence and the resulting feeling of desolation.

If it wasn't for that experience, I thought dreamily in the bright sunlight reflecting off the water, *I would not be here today. Everything in my life that has led me to this place right now has been worthwhile,* I decided.

I was just grateful to *be here now.*

20.
Lakota Sweat Lodge 2010

The flap shut and pitch black descended, a faint red glow turning the black to deep brown just above the hot stones. Fear spiked through me, raw panic.

Blindness. Claustrophobia. Isolation. Suffocating heat.

"Please," squeaked my little voice, "can't we leave the flap open just a little crack?"

"No, we need to seal the space," was the reply. "Do you need to sit next to Asil for comfort? Do you need to leave the lodge?"

We were buried in the earth, under a small dome structure covered in layers of burlap and skins, circled around a broad fire pit piled high with rocks that had been baking for hours in the huge bonfire outside. Ten men were crowded together on one side of the circle, a similar number of women kneeling in the dirt on the other.

"No," my voice squeaked getting slightly stronger. "I honor the intention and sacredness of this space, and will be alright." Sensing the two women bracketing me in the blackness, I asked, "Can you hold my hand?" Warm hands immediately clasped each of mine.

I was not alone trapped in the dark. I was supported. I released the electric current of my fear, and could feel the others immediately relax in the darkness. All energy was now available for focus on the healing intention. Adjusting my body into Child's Pose, pulling the towel over me to trap cool air near the earth, I surrendered to my breath and the searing heat. With *The light is within* as my mantra to occupy the mind, the visual of a glowing white lotus blossom in my heart to occupy my other senses, and the sound of my breath flowing in and out, I overcame fear.

White light slashed into the space, brightening the inside of my towel to a monochrome grey and bringing me back from wherever I had gone. What happened? Did someone have to leave?

I struggled from under the towel, as the cool air flowed into the cramped lodge and washed over my wet skin. Fifty minutes had passed and the first healing round was over. It felt like five minutes. Where had I gone?

"Will you be alright?" asked the leader before closing the flap again for the next of the four rounds.

"I'm perfectly fine," I replied. I was better than fine, I was giddy with my strength.

21.

Role Models

When you take on leadership of another human being, you have a responsibility to be conscious: to consider the impact of your actions on those you have been chosen to develop and the greater community of which you are a part. If you do not have the emotional intelligence needed to guide responsibly, it will be reflected in the responsibility of your charge.

Parents are the frontline of developing conscious citizens, and they are also humans on their own journey through life. They are a product of their own upbringing, and the lessons they have chosen to learn or not in life are passed along. Bottomline, they do the best they can from where they are.

❧

The most important thing that a mother can teach her daughter is about love. I could not have had a better teacher. My mother is a woman who embodies that virtue. I will be forever grateful for the gift of her in my life.

My mother is a beautiful woman, tall in stature and in presence, and with a solid warmth that emanates from her heart and shines through her hazel eyes. She is an artist who filled our home with funky little treasures, as well as many projects to support her children in developing our own creativity. She is a good and generous woman who regularly practices many small and selfless acts of kindness, deeply committed to her family and her faith. She holds a deep love of others that grieves to cause harm, discomfort, or offense by word or deed. She has been a bedrock, a confidante, and my biggest fan throughout my life. She is also the responsible oldest of five siblings in her own generation, a product of the '50s, and in many ways an innocent.

The second most important thing a mother can teach her daughter is how to set boundaries. Without that skill, life will be challenging. When a mother does not know how to set her own boundaries, the daughter learns by example.

Boundaries not set and held almost always mean that needs are also not communicated, and the anger and frustration built up from unmet and unexpressed needs must be released somehow. The women of my family learned to do so by flinging verbal daggers when triggered. Small, passive-aggressive comments helped to release the tension in small bursts, in a reflexive way that allows the one wielding the knife to ignore the true impact of her words. I saw them fly between my grandmother and mother, felt them hit their mark with me, and took my own collection of knives out into the world.

When words and behavior don't sync up, integrity and, therefore, trust can be lost. Then the daughter has learned two important lessons poorly: boundary setting and trust. Life becomes about sacrifice and fear. I learned that there was pain associated with love, that protection was required even from those closest to me.

Each child is different, and needs different things. When a mother stops seeing her daughter for whom she is and sees her instead through the filter of her own insecurities, she stops seeing what the child needs. Because of the bond between the two, it can be easy for the mother to make every action of the child be about her instead of recognizing the daughter as a separate entity with her own motivations, thoughts, and feelings. I fought for many years to be seen for myself, not as my mother's interpretation, and learned to make the actions of others be a reflection of me.

My mother and I have wounded each other deeply throughout life with our careless and unconscious words. Through the practice of forgiveness, we have remained unshaken in our love for each other. However, by modeling some of her behaviors, I have wounded others in my life.

A father has the responsibility of teaching his daughter about many things, including love, self-expression, and trust. Based on the relationship between the two of them, she learns how to relate to all of the men in her life.

My father is a quiet man, with smiling Spanish eyes and a big, sweet heart, painfully shy in the spotlight, but warm and loving and kind at home. Like many shy people, he adopts a persona to mask his vulnerability when uncomfortable or just sits quietly observing those around him, his brain actively working. He takes joy in the accomplishment of those he loves, and it is a joy to behold. He has an encyclopedia for a brain, a quick wit, and a thirst for knowledge that has stayed with him through life.

From my father, I learned about love and relationship, but also about rage, for he is a man of many unexpressed feelings and expectations, given to sudden angry outbursts that scald like the steam released through a high-pressure valve. True feelings were bottled up inside until they reached the boiling point and then blasted at those in the vicinity. When it was a focused blast, the effect was devastating.

The finer arts of family communication had not been part of his background, growing up as he did in the uneasy marriage of two very different immigrants. English was the spoken language in his household because it was the only common one—his father coming from the rugged Galician coast of Spain and his mother from the countryside outside of Bratislava, Slovakia. I never had the chance to know either of my paternal grandparents and gain more insight into my father.

In many ways, I am my father's daughter. The behaviors I modeled from him have cost me important relationships, as I, too, have struck out in anger. Other qualities, both inherited and learned, have made me the success I am today.

22.
Wrong Place, Right Time

Silence on the other end of the line. I could see from caller ID that it was Tom, could hear him breathing, but no words came out. *Uh-oh.* This was not going to be a joyful happy birthday call.

"Just tell me," I said into the phone, the familiar pit in my stomach twisting.

Tears evident in his voice, he replied, "I'm not coming. I can't come. I turned down the job."

This is not turning out like I planned, I thought in shock. How was this possible?

Over the past four years, I had poured all of myself into our relationship, determined that it would succeed and that our hard work and counseling would eliminate the problems between us. Everything I wanted in life had come easily to me up to this point, and this was the hardest I had ever worked to make anything happen. I could not possibly fail.

Guess what? Our relationship just failed.

I had left Tom and our home in Baltimore several weeks before, moving across the country to Arizona to attend Thunderbird. When confronted with my decision to go, Tom had immediately generated a job interview in Phoenix ready to follow me out west. "Not so fast," I had told him. "You can only come if we finally resolve whether we have a permanent commitment to be together. If not, I am using this as an opportunity to move on with my life."

When I answered the phone on this particular day, I had expected to be getting engaged. Every time we had come to this point before in our relationship, he had chosen not to lose me. For the first time, he chose not to choose me.

Picking myself up off the closet floor, where I lay curled in a tight fist, weeping, I changed into my bathing suit. Time to float in the pool and clear my mind of everything other than the gently lapping water and the orange sunlight on the inside of my eyelids. Two weeks into the breakup, these two places—the closet and the pool—offered me the most solace as I grappled with the blasted moonscape of my pain.

Coming out of the pool on this particular day, I was accosted by a pervert wanking his exposed penis while watching me float, and then trailing me through the apartment complex all the way back to my door still fondling his goods. Freaking out and feeling very alone in the new city, I locked the door and immediately dialed Tom, my best friend and primary source of support for the last four years. "Hang up," he said taking charge. "Call the police to file a report. Call me back when they leave."

The event ripped the scab off the wound, bringing Tom back into my life as we began to speak again every day or two. He offered to come out for a visit, to help me move to a safer apartment complex and to discuss what was happening between us face to face.

Tom was one of the good guys, long and lean, with a runner's build and strong arms, a Wisconsin boy who still drank milk in his thirties. He was steady and reliable and had always shown his love by the little things he did to take care of me instead of expressing it verbally. Dark hair and thick Lebanese eyebrows framed a mobile face and beautiful, warm sherry eyes. He showed up in Phoenix, and with his engineer's brain, quickly had the move sorted out and organized efficiently.

The first night in my new apartment, Tom slept on the couch, both of us feeling traumatized and cautious. The next morning, we drove to Sedona for the mid-October weekend, and checked into a beautiful little bed and breakfast in the red desert countryside. Following a long hike in a surprise snowstorm through a white, red, and green canyon, we soaked in the secluded hot tub as the full moon rose. Chemistry took over. Sex had always been our most direct, effective, and highly satisfactory form of communication and our time apart had only intensified it. The well of emotion that had been bubbling below the surface boiled over.

"Did you hear that Angie and Rob are getting married?" Tom asked me the next morning as we followed the steep trail to the top of the mesa.

Cut to scene of building exploding after demolition switches are triggered. "Is that so?" I snarled sarcastically before spiraling into a rage that tore both of us apart, and sent the desert critters scurrying for cover.

Reaching the mesa's top, I stumbled to the edge of the cliff, spent with shame and desolation. Why did we do this when we loved each other? Nothing left to lose, I surrendered and spoke from my heart about my fears, sadness, and regrets.

Tom held me close as I wept. "Why couldn't there have been more of this?" he asked sadly, "This openness and vulnerability? This communication?" No answers were forthcoming, just the wind circling up from the desert floor far below.

We held each other like fragile eggs through the night, my nose nestled into his chest hair, breathing in his scent, and made love for the last time in the morning. Later, I walked him to his gate at the airport, hugged and kissed him goodbye. Tears streaming down my face, I retraced my steps across the circles and squares on the orange terminal carpet, knowing that I would not taste his taste again.

"So, there *are* some knots you can tie," Lee had commented caustically to Tom about his neckwear at a wedding reception a year or so earlier. I quickly separated the two, and turned to toast the union of my college roommate and her new husband. Yes, another couple who had met well after Tom and I, who were moving forward with their life together while we stood still.

Lee had always been a bit of an enigma to me, the charming boy from Memphis, divorced, dilettant, and usually dramatically involved with some high-maintenance woman or other. He was straightforward about the fact that he was waiting in the wings for me, sometimes more sometimes less patiently, as Tom and I acted out our own ongoing drama.

It all began with Lee soon after Tom and I returned from our first trip abroad together, visiting a former roommate living in Madrid and then touring Galicia, the region of my grandfather and ancestors. The trip had featured a low point in our relationship, and we had driven angry miles along El Camino de Santiago bitterly arguing about everything and nothing at all. The desperate need to get away from Tom, and from the me I was when with him, first surfaced there and was still a strong underground current several weeks later as we separated for the Thanksgiving holiday. Deciding not to stew alone, I had dashed through the wet Baltimore streets to meet my friend Angie and her new housemate, Lee, for dinner. The three of us surfaced from our meal in the midst of giant fluffy snowflakes, and played in the winter wonderland all the way back to their brownstone.

"Are these your photographs?" I asked Lee as we were drying off and drinking wine in their warm house. They were amazing, I thought, as I saw him in a new light, connecting to the artist in him after being so long paired with a clinical engineer. He stepped close to sort through the stack and show me a few photographs that he particularly liked. The house got warmer.

Later, I climbed their spiral staircase to use to the bathroom mid level between his top floor room and the ground floor. As I came out in the narrow space, Lee blocked the small landing with his body. Mercy, this house was warm. We stood in the dark facing each other for a long moment. *Oh god, kiss me,* I thought as energy flared and awareness pulsed. As he leaned in, fear drove me to duck under his arm and down the stairs. Tom's girlfriend had slammed the door shut. The discontented woman in me shoved my foot out and prevented the door from closing.

Tom and I broke up, reconciled, and then started couples counseling soon after.

"You look angry and your words and tone suggested anger, yet you deny it bothers you," our therapist observed. "Tom, what is the truth?"

Out spilled a year and a half worth of unexpressed opinion and judgment, like a sack of coffee beans suddenly split open.

Where is there to go from here? I wondered numbly. Tom was the first man who had accepted and loved me for myself. Or so I thought until the therapist helped puncture that bubble. Was it possible to trust him again?

By withholding his thoughts, he had denied me the ability to participate in our relationship. Could I forgive him for that?

It had been his choice to begin couples counseling and to work through whatever was blocking us from building a future together. I just wasn't prepared for what I found.

We worked on building open communication and honesty, knowing they were the foundation of any successful relationship. Tom moved in to my apartment and we built a home together. But as time passed, I became more aggressively angry at being in a permanent state of limbo, and he took to flinging disguised verbal knives in a passive-aggressive manner remarkably similar to my mother's. Frequent rages would result in explosive sex and a clearing of the air for a while.

And so we went on. And all of our friends started getting engaged and married. And he continued not to know. Finally, I had taken matters into my own hands and moved to Arizona.

"Hi, it's me. Can you talk?" Tom asked, after I finished my comment to the marketing group gathered in my apartment and said a delayed hello into the phone. It had been almost a month since his visit to Arizona and this was the first time we had spoken.

"No, I can't right now," I replied. "I have five people over working on a class project. Can you call me tomorrow at nine?"

When the Thunderbird project team finally left that night, I returned to my trusty walk-in closet floor and assumed the fetal position as the waterworks began. *Wow,* I thought, *it's been nearly a week since I was last in here.*

The next night, the crowd was gathered again putting the finishing touches on our final project, and I began to get agitated as we approached the witching hour. Rushing everyone out before nine, my friend Nancy said she would be up late if I needed to talk.

"Can I see you when you're home for Christmas?" Tom asked. I still had a carload of belongings in our former, but his current, home and was planning on moving them during the holidays.

"No, what's the point?" I replied, "It would just be painful for both of us." Somewhere along the line, I had begun to accept the idea that our relationship was over and realized that I was surviving, making new friends, and even laughing occasionally. Seeing each other again would only rip open the wound. After years of energy and effort directed at a future together, it felt like enormous progress to begin to see a life beyond him. I felt too fragile to risk that by seeing him. Saying so out loud to him made me feel powerful again, it felt like a huge risk and a major accomplishment.

Fear flared up a few days later. *Wait a minute!* I thought as loneliness and uncertainty washed over me, *Maybe there still is a chance for us! Of course, we should take this opportunity to see each other.* I called him back to reverse my decision only to have him support it.

"No, you were right," he said reasonably, "we've got to keep moving forward." Fear-fueled anger took over again and blasted him through the phone, until we finally agreed on a day for me to move while he was still with his family in Wisconsin.

Final exams and end of semester parties distracted me for the last weeks before the holiday break. One night at the pub, I engaged in some heavy flirting and actually kissed a man other than Tom for the first time in over five years. *This feels really strange,* I thought, *but I kind of like it.* Then I flew back East.

Turning the key, I stepped into the apartment in Baltimore, and collapsed weeping on the stairs. It smelled like home. Flashes of the life we had built and lost overwhelmed me as I wandered from room to room, noting what was the same and what was different. I lay down on the bed we used to share and howled silently with pain. Looking around for a tissue, and unable to prevent myself, I peeked in his nightstand drawer and found a list of pros and cons he had written about me. Looking down, I was surprised the white paper and blue comforter did not turn red as my heart bled out its last few drops.

A door opened and closed downstairs, footsteps stamping off snow in the entry. A major snowstorm had made travel treacherous on my allotted day, and I had hoped to get in and out before Tom arrived today. Not so lucky, it seemed. I collected myself and went down to see him.

After packing up the car, we made one last trip around the apartment checking for forgotten things. We spoke of Angie and Rob's upcoming wedding in February. He agreed that if I went through the expense and logistical challenges to make the trip back to attend, he would not go. It would be easier that way for both of us.

"I'm sorry for everything," Tom said, as I prepared to leave. "Don't ever accept it when a man tells you he doesn't know. Not knowing does not, and never will, mean yes."

The phone rang. When the answering machine clicked on, a woman's voice floated out saying how much she had enjoyed meeting him and looked forward to their date on Friday. She was a setup from the couple we had been closest to.

I left the apartment for the last time shortly afterwards, with a knife hilt embedded in my chest, no blood left to bleed, no energy left to rage, only a deep sense of shame and sadness.

"We had an agreement," I said into the phone through gritted teeth a few weeks later.

Apparently that agreement had been nullified in Tom's mind when I had arranged to attend Angie and Rob's wedding with Lee.

What followed was our last conversation ever, consisting of two hours of previously unexplored rage and recrimination. Gloves off, nothing left to lose or gain, we annihilated each other.

"You are such a positive person! do you ever get angry?" my friend Carrie said, laughing, as our group perched on the sunny rock. We were midway through the day's hike and taking a lunch break on a warm Arizona day in February.

Looking out at the Superstition Mountains, I made a commitment to myself. *I will never stay in a situation that crosses all boundaries, or that distorts and mangles me again.*

I realized that it wasn't Tom who had made me so unhappy, that it was my choice. I had chosen to stay with him, attached to the relationship because it came at the right time in my life even though he wasn't the right person. While he had many of the qualities that I wanted in a life partner, we lacked the essential foundation of good communication. Without that, no real relationship was possible. If we couldn't discuss our needs openly, then how could we ever have them met? And denying needs doesn't eliminate them, it just distorts and drains you, makes you unhealthy and incapable of a real connection with another.

By allowing myself to be powerless in the face of his ambiguity and my attachment to the outcome of marriage, I had disappointed myself. I had become a person that I was ashamed of, and let that shame be the driving force in my life. Being stuck filled me with anger, which I then inflicted on him and perpetuated the destructive cycle that we had been caught in for years.

Finally remembering that I had the power to make a different choice for myself was what freed me. I had expressed my needs and walked away instead of trying to force the situation to be something that it was not.

I let go of control. It was the beginning of finding my way back to myself, the joyful me that my friends now saw.

23.
Full Moon Sweat Lodge, Costa Rica 2009

We bounced up the dirt road and through the puddled river beds on our way to San Juanillo. I drove while Carlos rode shotgun and another yogini clung to the back of his seat for balance from the tiny rear seat in the rental car. Turning sharply left, we crawled down the broken up dirt trail through the thick jungle to the meeting point, a rustic pizza place with tables made of tree slabs sanded to smoothness and telling their own stories with thick rings of grain.

A group gathered and chatted until it was time to walk the steep and muddy path down to the black sand beach. It was rainy season in Costa Rica, and we were taking advantage of the rare dry evening to celebrate the full moon with a sweat lodge.

Marcelo, the Argentinean shaman leading the lodge, was already on the beach and had been heating the rocks in a large bonfire for the past hour or so. Carlos assumed responsibility for the fire and the stones as we gathered together for brief instructions and then an intention-setting ceremony. We laid out our straw mats on the dark sand around the fire pit and watched as the sun disappeared behind a bank of clouds over the ocean's horizon.

Filing into the tent, ten women and two men gathered around the sides and perched on the stones provided as stools. The flap was closed and we sat in the murky darkness, the fire pit and the full moon outside the tent providing enough light to make out the glow of faces in the crowded space. Water and herbs were poured on the hot stones and the heat intensified, steam rising from the rocks and from the inhabitants as we began to release toxins. After twenty minutes, we ourselves were released from the lodge onto the beach for a ten-minute break.

Ducking through the flap, I straightened and walked slowly to the water's edge treading carefully on mossy stones. I sank to my knees in the dark ocean and submerged to float on my back, caressed by the glowing light of the full moon and the cool waves of water flowing over me.

Returning for the second round, I went several levels deeper. As the heat grew more intense, I dropped my head to my knees and focused on my breath. Words formed in my mind and then repeated. A new mantra was born, "*I release the need to seek, and trust I will be found.*" The phrase followed me across the rocky beach as I once again submerged and floated, carried me through two more rounds in the lodge, and repeated as I lay trembling and weak on my straw mat in the black sand by the fire. Tiny hermit crabs scuttled on the straw and tickled my legs and arms as I bathed in the moonlight and drifted in a trance.

Surrender and release the illusion of control. Trust that you have and will receive all that you need.

Sandy, salty, and sweaty, we climbed back up the hill to the strange little pizza place carved out of the jungle. Clouds moved in and eclipsed the moon, a storm was brewing. We made our way to the car for the drive to Guiones, before the rains hit and the river beds filled and were too deep to cross.

Carlos took the wheel, and steered us back home.

24.

Hurray for Hollywood

Bally's casino, Las Vegas. A year out of graduate school, and I was sitting at a slot machine with an old man feeding me quarters.

It was my first time at ShoWest and I was awed by the circus-like atmosphere and the glamorous sheen. Nine-figure deals were being made in all corners of the casino, as movie studios previewed the coming year's lineup of new films for theater owners with an abundance of fanfare and star power.

Jack Valenti leaned against the slot machine as if my playing and winning was the most important thing in the world. Never mind his international press conference and keynote speech the following morning, or the parade of industry power players. It takes a born gambler to get to where he had ascended in life and he did enjoy each and every game. For over thirty years, he'd held the position of most powerful lobbyist in the world, at the helm of an industry famous for preying on any sign of weakness.

Even in his late seventies, he was the most brilliant person I had ever met. A diminutive man, what he lacked in physical stature was more than made up for with power of the brain housed inside his meticulously coiffed silver head. Quick on his feet and with an easy charm, he had a mind that recorded, catalogued, and recalled minute details, and that, at a split second's notice, could clearly articulate a spot-on strategy for any situation.

He turned to exchange greetings with a big Hollywood mogul while I sat pushing buttons, and then I was introduced. A long, slow assessment ensued, the kind that I was starting to really hate, but that happened with just about everyone in LA. Who was I, besides another woman on Jack's arm?

For you were never taken at face value in the high stakes world I had entered. Your sum value was equal to what you could provide to another on their journey to the top of the heap. Without looking for it, I had landed in an enviable position with control over critical industry information, working for an organization at the pinnacle of national, international, and movie industry politics. I was a newcomer to the established power game and had no known agenda. The shrewd players could sense that and found me an enigma at first, albeit a relatively unconnected one.

So, I sat and listened and observed. And tried to hide how much of an outsider I felt, playing slots amidst the dinging and buzzing and ringing casino, once again feeling befuddled by Jack's energy and attention.

For in the language of my new reality, Jack was endorsing me, introducing me around, bringing me into the world of green rooms and movie stars and the power elite. This would all make doing my job easier and was supposed to provide the candy to keep me satisfied and addicted. Unfortunately, I was learning that there was always a price to be paid for any favor, and I was not prepared for the form it would take.

It had all begun with a folksy voice on the phone, asking how I had heard about the job and reminiscing about the career services center on campus. Ah, another Thunderbird alumnus. "Sure, I'd love to fly out for an interview on Monday."

A limousine collected and then deposited me at the peach building on Ventura Boulevard for the first time. On the outside, it looked innocuous enough. Wrought iron rails guarding walls of a bright cotton candy peach looked into a central courtyard with a fountain, around which the U-shaped building was arranged. The only hint that it was something other than a shopping mall or regular business complex were the tiles of old films embedded into the wall facing the sidewalk.

Immediately clicking with Tbird Ben, we talked about what the Motion Picture Association did for the movie industry in the U.S. and around the world, went over the story of why the position was open, and discussed my previous experience. By the end of the meeting, it was clear that Ben was very interested and I was very curious.

A second interview was arranged for the following Monday. A packet of information on the company, as well as examples of the types of things I would be working on, was sent, and I plowed through them as if preparing for an exam. An informal offer was made at the end of that interview, pending meeting and approval of the organization's titan and head, Jack Valenti.

On the third Monday in a row, I was again transported to Los Angeles and introduced to the Peninsula Hotel, an institution of opulence and power in Beverly Hills. Ben and I sat in the breakfast room amid the power elite who were making contacts and finessing deals, drinking coffee, and awaiting the maestro's grand entrance. Beautiful waiters filled coffee cups the moment the dark liquid dipped below sight level, conversation buzzed all around, and people preened and pretended. Like a virgin on the block, for the very first time I felt the room avidly focus attention on me as I entered, endured the quick assessment of my assets, and suffered the dismissal as the crowd then looked beyond for the next offering.

After half an hour with no grand entrance, we were instructed to come up to Jack's suite. An emergency conference call had sprung up! The interview would be conducted en suite and en call.

"Hello, darlin'," he said, the first of many such endearments directed at me. The master of multitasking asked me a series of innocuous questions, one ear on my responses, one on the call. Ben, who had prepped me for the meeting like the skilled attaché he was, sat by approvingly as I answered like an unruffled bird. Jack pronounced his acceptance of me in a flowery speech and then dismissed us to focus on the phone call at hand.

When the offer came, I felt unsure and rushed. A voice inside me was protesting. Only one other location ranked lower than Los Angeles as a place to live. I was still too fragile to even consider returning to the D.C. area with fresh scar tissue from the break with Tom. *Well, LA is certainly a world away from him,* I thought, looking at the bright side. No chance of running into him there, or any other painful reminders of our recently failed relationship.

Once news of the offer became known, my dean and mentor spread it about and put me up as a candidate for a number of other jobs. When you're wanted, you are wanted. The buzz got around campus, and people were interested and intrigued. "How cool, Hollywood! Jack Valenti is a legend! What an awesome job! This will guarantee your career! Let's keep in touch!"

But some inner voice warned me, *Do I want this superficial world? What do I really know about what I'm getting into? What kind of person thrives in the power structure? Am I that kind of person? What about wanting to refocus my career on marketing products for children and developing better humans?*

And so like a prospective bride considering a questionable suitor, I delayed, requested more time to decide, asked for more money and more benefits. I was granted whatever I requested. An offer I couldn't refuse? It began to feel that way, as I considered the repayment of my towering stack of student loans.

Sitting in my Thunderbird nest, watching *Party of Five* before meeting friends for our regular pub night, the phone rang. "Hello, darlin', Jack Valenti here. What can we do to have you join us?" drawled that famous voice into my living room, after a week or two of my stalling. It was a voice that knew how to get what it wanted, that paralyzed me for the first of many times with its utter confidence and power.

In the end, I accepted the job offer. It meant a tripling of my pre-MBA salary, a nifty new title, and entry into a world that many people fought tooth and nail for. It meant that I didn't need to worry any more about what was next. I could put aside my gnawing fear at leaving the sheltered world of school and having to build a life without Tom, alone in a world without parameters. Movers were arranged, temporary housing provided, and an offer letter supplied to smooth the way to purchasing anything that I might need in advance.

I decided that I needed a new Saab to ease my way into the world of valets and power lunches and maintaining the right appearance.

"How long will Barry be retained as a consultant?" I asked Ben for the tenth time.

"The terms of his 'retirement' keep him on for three more months," Ben replied patiently. Unknown to me, I had assumed control of my new department following a bitter and hostile takeover. My predecessor had been forced out after twenty years on the job, the last five of which he had cruised on autopilot. A very public mistake at the last ShoWest had finally given Ben the ammunition needed to expel him from his position.

"He's meant to be a help to you," Ben explained again. And I explained again to Ben how Barry was anything but a help.

A portly and pretentious man, pure old school and adverse to change, my predecessor had allowed years of dust to accumulate on the department and its projects. He was not inclined to help in the slightest, but rather waged a guerilla war to ensure my failure. No one could replace him—and certainly not a woman in her early thirties. Helped in his efforts by his trusty right hand, who was now to be mine, absolutely no information on practices, processes, or policies was forthcoming. When pressed, I was given just enough information to hang myself.

But little did Barry know who he was dealing with. Since a wee tiny girl cruising the floor in a hip brace, I've been known for my super-sized strong will. A challenge will never beat me, once I've committed to the project. Okay, that was until Tom, and while my failure with him had deeply shaken my confidence, it was a personal failure that dealt with relationships. This was professional.

I had arrived in LA fresh from a blissful year of healing in the deserts of Arizona, top of my class, excelling at all projects, and kicking ass on a consulting assignment in Luxembourg and Germany. My confidence professionally was stronger than ever: I was back in the flow of doing well without conscious effort, the key part of any team. If no help was forthcoming, I would solve the puzzle myself and build a better, more efficient process for doing things. And I would make the old schoolers document every single thing they told me.

A small chink in my armor began to grow, however. Relationships were critical to the success of my job, and although I was a skilled facilitator, I was a baby dropped into a pool of sharks. If I had been a different person, I could have thrived on the swimming.

But I had just come from a personal relationship where the truth was rarely spoken, and I did not like the pool one bit. It triggered fear in me, the same fear that I had tried to leave behind with Tom, the kind that came from not knowing when the next knife would be thrown, not knowing if the ground was in fact solid or if it would disintegrate under my next step.

He crowded in close to the desk, flicking the adding machine paper back and forth like a lion twitches his tail. His breath was heavy with wine from his lunch meeting.

What does he want from me? I wondered nervously. Curt felt like a predator at large. Sexual tension hung heavy in the air.

Wait. He's with Marty and knows we are friends. I diffused the situation with professionalism, distanced myself from the foot-wide strip of my desk he was pressed against.

But deep down, well I had been attracted since our first meeting a year before.

From the first conference call, the sound of Curt's voice and his intellect had attracted my attention. His agile mind and affability came through the phone line, even though it was the end of a long day in his part of the world. He was another professional, someone grounded in smarts and skill versus position to gain him respect.

An observer like me, he sat and he watched, gathered information and used it astutely. *What information does he have on me?* I wondered.

Sparks first flew between us at a dinner at an exclusive restaurant in Sherman Oaks, following a meeting of regional presidents. The private dining room, looking like a cross between an important bureaucrat's office and an affluent study, was done in heavy oak and blue draperies. The table was set with all of the male players and me, the token female, sharing the head with Jack's arm resting along the back of my chair.

Curt presented a very attractive package. Recently divorced head of European operations, he exuded the kind of Mediterranean charm I found irresistible. He was a consummate political player, having grown up professionally in Washington's diplomatic circles, and had a brilliant strategic mind. His slight build was clothed in expensive and well-tailored European suits and his dark hair, slightly longer than was fashionable, flowed and curled behind his ears. He wore his intellect as casually as his clothes, and his dark eyes assessed, observed, and catalogued everything he saw for future advantage.

The dinner went on as many did, a sharing of the political issues in their regions, and broke after a dozen bottles of excellent wine. From my perch next to Jack, I also observed, catalogued, and recorded information.

Excusing myself to go to the ladies room as the party broke up, I said my farewells to each player on my way. When I came out to the valet alleyway, I observed Curt seeing the last of the others into a car. He pulled his valet ticket out of his pocket as I approached, turned it in with mine, and we connected under the dimly lit canopy. Tingling and a bit tipsy, I thanked him for his invitation to Brussels as my car arrived, said I would plan a trip soon. Swooping in for the traditional Belgian three-part kiss, he grazed the outer corners of my lips in a distinctly unprofessional manner, one side then the next, coming in for the third.

I drove home with a smile on my face and a sizzle in my belly.

Out to lunch a few days after the executive dinner, at a funky little strip mall sushi place down Ventura Boulevard, I first learned of his involvement with my friend Marty when she confessed her ongoing affair with a co-worker.

Ours was a burgeoning friendship, a rarity in Los Angeles so far. Another single female professional in a similar position as mine in a cold city, Marty was a quirky, intelligent woman around my age with white blond hair. Thin and angular, hers was an attractiveness based more on stylishness than any particular physical attribute. She was spunky in a cold and sophisticated way. We had begun going to lunch, for drinks here and there, and sharing light confidences. She was an industry friend, if that was possible. Still careful, because it was necessary for business, but we were beginning to cross the line into trust.

Marty spoke of a recent trip to Brussels, of staying at a lover's apartment last minute, and his embarrassment at having his laundry hanging around the place. Then it came out: Her lover was Curt, they had been sleeping together for the past year, but it had been cooling off lately. The sexiness of its hidden nature was an allure for the both, but a recent conversation with him suggested it was ending, there was no future.

Ah, I thought, as a wave of disappointment sloshed me. *This one is not available, put him away. Your friend is there first.*

Interesting timing, though, this revelation.

A month or so later, Marty and I slotted in a trip to Barcelona and Mallorca for some fun and flirting. Our first night in the city, Marty casually mentioned that Curt would be joining her for a night. On the anointed day, I relocated to a local Spanish hotel on Las Ramblas to leave the couple the suite in Le Meridien. All was done quietly, to hide my presence and appear as if Marty was travelling alone.

Meeting for brunch the next afternoon, Marty mentioned Curt's upset when he found out that she was travelling with me and my knowledge of their relationship. To appease his anger, Marty told him something I had shared with her in confidence: that I was actively looking to leave my job and interviewing for positions in New York. Tit for tat, now we were all back at an even playing field. Didn't I understand that Marty had to give him that?

And so we came to the predator in my office, flicking the adding machine tape.

As Curt left the office trailing fumes of wine, I thought, *Another level of the game has been engaged.* I sighed wearily and thought wistfully of a time when attraction and flirtation was a simple and open thing.

Walls, it seemed, were needed with everyone.

By my second ShoWest, I was no longer in awe of the industry. Except—wait a minute—was that really Sean Connery walking into the casino and towards the green room? I'd never seen a crowd actually physically ripple in the wake of someone before, and I had seen many celebrities at this point. Drawn by a palpable magnetic force, I took several steps after him before shaking free and resuming the wait for Jack's arrival. *Oh, I hope we go to the green room, too!*

I had tried desperately to find a way out of attending this year's event, but I was needed. After two years on the job, my duties as Jack's arm candy and statistical support at this and other major events were well defined. Whose fault was it that these duties came with additional unwanted attention? He was infamous for his lecherous activities and I should have put a clear stop to them at their first appearance. His ability to befuddle me had not diminished, and while I always managed to escape with my virtue intact, my boundaries as a woman and a professional inevitably felt violated. It was just another game he enjoyed and was determined to eventually win, but for me it was always an uncomfortable and shameful experience.

"Darlin', come up to my suite an hour before dinner, and we'll have a drink," Jack drawled when I deposited him at his afternoon meeting.

Desperate for a way out, I went in search of Ben. A business meeting with my boss surely supersedes a drink with his boss, I strategized. Walking through the casino, up the escalator to the concrete bridge outside, Ben and I spoke in code about the situation and the different ways I might handle it. We would present an important business issue that needed immediate attention, and have dinner together instead. As we prepared to depart, Ben's cell phone rang.

"Yes, Jack, Robin is here with me. I'll send her directly up," Ben spoke into the mouthpiece.

Right. It seemed that Jack had power over everyone. I was alone in my dilemma, no allies to trust or to help.

"There's another school shooting and it looks like a big one. "

"Pull out the report on violence in the media and begin updating it," I told my staff as news reports on Columbine started coming in. Two teenage boys armed with automatic weapons and explosives had laid siege to their high school in Colorado.

We had empirical data demonstrating from every angle how violence in movies could not be conclusively linked to violent behavior in youth.

The MPAA's party line was that the rating system was in effect to give parents the tools to control and monitor what their children were viewing. If youth were watching inappropriate movies, then it was the responsibility of their caretakers to more closely control their viewing habits. Film makers must not be censored in the content they provided because of the lack of appropriate supervision. In fact, parents consistently cited sexuality as the most disturbing content in movies today, at least twice as often as violence. If parents were not overly concerned, why should film makers be? Valid points, all of them: Just none of them contributing to understanding or solving the problem, a purely defensive positioning.

By early afternoon, it was apparent that Columbine was not just a school shooting, it was a massacre organized with near military efficiency and resulting in twelve dead and twenty-one more injured. The public outcry was deafening, outrage and shock at how our youth could be capable of such horror.

Congress seized hold of the issue, and initiated investigations into all possible causes for the shooting. Links to the violent video game, *Doom*, were explored first and an investigation of that industry launched. When journal entries from one of the shooters about the uber-violent movie *Natural Born Killers* were brought to light, as well as the similarity of the shooters' Trenchcoat Mafia clique to a school shooting scene in *Basketball Diaries,* national attention began to focus on the movie industry.

A Federal Trade Commission investigation was launched into the marketing practices of movie studios, claiming that the rating system was in name only and not enforced in either viewing or marketing practices. The MPAA went through a massive legal investigation, and my department took a starring role as a potential area for discovery in its years of research results.

"We would like you to swear to an affidavit saying that we have no evidence linking violent content to violence in youth. Would you be willing to do so?" I was asked by our General Counsel.

What choice do I have? I asked myself. Personal views must be put aside, and only empirical data considered. It was my job and I was a team player.

Another boundary was crossed, my word given to something that was technically correct, but instinctively felt false.

Everything we take into ourselves influences who we are, who we become, particularly for impressionable youth. But not, I guess, if it can't be statistically proven.

A part of me died that day, a delayed casualty of the shooting. Another nail was hammered into my personal coffin.

❧

The world of entertainment was changing around us. The year was 2001. The dot com bubble had inflated rapidly, Napster and other file-sharing services were popping up everywhere on the Internet. Reality TV had made a very successful debut exhibiting the worst of human behavior with the first season of *Survivor,* and the explosion of new cable channels offered a distribution outlet and viewership for every specialty under the sun. News had become entertainment, all of the major information and news providers acquired and folded into larger media and entertainment companies with a bottomline emphasis on increasing viewers at all costs.

It was an interesting time to be sitting in a job like mine, which kept its fingers on the pulse of what was happening. Or it could have been, if not for several things.

The movie industry as a whole was just not that interested in changing. They were making lots of money just the way things were. *Titanic* had recently blown any previous box office records out of the water. DVDs and home entertainment were driving revenues sky high. There was no way to control content rights on the Internet, and the movie business wanted no part of it until those rights could be protected, except to prosecute those who dared pirate their films.

To understand and address the changing world of technology, I proposed and rallied support for a groundbreaking, industry-wide research project. One of the major technology research firms was so excited about it that they offered us a partnership deal, offering their extensive capabilities at a heavily discounted price.

I was excited to have a challenge. Things had gotten pretty dull in the job since I had reorganized my group into an efficient and productive resource, and day-to-day management and the politics associated with it were not enough to keep me engaged. This project gave me something to sink my teeth into, with the potential to expand industry knowledge in a useful way and provide something that would help to create the future. It more than made up for all of the other pockets of ugliness in my job.

My contacts at the technology research firm were as excited as I was. We began the strategy and planning phase, with a task group of executives from all of the major studios, and agreed on approach, design, and timeline. As we moved toward implementation, the executives began to drag their feet. Deliverables were missed, contacts were unavailable. Finally, my boss Ben called me into his office to say that the project was being killed.

There was concern that the results could not be managed properly if anything was found that did not support our industry positions. With the research firm as heavily involved as they were, iron clad legal control of all results would not be ceded to the MPAA. The information could be used against us. From a strategic perspective, we just could not afford to have our name associated with something we couldn't control.

In other words, there was no interest in building a brave new world; they would fight progress as long as they could while still maximizing revenue. It was business after all.

No more, I told myself. *I am out of here. There is nothing left for me. My energy needs to be put into something that looks forward instead of defending the past.*

25.

September 11, 2001

I woke that morning and showered as usual, unaware that the world had already begun to change.

Following my usual routine, I came out of the shower, opened the blinds to the bright Santa Monica sunshine, and turned on "Morning Edition" on NPR. The words slowly began to sink in as I applied my makeup. Was it the anniversary of the World Trade Center truck bombing? What were they talking about?

Suddenly, something the commentator said struck a chord. I realized he was talking about today, right now.

I ran into the living room and turned on the TV in time to see the top corner of Tower 2 gracefully slide off and crumble into the air high above Lower Manhattan. Sinking onto a stool in my robe, I sat stunned in front of the television for long enough to see both towers crumble and the airplanes smash into the buildings from every possible angle.

What the hell is happening? HOW *could this be happening?*

Mind wrapped in cotton gauze, I dressed for work and numbly completed my morning routine. Autopilot saw me up the 405 and through the Sepulveda Pass to the Motion Picture Association headquarters, only to be turned around at the parking garage gates. The office was closed. Hollywood, it seemed, was under high alert of a potential attack. If terrorists were attacking centers of U.S. power—financial and military—then of course they would go after the center of American culture, or so thought the great minds of Hollywood.

Rather than retracing my steps to an empty apartment in Santa Monica, I continued on to a scheduled hair appointment at my salon in Beverly Hills. I was flying through New York in four days to attend the wedding of dear friends.

Arriving at the salon, I was absorbed into a community in distress. Five television sets blared the latest news, cell phones rang constantly as stylists and customers called family and friends back East, and shared worries about those not reachable. We watched as home videos showed even more angles of impact, all echoing the wrenching sound of shattering glass, smashing concrete, and grinding whining machinery combined with human shrieks of terror. We saw films of small shapes plummeting in the air, and gasped in horror as we realized those were people jumping, choosing to fly rather than fall to their death. We viewed the towers collapse again and again, people running for their lives from the giant roiling cloud that darkened the streets like in some blockbuster horror movie. We cheered brave first responders and firemen everywhere taking action and making enormous sacrifices to help the suffering and manage the emergency. And we saw our President sitting in a grade-school classroom looking like a paralyzed and frightened rabbit upon hearing the news.

Into the midst of this turmoil, walked two secret service men, quietly but immediately recognizable by their dark suits, their stoic demeanor and their stealthy eyes. A signal was given and another two came through the salon door escorting an elderly woman into the now eerily quiet salon. Nancy Reagan, former First Lady, had arrived for her weekly appointment.

Ah, I thought, *some leadership, some counsel for the traumatized and frightened citizens.* What words of comfort would she have? What example would she provide in this time of crisis?

Well, she just said no, or rather nothing. Not five feet away, I sat stunned under a hair dryer, watching as she calmly blocked out the community in desperate need, ignored the blaring televisions and frightened conversations, and casually flipped through a fashion magazine.

Watching her, I could empathize with how sometimes, just to be able to live the life you find yourself in, it can become necessary to separate yourself from noticing things. That practice can both serve you and kill your humanity. I could only imagine the life that she had lived with the world's eye fixed firmly on her and what she had to do to survive it.

I also thought about choices. You can choose to stay inside a protective bubble no matter what happens, or you can choose to reach out and contribute to others in a time of need, providing leadership and comfort in tragedy.

Nancy Reagan chose to remain separate on 9/11. I made up my mind that I would not.

"When can I rebook my flight to New York? You say the latest estimate of airports reopening is now for tomorrow, Thursday the fourteenth?" I asked the beleaguered airline representative. "Is it possible to get on a wait list for the first flight?"

After three days wandering the sunny streets of Santa Monica in a crowded daze and media stupor, I was feeling desperately trapped on the wrong coast. *Tell me what I was doing out here again, working at a job I disliked in a city I disliked far from family and friends? Oh yeah, the money was good and the job impressive.*

Feeling trapped was a national experience during the days following the collapse, as travelers everywhere dealt with the tragedy stranded far from home and loved ones. A friend's sister was not enjoying her extended visit to LA, a Texas panther separated from her cubs in a crisis. Other friends were stranded on business trips throughout the country and the globe, all desperate for news and connection and reassurance. Each day, we would sit with the nation and worry and morbidly watch for new pictures of the disaster, avidly grasping for clues as to who would do this and why.

Despite the total transportation disarray, I was still determined to find a way to make it to Maine by Saturday for the wedding of close friends. *I will celebrate love even in the face of this catastrophe,* I promised myself. *This violence will not diminish me, or change who I am and what is important. I will help to shield my friends and prevent the tragedy from tarnishing their long-awaited ceremony.* I needed to know I could get back home when I had to.

On Friday morning, a last effort with the airlines was rewarded: There was one seat on a flight leaving from John Wayne Airport in

Orange County in four hours. Without thought, I booked it, threw my clothes in a suitcase, and jumped into a taxi for the two-hour drive down the coast to the regional airport.

I emerged from the sunny dream land of Southern California to a world that had changed.

Entering the airport, taxi cabs were stopped at a bomb-safe distance and driver and passenger papers were checked. When approved, we proceeded to the drop-off zone at a metered pace. Heavily armed soldiers patrolled all parts of the terminal and made their presence felt with intense and scowling energy. Tables had been set up for hand search of all baggage, which was then directed to x-ray machines and eventually checked in. All documentation was verified and authenticated at least five times, and all passengers were subjected to full body searches.

A thin edge of suspicion and hysteria blanketed the boarding area. Once on the plane, skiddish passengers watched each other with open vigilance, flinched whenever someone stood or opened an overhead compartment, prepared to tackle at the slightest questionable activity, and chatted nervously with each other for five hours.

Upon landing, we were informed of a bomb threat in Newark Airport and deplaned in the midst of a massive evacuation. Thousands of people shuffled like cattle through the narrow terminal hallways, and massed on the sidewalk outside of arrivals, still close enough to be devastated if a bomb went off, but with no other place to go. After several hours, the airport was finally given clearance and the mass of humanity slowly began to merge back through the buildings and the security check points.

When I finally boarded the puddle jumper that would take me to Maine, I felt as if I had aged years in that one day. Another decade was added when the plane flew up the river and passed the mangled skyline on the lower tip of Manhattan. The gaping hole of Ground Zero glowed like a grisly beacon, stadium lanterns lighting the ongoing search efforts and illuminating the curling vapors of dust and smoke rising from fires that were still burning four days later.

At two in the morning, I was finally deposited in Portland, Maine, and into the arms of my dear friends, who then whisked me to the bucolic inn on the sea for the wedding festivities.

Three days were spent on the sunlit rocky coast of Maine, celebrating the couple who had been a solid partnership since age nineteen when they had met as camp counselors. Ten years of love, support, and commitment had led them to the weekend's ceremony, and a joyous community of world citizens had gathered to commemorate their union. We formed a human shelter around the newlyweds, blocking all news of catastrophe and sorrow, and finally found some peace for ourselves after the devastating week.

Upon returning to Los Angeles, I made several decisions about my life. Time was precious and life was short. I would no longer spend it in a place I did not want to be, devoting my time and energy to an organization whose positions I found questionable. For almost four years, I had suppressed the little voice inside of me that shouted in outrage with each personal and professional boundary I let be crossed, afraid to take a stand. With or without a job, I would move home to New York. Luckily, I was approaching the end of a long interview process with a large international public relations firm based in Manhattan, and an offer seemed inevitable.

"I'm not surprised," said Ben, my boss and mentor, after I told him I was resigning. "You haven't been happy for a while. But is now really the time to be moving *to* New York?"

"Well, darlin', I'm real sad to see you go," drawled Jack Valenti after I told him of my resignation while speeding down the 405 to LAX on a bright October morning. My last and most difficult conversation was now complete, and all that remained was to celebrate with friends in Phoenix at a Thunderbird homecoming reunion. I was free!

Thunderbird was more than just a graduate school to me. It had been a place of tremendous healing and growth. For the first time in my life, I had felt truly connected to my passions and discovered a diverse community of like-minded people who shared them. As Tbirds, we called ourselves citizens of the world, and I planned to reconnect with that part of myself through travel and open up again to the dreams I had before becoming bogged down with the LA lifestyle. It felt particularly important given recent events, which had demonstrated that what impacts the U.S. also affects the rest of the world.

With the economic fallout from 9/11, the PR firm I had been interviewing with had frozen new hires for the remainder of the year, so I took the time for a much-needed personal recharge outside of my traumatized country. My new freedom enabled me to spend a month in Milan helping a good friend realize her dream of living in Italy, and celebrate pre-Christmas festivities with other friends living in Munich. Drinking endless cappuccinos in Italy, I heard the world perspective on what was unfolding in the aftermath of 9/11 from the animated discussions of locals, CNN International, and BBC World. Practicing my German in Munich, other viewpoints were offered in conversations in the wintry Christkindlemarkts, drinking *glu wein,* and chatting with an international assortment of characters, and also by reading about the hunt for Bin Laden in *Der Speigel.* The world was poised to help the U.S. in our fight, and offered sympathy, support, and solidarity in candlelight vigils honoring the fallen.

I returned to the U.S. to spend the holidays with my family, relieved that we had not lost a loved one in the tragedy like so many others had. I felt full of hope and optimism for my new life in New York, glad to be free of the stress and unhappiness of my time in Hollywood.

"Still no news on his remains?" I asked Michael, looking across the street at the house festooned with flags and other patriotic symbols and a steady stream of visitors.

"No, they're hoping for some kind of closure, any kind of news at this point," Michael replied. Three months after the tragedy, and the firefighter's family was still in limbo about their disappeared loved one. So many bodies from the disaster could not be found or identified, leaving countless families with a gaping hole and no formal confirmation to begin the healing process. In the absence of certainty, hope was a difficult thing to lay aside.

A group of Thunderbird friends were celebrating a mellow New Year's Eve at Michael's home in White Plains, a suburb north of the city. The first morning of 2002 dawned with bright sunshine, and I took a train into Manhattan for my first visit since the Twin Towers' collapse. I would pay my respects to the fallen innocents at the giant cemetery of Ground Zero before officially becoming a resident.

Stepping out of Grand Central Station and into the crowds on 42nd Street, I decided to walk all the way down to Ground Zero rather than go underground in the subway. I walked down Madison to Broadway through Union Square, Greenwich Village, Soho, and Chinatown, and then approached the Financial District, covering miles of city blocks and passing numerous impromptu memorials to the dead and the missing. "Have you seen this person?" asked tattered sheets of paper with xeroxed faces tacked up next to drawings, farewell notes, and photographs of the fallen.

Torn up pavement with utility and construction barriers blocking access became the norm as I got closer, providing some preparation for the destruction ahead. Disoriented without the Towers to serve as a landmark in Lower Manhattan, I wandered in circles around the devastated area. Eventually I found my way to the chain-link fence covered with torn green burlap, which provided glimpses of the pit of rubble that had previously housed the city's tallest buildings. Following the barrier like an outdoorsman follows a river to his destination, I found the entrance to the area at last and joined in the long line waiting to walk past the temporary viewing shelter that had been erected for those wishing to pay their respects.

Concession stands were set up all along the main artery into the site, selling tee-shirts and other memorabilia. *Would other countries capitalize in this way?* I wondered before I turned a corner and registered the full effect of the devastation.

I was expecting the gaping crater filled with debris on the WTC site. I wasn't prepared for the surrounding circle of skyscrapers with blown out windows and blasted facades, and the echoing sense of haunted emptiness. The place screamed with remnants of violent energy and tragic loss. It was truly an empty field of battle.

❦

"The smell of decomposing bodies has finally cleared," said the doctor's receptionist, "that was the worst thing for me."

I was waiting to escort a friend home from laser eye surgery, and was getting used to the conversations that constantly took place as New Yorkers tried to come to terms with what they had gone through. Cocktail and dinner conversations still centered on where each person was during that fateful day. Stories ranged from making it out just before the Towers fell, to being saved by a freak meeting cancellation, to running from the dust cloud and hiding under deli counters, to being trapped in subway tunnels and finally coming up into chaos, to watching the airplanes hit from the commuter trains approaching the city. Everyone knew someone who didn't make it, and a few were the only ones who made it out while the rest of their colleagues perished.

Post-traumatic stress disorder counseling and support was advertised in all of the subways and public places, and provided at no cost to those who lived and worked below 14th Street and bore the brunt of the hardships as the city recovered.

Public transportation, the circulatory system of the city, presented a challenge as many feared going underground and being buried alive in another emergency. Subway service was disrupted by unstable or destroyed tunnels in the Financial District, and commuter lines in from New Jersey were not running. Many businesses moved from Lower Manhattan to the suburbs, causing trouble for mainly carless city workers and causing city planners anxiety over whether they, and their tax dollars, would return.

But New Yorkers are a resilient and hardy bunch, which is both a great strength and a necessity, living on top of each other as they do. The city took the changes in stride, shook itself off, and began to move forward again. And as with many survivors of a great tragedy, they began to pull together as a community, letting the tragedy unite them instead of divide them.

The city rose from the ashes as a stronger and more humane place. I was proud to call New York my home, and excited to build my life there.

Outside the New York metropolitan area, however, the nation, which was already split by a divisive presidential campaign and questionable election results, began to fracture. Instead of using the surge of post 9/11 patriotism to positive end, politicians used the tragedy to pass questionable legislation by playing on the country's fears. Racism and atrocities were justified in the name of self-defense and national security.

And seeing how successful the strategy of fear was, the president and his advisors began building the case for an unnecessary and unwinnable war. A war that we were still embroiled in ten years later.

Fear had become the national rallying point, even as community became the connecting force for those most impacted by the tragedy.

26.
Relearning Some Lessons

A year of bouncing from couch to couch, homeless and unemployed, following 9/11 had made me a bit desperate. In fact, my desperation had nearly driven me to the point of selling myself out for safety.

With the scarcity of any strategic marketing jobs in the economic fallout, I was taking interviews wherever I could find them. When a major tobacco company called about a position to run their strategic research group for the Americas, I decided to accept the meeting just for the practice. My background working for the MPAA during its controversial times with Columbine and Napster had attracted them, seeing transferable skills and a willingness to consider a more ethically challenged industry.

When the first interview turned into an offer to fly me to Geneva to meet the entire global research team and my prospective colleagues, I told myself that I was just taking the trip so that I could get a free visit to my best friend in neighboring Italy.

Wading through the smoke-filled hallways and offices, I spent two days of interviews at the headquarters in the beautiful and elegant Swiss city. I couldn't help being impressed by the sophistication of their consumer research practices and the thoroughness of their global data set. The sheer volume of resources devoted to understanding consumer behavior, motivation, and segmentation was staggering. The professional in me was attracted to working for such a highly funded, state of the art group after years of working in organizations where every research dollar had to be squeezed out of the budget like blood from a stone.

Over dinner, my would-be boss described a new technology being developed that enabled you to inject a tracking device into your children so that you could always know their whereabouts. As a father of two small girls, he was all for it given the increasing number of missing children being reported throughout Europe and the rest of the world.

I listened to him appalled at the casual acceptance and approval of controlling another human being in that way. "What about the freedom of the children, their ability to grow up learning autonomy and good decision making, their own sense of separate self and individuality?" I couldn't help expressing some of my opinions. I'm pretty sure that's what lost me the job.

When the word finally came that they had chosen another candidate, I must confess to some disappointment. While I had never truly considered accepting the job and devoting my energy to a product that was proven to physically harm people, who knows how I would have responded to the offer given my growing desperation and need for security.

I had been given me a clear lesson in being true to my principles no matter how desperate my situation, as well as the support not to force a difficult choice.

Two months later, with the dawning of the new year, the economy rebounded and I interviewed and received three job offers before January was over. I chose the one that most closely matched my needs for salary, location, and lifestyle, despite the fact that the job responsibilities were similar to a position I held six years before, prior to receiving my MBA. At least the products sold were not harming anyone, and I could begin to build a more stress-free life and enjoy the city I so loved. I told myself that I would get settled, pay off some debt, and continue looking for a more stimulating and inspiring job.

The atmosphere was comfortable, did not expect a lot or reward extra effort, so I settled in and focused on other areas of life. Not a bad gig, huh? Well, maybe not, except I was born with a deep need for challenges and a drive to succeed and grow. I once again found myself in a situation where 1) I wasn't seen, 2) I was forced to comply to edicts that did not make intuitive sense, 3) I was charged with maintaining the status quo instead of building a better future, 4) I was guided by ineffectual "leaders" whose words and actions did not match, and 5) I was not rewarded for my achievements.

A recurring pattern in my life, I noted.

Perhaps it was time to shift that pattern around into finding a situation that did provide what I wanted: visibility, intuitive management, positive impact and service, strong and smart leadership, and meaningful rewards for accomplishment.

27.
A Different Kind of Work
2009

A family of monkeys was draped along the thick branch of the Guanacaste tree, long arms hanging loosely over each side, a baby resting sprawled on its mother's back.

"Look at the balls on that one!" Amba crowed with laughter as we sat on her patio and watched them in the midday heat.

Minus the male equipment, my last four months had been spent pretty much the same way, swinging in total relaxation in my hammock on lazy afternoons when not in yoga training. It had been an incredibly healing time of completely listening to my body without stress or any requirements other than what I myself chose.

Amba Stapleton, one of my teachers and the co-director of the institute where I was studying, was pure warmth, laughter, and feminine power packed into a tiny frame. She was offering me an opportunity to write the newsletter for the Nosara Yoga Institute, so that she and her husband, Don, could stay engaged with their students and alumni after they left Costa Rica.

Words were flowing fast and furiously out of me since I had started writing creatively again after solving my ten-year writer's block during the first teacher training. But was I ready to start focusing them on something other than my own personal creative expression? Amba was very clear that it was my choice. I needed to listen to my own inner voice and see if this fit with my healing process.

One thing that I had learned about myself was that I needed to have the time and space to think about things before making a decision. In my fast-paced corporate life, I had always felt rushed, spread too thin by an overload of priorities, deliverables, and staff personalities that precluded quiet time for reflection.

I asked Amba for a few days to think about it.

I was ready for something to occupy my time, especially since the yoga teacher training programs I'd been taking during my first few months in Costa Rica had ended and I now had unlimited freedom. But was I ready for a monthly project, for working again? Deadlines, timelines, deliverables. They scared me. What impact would they have on my healing? Did I want to work, be accountable to someone or something else, on my sabbatical?

It's a muscle needing a different kind of exercise, I finally decided. I would strengthen my focus on accomplishing a specific goal like the newsletter again, and experiment with the process while in a supportive environment. I could create my own style of work that, like the yoga trainings I had completed, provided the discipline to be strong and creative, and gave me the freedom to do what worked best for me.

During our first editorial meeting, I couldn't stop smiling. I was actually going to get to write about this!? The topics we discussed were a perfect extension of the teaching I'd experienced during the training programs that had so inspired me. I couldn't wait to dig into the ideas for the articles in order to continue my learning process.

Amba was clear that she wanted me to introduce myself as the new editor, to have my own byline, and to create something that was my own personal expression in addition to featuring expert articles by her and Don.

I loved my new job!

At the same time as I took the writing position, I began teaching my first yoga classes. When my friend Dana returned to the States, I took over her time slot on Sunday afternoons and began teaching my own version of Yin Yoga. Because that type of yoga had been my personal practice for years, I was able to immediately bring my own unique therapeutic elements to the class.

Using the breath as a tool to sweep tightness from the body, and guidance from yoga masters, Taoist masters, and other masters, I led my students through the long holds of positions and into meditation. The peaceful energy generated in Tree Tops pavilion, supported by magnificent ocean views and abundant wildlife visitors, engaged the senses while I read the following poem by Rumi to focus the mind.

This being human is a guest house,

Every morning a new arrival: a joy, a depression, a mean-ness.

Some momentary awareness comes as an unexpected visitor.

Welcome and entertain them all even if they are a crowd of sorrows,

Who violently sweep your house empty of its furniture.

Still, treat each guest honorably; he may be clearing you out for some new delight.

The dark thought, the shame, the malice; meet them all at the door laughing and invite them in.

Be grateful for whoever comes because each has been sent as a guide from beyond.

"Here, take my phone number and email," my student said, "my sister and I want to do private yoga classes with you when you get back to New York. I've never been able to quiet my monkey mind so well. I need this with my stressful life in the city. Thank you."

Wow. I had made a difference for someone.

I loved teaching!

⚜

A hand reached out and grabbed my arm as I walked past the first-class seats on the airplane from Liberia, Costa Rica, to Newark, New Jersey.

"You're from Nosara, right?" said the woman attached to the hand. "I took your class at the Harmony Hotel last week. It was great. Where do you teach in the States?"

I explained that I was on my way back to New York after eight months studying in Nosara, and hoped to start teaching in the States soon. "Best of luck to you," she exclaimed, "I hope to take another class with you someday!"

Smiling, I walked back to my seat and meditated on gratitude. I didn't know what was next for me, but knew that I had found a way to make a difference.

Person by person.

28.
Transformation

Soon after my Granny died, I began to question who I had become in life. I had passed one milestone and then another, had attempted to change my life and find happiness several times, and it somehow kept eluding me.

"You really should try The Landmark Forum," my friend enthused. "It changed my life!"

I began my journey into the transformational world along with several hundred other people in a conference hall in Midtown Manhattan. The basic premise of the Forum is that there are several key moments in our youth when we make a decision about how the world is, and then that world becomes our reality. Our belief system is born and we live our lives according to it. By understanding and accepting responsibility for how we created our world, we can open up possibilities to create a new one.

This made sense to me, so I continued through several Landmark programs, learning more about myself and practicing making distinctions between what happened in reality and the story I made up about it. By changing how I reacted to situations, I could begin to build a different life for myself.

The key was to take responsibility for your own choices.

"I don't know if I'm doing it right. Am I doing it right?" I asked the circle of open and concerned faces crouched around the mattress, my small voice quavering and vulnerable.

Exhausted and spent, I had just finished releasing a good chunk of stored anger into a makeshift punching bag laid out on a mattress on the floor. I had quite enough of letting other people tell me what to think and how to be. It was time to start trusting my instincts.

Friends of mine from Landmark had recommended doing the Arete Experience as another, more personal and interactive transformational workshop. "You really get deep into your own shit," my friend Rich told me. "It's the most powerful thing that I've done." Well, I was really sick of my shit, and if I had to get deep into it to get past it, well then I was all for it.

It had taken quite a while to get me to the point of opening up, scaling the thick and sturdy wall between me and my emotions. An hour had been spent, pressed against the wall in front of the room and the circle of participants, deflecting queries and fiercely defending my vulnerabilities from exposure. I was strong, things didn't bother me.

"How do you feel when Robin says it doesn't bother her? Where do you feel it in your body?" the facilitator asked the circle. "I feel an ache in my throat," said one participant. "I feel a tightness in my chest and burning in my eyes," said another.

What broke through my armor, ultimately, was not the impact of life on me, but my concerns for the two people I loved most in the world: my niece and nephew. The thought of them growing up crippled by insecurities and fears that I had faced in my life drove me out of my self-imposed prison and into expression. I wanted to save them that pain by providing a balanced example.

As a child, I had learned that there was a right way to do things, and I spent my life trying to find that right way externally rather than listening to what my intuition told me. I looked outside of me for answers and built walls around what was inside because it rarely matched up with the answers I found.

Recognizing my need to conform to some perfect external ideal, I was able to start dismantling it. I began finding ways to release the tension and anger that had built up from not expressing the truth of what I felt. And I began the practice of speaking my truth in the moment.

Another angry woman took the floor at the Arete workshop. She had no trouble unleashing her emotions as she blasted the room and everyone in it. In the space of five minutes, she had lost any sympathy from her fellow participants and had converted it into outright dislike.

She read the energy and turned it up a notch.

Abrasive, attacking, arrogant, and acidic. No one was rooting for her, except for her to get off of the stage. We just wanted to be far away from her.

Kevin, one of the facilitators, took a deep breath and stepped to the front of the room next to her. "Do you mind if I stand here beside you?" he asked.

She was puzzled.

"It seemed like you could use someone on your side," he said. And throughout the next hour or so, he stayed by her side helping her to feel like she wasn't alone. Gradually her anger and her attacks toned down, and she slowly opened up.

He was able to see past her anger to the vulnerable person who desperately needed connection at the same time as she shoved it away. He helped someone to feel less alone.

By his actions, he changed her world. He enabled us to see her as well, past her self-protective, abrasive exterior and appreciate the vulnerable human she was inside. She was able to open up, probably for the first time in her life, and receive the support from others that she so desperately craved.

Wow. That's what I wanted to do with my life. I wanted to make that kind of difference for someone.

I walked to the middle of the circle, crouched in a squat on the floor, and curled into a tight ball with arms protecting face and head. A low, continuous moan escaped from my lips as I rocked back and forth.

Midway through the first intensive weekend of my life coaching training, we were working with our shadows and asked to act them out alone in front of class. What belief was it that triggered our deepest fears? We had already gone through a day's work of exercises systematically drilling down to that point: I am defective. Don't see me. Don't judge me. Don't hurt me.

Yup, that was mine.

When the opportunity to train as a life coach and facilitator for workshops like the Arete Experience graciously presented itself in my life, I jumped on it. Never mind the fact that it would involve a significant investment of time in addition to my full-time job, as well as seven trips to San Francisco for long intensive weekend courses over the next year. I remembered the difference that Kevin had made during my Arete workshop, and was still inspired to do that with my life.

The process of training to be a coach necessitated getting yourself really clear of your own garbage so that you could be present for others. That meant facing and working through all of those things that I had been hiding. It also meant being open to others pointing out my blind spots and calling me on it when I started defending a position.

"Oh, I see...you're *unavailable*," said my friend John less than five minutes into in our first joint coaching session. "Your heart is a closed door," he continued. "You may say you want love, but you aren't allowing it." Like a surgeon with a scalpel, he got straight to the core of it.

Now just what was I supposed to do to become available? That was a tougher question.

Another practice we learned changed my world: the clearing discussion. So simple, yet so powerful and essential. For a person who grew up in a family that swept under the rug instead of out the door immediately, the effectiveness of it started a landslide.

The practice of it is simple and very powerful. Clearing is a one-on-one discussion about any issues or feelings that had come up over a period that needed to be expressed in order for both parties to be present. By releasing any minor irritations, feelings, and emotions, they were not allowed to accumulate and build up into something greater. Relationships were able to stay present because there was no backlog of unexpressed personal resentments fueling discord. Key to the process was being able to actually hear what the other person was saying without defensiveness, giving them permission to have their opinions and thoughts without making it be about you.

Wow. If only I had known this growing up, life would have been so different.

29.

Light in Your Eyes

My father and I had been at odds for years about two things: respect and responsibility. We had been judging each other for not having enough. Being similar people, our tendency had been to store up grievances, without communicating them, of course, and then explode when they reached critical level with a rage totally out of proportion with the immediate circumstances.

For many years, we had been blowing up and walking away, and never addressing the underlying issue. We stopped listening to each other because we only heard what we wanted to hear, which was whatever supported our own position. We stopped seeing each other.

If there were anything productive in the activity, I would lay the some of the blame for our estrangement at Rush Limbaugh's door. He and the other ultra-conservative talk show hosts had become my father's main "advisors" in his retirement. But this is not about laying blame. We've had too much of that.

However, a steady diet of divisive rhetoric, ridiculing, and labeling turned my father into a man who focused his considerable intellect and energy into sneering at people. Basic psychology, programmed behavior from repeated stimulus, he was brainwashed with a message of hate and enfolded in a big black cloud of negativity. It was us against them.

"Can I borrow the car on Tuesday to move the rest of my things from the old apartment?" I asked my mother on Christmas Eve. I was back from Phoenix for the holidays after my first semester at Thunderbird, and had a few remaining items to move out of my former home with Tom. It was my last painful step in ending our relationship.

"Yes. We'd offer to help you," my mother replied, "but your father vowed never to step foot in that apartment. You know he didn't approve of you and Tom living together."

Ouch. I looked for the dagger lodged between my ribs. No, I didn't know that, but really appreciated learning it now. I didn't quite feel bad enough yet about the smoking ruins of my relationship, and hearing that my father had pronounced a boycott on our home hurt a lot. And it made me angry to think of him sitting silently in judgment of us. And why did my mother feel that now was the best time to inform me of that fact?

F-A-I-L-U-R-E on a triple word score in the Scrabble game we were playing with Granny at the kitchen table. How many points for that? Was I winning now?

Ding, ding went the timer. Saved by the bell, my mother rushed to the stove to check on dinner.

My father passed through the kitchen, headphones covering his ears as the latest broadcast of Rush Limbaugh's radio program blared negativity into his brain.

Granny's age-spotted hand reached out, covered and threaded its fingers between mine. "Dear, I know it hurts and that you miss Tom. I still miss your grandfather and it's been over ten years." We sat quietly watching the tear drops fall on our joined hands.

⬥

She was a pistol, my ninety-year-old Granny. Five-foot-two with a Brillo pad head of wiry grey and white curls, and a twinkle in her eye, she knew how to put an outfit together and could charm the pants off men twenty years her junior. Being a good Catholic, she never literally tested that skill, but men of every age admired her sass as she sauntered into a room with her hat at a jaunty angle.

We had grown very close as adults in the five years since Tom and I had split, and I had stayed with her frequently when 9/11's economic fallout had kept me unemployed for my first year in New York.

Nights were spent tucked into the little twin bed in her guest room bearing my rose-covered childhood bedspread, then the days unfolded job searching and doing Internet research while she watched her television programs. "I can't believe how much water you drink," she would say every day as she was setting the table for our meals. Two peas in a pod, we would settle companionably onto facing sofas after dinner and read our books with a blanket thrown over our legs.

"Put some lipstick on, dear. You look a bit pale," Granny instructed before we went out food shopping or to run errands. "Never tell them how old you are, you look much younger," she advised. "This is my granddaughter, Robin, back from Hollywood," she would proudly tell all her friends.

A bad fall resulted in a broken hip, and then a speedy trip to her end the next year.

"Oooh, Robin...," Granny moaned, "Oooh, Annie..." Heartbroken, my sister and I sat on either side of her hospital bed as she struggled with the pain medication and her slow journey toward death. *Oh, Granny,* I thought as I stroked her white curls. My first close experience with a loved one dying was painful to watch, but I was glad to be there to say goodbye and ease her transition.

"I'm home safe," I told my mother when she picked up the phone after the long day at the hospital.

"What should I do about Thanksgiving?" my mother fretted, in pain and rambling. "Do you think I should call it off? What do you think everyone would think? Can you call Jenny and sound her out? What do you think she would think? What do you think? What will the others think? Maybe I should just do it? But it really doesn't seem right. I don't think I have the energy. What if we still need to be at the hospital? What should I do? Nobody will have anywhere to go if I don't have it..."

"Mom, please stop worrying. I think everyone will understand no matter what you decide. It doesn't matter," I replied, anxious to soothe her nervous pain. No one knew how to handle what was happening to our dear Granny, family matriarch and last of her generation.

"Why are you criticizing me?" my mother flared and began weeping.

"I'm not," I said, "I'm..."

A snarl of rage erupted into my ear. My father had grabbed the phone away. "How dare you make your mother cry at a time like this!" A stream of venom detailing what a selfish and ungrateful child I was stabbed into my shocked brain until the phone was slammed down with a violent crash and the dial tone blared in my ear.

I sat stunned. This was what my father thought of me? This was what he saw when he looked at me, someone who was capable of deliberately making her mother cry when her own mother was dying? Despite our ups and downs over the years, I had always thought that he saw the good in me and loved me. I saw now that he had made me the enemy.

My heart, raw bewildered and painfully engorged from the day at Granny's deathbed, broke that day. I sat on the couch in my Manhattan apartment, totally alone in a city of millions, an occasional siren and car horn accenting the sound of my weeping.

Was that who I was? Self-doubt crept into my heart, though I knew my motives to be pure. Such is the power that a father has over his daughter's opinion of herself.

The incident was never mentioned by either of us. Many times in the past, I had forgiven him for his scalding blasts of rage. I probably could have forgiven him this one, too, in compassion for the pain we were all experiencing, if he had ever taken responsibility for his words. He never did. And so I chose to model that lesson from him as well.

I chose not to forgive.

"You owe me 84 cents for the screws to fix this bracket," my father informed me as he finished fixing the shelf in my Manhattan apartment.

For as long as I could remember, my father had kept lists: lists of mileage and the price to fill each tank of gas, lists of tasks to accomplish, lists of items to bring on his next camping trip. The lists stacked up next to the accumulation of things he refused to throw out—old magazines, plastic containers, anything else that may possibly have a future use—and began to overwhelm the basement and office where my mother attempted to keep it confined.

One day, he started keeping a list of everything that I owed him.

This first list also coincided with the national debate that had been heating up since the divisive and questionable election of George W. Bush and his response to the 9/11 tragedy. My father and I had come down on very different sides.

"Treehugger," he sneered at me when I criticized the U.S. participation in the Johannesburg Summit, the UN conference on sustainable development. The Kyoto Protocol, a plan for converting world energy production from fossil fuels to solar and wind power and other renewable energy sources had been significantly watered down thanks to the influence of the Texas oilman who was also our president.

"Bleeding liberal," he scoffed derisively, when I suggested that national security was better served by working with the international community rather than attempting to bully them.

How was it possible to respect a man who saw only separation? Who did not see how our actions personally and as a country impacted each other? Who spent more time with his headphones listening to Rush Limbaugh and the new crop of dividers than speaking with his own family?

I did not respect his opinions or his lists. Who was this man? And where had my father gone?

I began to dread going home for visits. A wall of sound struck my ears every time I entered my parents' house. Two televisions and three radios blared downstairs, and often another one and two respectively upstairs. Fox News and Rush Limbaugh were the content providers, spreading ridicule over the air waves and nasty energy throughout the house. It was not a place to find peace and quiet, it was a place to be endured.

Did you know there was a war on Christmas? A new charismatic opinion leader had entered the fold of media personalities, and Glenn

Beck was making it big by whipping public frenzy over an imagined slight to Christians during the sentimental holiday session. He, Bill O'Reilly, and Rush Limbaugh were my Dad's closest friends and companions through each day of his retirement.

Anything to rally the troops against the enemy was permissible. But just who was the enemy? Our family, our neighbors, our fellow citizens it seemed. Anyone who disagreed.

What happened to the separation of church and state, a key foundation of our constitution? I questioned. And how was it socially responsible to use people's fears to turn a national tragedy into a religious crusade? It was certainly a successful strategy, as I watched our president and his advisors override international objections and lead my country into an unnecessary and unwinnable war against the Axis of Evil.

"You just don't understand the issues," my father sneered condescendingly.

"No," I steamed, "why aren't you seeing me?" I guess my master's work in international political economies and diplomacy, my ten years of direct work experience in politics, and a life lived traveling extensively and experiencing other cultures disqualified me from having a valid opinion.

My father's other primary occupation in his retirement was spending time with my sister's twins, and it was only with them that occasional glimpses of the loving father I grew up with showed through like sunlight through a break in the clouds. In particular, he had a special bond with Tomas, who came into this world talking and was quite the conversationalist by the ripe old age of seven.

"Did you hear what Tomas said at school today?" began many of my father's conversations, before he would launch into a detailed story of the boy's latest escapade, chuckling with affection. A lightness came over his face and shone through his eyes, and his whole energy changed when he was focused on expressing love.

I miss this *man,* I would think. *Can I please have more of him? How do I get him back?*

The bond went two ways, and Tomas would spend hours chatting with my father, trailing him around the house and asking him questions. "Grandpop, can I use your computer? When can we go canoeing? Can you show me how this works? Look what I made, what do you think?"

Unfortunately, so much time with my father also meant that Tomas absorbed a lot of the divisive messages blaring from the television and radio.

"And why aren't *you* married anyway?" Tomas snarled at me as he passed the open driver's side door.

What the f—-? How does a seven-year-old know precisely how to stab a single woman in the heart?

I looked at him in shock. Where did that come from, that instinct to wound?

While driving the twins home from school, my mother and I had been discussing the war and I had criticized Bush's slow reaction to Hurrican Katrina. Tomas and Clara had listened from the back seat, and he had chimed in that he and Grandpop loved President Bush.

Pulling into the driveway, I had replied that while some people liked him, many others disagreed with what he was doing to the country.

And what had been Tomas' response to my opinion? Stabbing at the enemy with rage and anger.

Knowing the way my father loved Tomas, I knew he would never consciously want to be responsible for exposing a little boy to the message that it was okay to strike out in mindless anger.

I know it's a hard thing to be a good example. There have been many times in my life when I have not been one. But when you have a child, you are obligated to be a good example in words and deeds if you want the child to learn to be a responsible citizen. As a leader of another's opinion, you have a responsibility to model behavior that promotes the greater good. And hate of any form only breeds more hate.

But when in the course of human events, you lose sight of what you're becoming, then you lose sight of what example you're giving. I realized that my father had become unconscious to the impact of his actions, just as I had by holding a grudge against him.

Instead of taking Tomas' comment personally, I committed to taking a more active role in the development of the twins, providing a balancing force based on positivity, love, and openness. And that began by becoming a good example myself.

I chose to forgive my father. The decision was the first step of a much longer journey.

Several years later, I sat on the back porch of my parent's house and listened to the crickets chirp in the dark night. The trees enclosed the patio and I could spot a few stars peeking through between the branches. *Wow, my dad really did create his own private little world back here,* I thought, appreciating the time and effort he put into the yard and his home.

The house was quiet and comforting, and for the first time I could feel myself settling into the place as home. I set up the dining room as my writing space and quickly got into a groove scoping out and then beginning to draft sections of material.

My transformational yoga journey over the past year and a half had shifted a lot of things for me since my parents had helped me pack up my Manhattan apartment and begin to build a different kind of life for myself. Though they hadn't necessarily agreed with my decision at that time, they had always supported me. The joy they showed in my new found happiness was all the proof that I ever needed that they loved me deeply and wanted only the best for me.

As part of my journey, I had decided to follow my life's dream of becoming a writer. When they took off on a cross-country adventure, they offered me their home as a writer's retreat for two months. It was there that my writing project finally started taking shape after a long creative and ideation process. Gratitude was my attitude.

I quickly settled into a productive routine. Morning meditation was followed by a hike under the tall trees and among the late spring flowers in the nearby state park. The rest of the day unfolded with writing, unstructured creative time, goals, and deadlines. Twice a week I went to yoga class at a beautiful little Anusara studio up the road, and two other times I had a Skype session with Mónica, my writing partner, to check progress and set new goals. Life was good.

When my parents came home in mid-July, I scoured the house from top to bottom in a two-day cleaning extravaganza. Lucy, my extremely hairy white dog, left traces of her presence everywhere and I tried to erase as much as I could, anticipating my father's reaction.

Yup. I received a list of grievances once he had a chance to look around, but this time I asked for a list of requirements for making the situation livable as I searched for another home. Somewhere over the past year and a half, he had seen the changes in me and he liked what he saw. I was taking responsibility. He was willing to work with me, if I would comply with his requirements for cleaning up after Lucy. Daily vacuuming was necessary to keep the house livable in his opinion.

Being the person I am, and given the time it takes to change behavior patterns, I forgot to vacuum for a few days. That triggered an accusatory explosion of rage at my lack of respect and inconsiderate nature like in olden times. And, it set off an answering rage in me. But this time, we didn't walk away from each other. When he slammed out of the house, my mother and I were able to have a discussion about what had happened, and I actually heard that it was about respect for him. And she heard what I was saying. "Yes," she said, "I know something about the feeling of never being able to measure up to someone's uncommunicated expectations."

I went out to the yard to find my father. We were both shaken up by the explosion, and sorry for losing our tempers.

"Dad, I'm trying," I said, "but I forget. Can you please remind me instead of bottling it up? My forgetting is not intended as an act of disrespect, I just have a lot on my mind right now. Please remind me, help me learn."

The next day, after sitting in a pile of Lucy's hair, my father wouldn't look at me, simmering with anger and resentment. I bustled around the house cleaning and checking items off his list.

He came in from the yard as I was preparing to leave. I stopped him, thanked him for all he had done for me. He grumbled.

"Ewe! You're all sweaty," I teased him, as I kissed each cheek repeatedly. "Thank you, thank you, thank you." He broke a smile.

Each time I saw him after that, his face became more open. He began to look at me again like he looked at Tomas, with light and love in his eyes. He began to see *me* again.

When I was leaving for Spain at the end of the summer, he joked, "You keep getting younger each time I see you! How's that happening?"

I got my father back by offering love and forgiveness, both to myself and to him, and by releasing the past. By responding to his anger with love and gratitude, I had the power to transform our relationship.

Love is the most powerful force in the world, and the only way to respond to hate and division.

Observe

"I love it when the moment of change comes, the open road and me."
—Luka Bloom

"Walk on, and leave it behind."
—U2

Wisdom Body (*Vijnana -maya-kosha*)

The wisdom body represents our ability to see life for the lessons it provides us, rather than seeing ourselves as the victim of circumstance. This skill of discrimination—witness consciousness, not taking personally what happens in life—enables us to see the patterns of reaction we have developed over the course of our lives. Our inquiry into these patterns allows us to release them and to incorporate new, more productive modes of behavior. We begin to make more conscious choices that influence the well-being of ourselves and others. We gain the power to create the life that we want going forward, by living from our spirit versus our ego.

30.
Intentions and Agreements

"Are you in shape for this?" my father asked.

My mind flashed to the difficult times last year in Costa Rica, when my body felt broken and used up by the hours of intense yoga training yanking me apart. I thought of walking hot dusty miles on dirt roads to the *supermercado* and back carrying my groceries, and of later riding my bike on the same paths and others bouncing over rocks and vines, food flying out of the basket. Memories of long barefoot walks on the beach: in the morning for meditation, becoming one with the sound of the waves; at sunset drinking in the colors of the sky and water and the community on the beach and in the waves; and then under the nebulous clouds of the Milky Way in the undiluted dark, each star pulsing life from beyond this tiny world. I recalled walking the jungle path at night, using only the light of the stars and the moon to guide me, fascinated by strange moon shadows and listening to night creatures crackle the trees and undergrowth. Later, walking and riding horses through the mountains and gorges of New Mexico searching for inspiration and peace, and even later climbing the hills and mountains of Southern Spain, talking into my voice recorder and meditating in the olive and almond groves.

I remembered the wizened old man in the Burgos Cathedral earlier that day, who had beckoned me over to show the marionette up in the corner giving the same show since the thirteenth century. I had cried thinking of my Spanish grandfather, whom I'd never had the chance to know, but who had shaped my father into the man he was today.

I could have told my father all this and more, but instead I thanked him for the time spent together over the summer and for all he had done for me. I told him I loved him, and that I would speak with him again in a month.

And then, calling all angels, I signed off Skype and cut contact with the world once again. Believing in them by now, but not realizing all forms that angels could take, I began walking my Camino.

For what is an angel, other than an entity that lifts you when you need it? Real or a figment of your imagination, it serves the purpose if you let it.

El Camino de Santiago is one of the world's great pilgrimage routes and also a UNESCO World Heritage site, with monuments of historical significance all along the way. Its origins predate Christianity, though it is best known as a path walked by Christians and others for over a thousand years to visit the tomb of Saint James the Apostle in Santiago. Once a Roman trade route following the Milky Way to the Atlantic Ocean, it also served as a pre-Christian Celtic ceremonial journey westward to the setting sun in Finisterre, considered the end of the world at the westernmost point in Spain. Legends and myths also link the road to prehistoric fertility cults of Aphrodite, Mari, Ishtar, and Kali, and designate the path as one of the great energy leylines of the planet.

Whatever cultural or spiritual significance given to the route, the Camino represents a powerful and highly travelled path to fulfilling one's intentions.

I was drawn to making the journey not only for the purpose of meditation, but also because it allowed me to walk and intimately experience the region of my grandfather and ancestors. Pilgrims choose to walk the way for many other personal reasons, as well. Some that we encountered included mourning the death of a loved one, petitioning for a pregnancy or new baby, curing a loved one's illness, working out one's sexuality, deciding on a life change, sparking creative inspiration, or just figuring out next steps.

Although there are many routes and starting points, most pilgrims begin El Camino in St. Jean Pied de Port in the Pyrenees and walk 500 miles across Northern Spain to Santiago. Some use guidebooks to plan and navigate their routes, while others go in complete trust, following the yellow arrows and scallop shell signs that mark the path the entire journey.

The way is rich with symbolism, offering many opportunities to release the burdens carried through life. "Imagine walking with people who have dropped the walls surrounding them," wrote one blogger who had recently completed El Camino when I was doing my research for the journey. He then went on to describe the deep connections made between travelors who continually lost and found each other again along the route. The blogger described the process of shedding personal belongings in each town as a metaphor for lightening your load and stripping down to what is essential in your life. He also wrote of his experience at the Iron Cross, erected in Roman times on the point of highest elevation, and the practice of pouring your regrets and concerns into a stone carried for hundreds of miles and then left behind on the towering pile at the monument. The final ritual of El Camino came at the very end of the world in Finisterre, a three-day walk beyond Santiago to the ocean, where pilgrims burned their clothing or other offerings to mark the beginning of their "new" lives.

My friend, Mónica, and I had discussed making the pilgrimage together during our adventures the previous year in Costa Rica when another friend dropped out, and had made the commitment to walk the path earlier that summer. We spent the month before embarking in Barcelona working on our writing project, planning our journey and buying our provisions.

The time in Barcelona had been an experiment for me. For years, I had threatened to move to the city, starting with a passionate declaration in the New York City subway to friends as we dispersed from marching against the 2004 Republican Convention in our fair city. "If Bush is re-elected, I am moving to Barcelona," I had stated dramatically. A country that could support and endorse the dehumanizing strategies of fear that his administration employed could no longer be considered my home.

Now that I was free and actively shopping around for a new home, I was grateful for the opportunity to explore fulfilling this dream, too. A friend from Thunderbird offered us his apartment in Barceloneta, the district bordering the Mediterranean beaches, and we explored the city from there. New friends, old friends, a few interesting men, and a neighborhood community had materialized immediately, along with an invitation to audition my Yin Yoga class at a beautiful Anusara studio in El Born. And, the government had recently changed regulations concerning the grandchildren of Spaniards, making it a much simpler matter to apply and qualify for citizenship.

But I had changed, too, over the last two years and while still enthralled with the place and its energy, I questioned whether city living was for me anymore. I had decided to defer any decision until after I walked El Camino, and explored more rural places along the route as potential homes as well.

Given the four weeks that Mónica and I had to walk, we chose to make our pilgrimage from Burgos to Finisterre, a total distance of about 370 miles or 600 kilometers. We were to learn later that we started at perhaps the most difficult point, adjusting to the initial physical wear and tear of the journey on the Meseta, a brutal landscape of golden, but barren high desert with absolutely no shade.

As Mónica and I began following yellow arrows through the Burgos arches in the early morning darkness, I formally set my intention for El Camino de Santiago and the next 600 kilometers I would walk. My pilgrimage was dedicated to the intention of "finding home," and for me, "home" included being united with the right man.

Little did I know in setting my intention that the experience would entail learning three critical lessons about personal patterns that had influenced my relationships with men throughout life. These were clearly demonstrated like a gift from the angels I had invoked in setting out on my journey. The men who would appear on my Camino taught me about allowing an open and playful energetic connection without taking it further than friendship, and about consciously choosing not to fall into the ambiguity trap of "does he like me?" thereby closing off to other possibilities. It also provided the opportunityto mourn the loss of a powerful connection, while releasing attachment to a man with many great qualities but several important things missing. My Right Man BATNA would come in handy, and prove as essential as my guidebook.

Mónica and I paused for a moment on *el Puente de Malatos* (the bridge of maladies) where, as I had so many times the past two years, I released all that no longer served me into the flowing water below and asked for courage for what lied ahead. I brought to mind my broader personal intentions for Spain, to be powerful and beautiful, and crossed the medieval bridge.

As we walked our first kilometers together in the late September sunshine, Mónica and I revisited our ground rules and agreements for taking the journey together. We would:

1. Speak the truth,
2. Be in integrity with our commitments,
3. Listen and be open to receiving even if it hurt,
4. Coach each other towards being the best we could be, and
5. Above all else, have FUN!

Having committed to our list, with lots of laughter and frequent breaks, we completed our first stage to Rabé de las Calzadas.

Our first night on the Camino was not to be a typical one, though we did end up making one of our dearest friends of the pilgrimage in Ann, a soul sister from Belgium. We stayed in an *albergue*, or pilgrim's hostal, run by a civilian mother superior who seemed to be French in the evenings for the communal dinner, but German in the mornings when she imposed strict breakfast regulations on us. There we shared a small dormitory with eight other women. Stringent restrictions were placed on who could stay in this albergue (absolutely no cyclists, as they were not considered to be true pilgrims), and on how we comported ourselves (for example, all packs, clothes, personal items must be bagged to prevent bedbugs).

All I needed was a plaid uniform and I could have been back in Catholic school. Not exactly what I had in mind setting off, but I surrendered to the journey.

Collapsing on a stone pylon marking the path, I read in despair the sign indicating that Hontanas was still another five kilometers away. After an "easy" first day of only eleven kilometers, we were pushing on for the full twenty on day two. It felt like I was carrying a small automobile on my back.

I threw my pack down on the barren field of tan dirt and unhooked the foam mat attached to the top. I needed some yoga desperately.

Catching up to me, Mónica crossed the municipal road and unstrapped her mat as well. We dropped down to our backs on the ground, groaning, and brought our knees to our chests. I segued into a deep, reclining side twist, while Mónica kicked her legs up into Happy Baby pose, sighs and sounds of pleasure releasing from us both.

Passing cars slowed on the road, a lone pilgrim wandered by scratching his head and cautiously skirting us.

"Buen Camino!" We called after him in unison.

The Mexican and the American, Mónica and I soon became a familiar sight on the Camino, as one by one, pilgrims passed us by, either smiling at our antics or shaking their heads in confusion. *"Buen Camino!"* we called to one and all. We were generally to be found doubled over in laughter with tears streaming down our faces, collapsed on benches by the side of the path examining new blisters, or stretched out on our improvised yoga mats, releasing tight muscles. Both fresh from the jungles of Costa Rica, we were walking the path our own way. *And* out to enjoy life while we were at it.

Who said a pilgrimage couldn't be fun. *Pura vida!*

We had made an agreement to take this journey together, united by the common purpose of coaching each other, and for various personal reasons individual to each of us.

When I had jumped off the cliff and left my previous life behind, I never imagined that two years later I would still be circling for someplace to come in for a landing. My time in Costa Rica and on the road had changed me in profound ways, and I was having trouble finding where the new me belonged. Time spent back in New York had left me feeling haunted, ghosts of my past reaching out to drag me back to an unhappy life, while at the same time filling me achingly with the familiar sense of home.

Each step I had taken so far on my journey had brought me more clarity and direction, and I was confident that by following the yellow arrows of El Camino to the end, I would find where I belonged.

Mónica, my dear sister, was standing at the edge of a cliff of her own and building up courage for the jump if she decided to end her ten-year marriage.

Whenever a serious decision is called for, the best plan of action is to relax, be in the moment and let the answers come to you. However, with such weighty issues on both of our minds, it was inevitable that our journey would take us down a bumpy road.

31.
Der Schönste Junge

"I have a brother when I'm a brother in need/When I feel myself going down/ I just call and he comes around/and for the first time I feel love."
—U2

(Week One)

Soaking my feet in a swimming pool at an albergue smelling of horse manure from the animals across the lane, I thanked my angels. This was paradise after twenty kilometers on the high desert, empty of everything but golden fields and glaring light. A wide and lush green lawn surrounded the blue blister bathing pool, populated by funky sculpture made by the resident artist and albergue owner, and bordered by a variety of old stone buildings and the converted barn that served as the dormitory. The town was Boadilla del Camino.

My angels had a busy fourth day on the road, supporting me through an endurance test with blazing sun, aching hip, heavy pack, and new blisters. At one point, I visualized that they had transported me to my Granny's couch, snuggled under blankets while a snowstorm raged against the windows. I actually felt a cold breeze as I walked. Even with their help, I had arrived nearly incoherent with sun stroke, walking into the courtyard past a mirage of my last lover, Antonio, blasting mojo at me as he exited.

My intent right now, resting at the albergue, was journaling, but the pool began to populate first with a very attractive man from Madrid and next with his fantastic friend from South Africa. Mónica migrated over and then four Catalans, including twin brothers from Terrassa, Jaume and Josep, and also Pere and Cesç from Barcelona. Jakob, a recent university grad from Berlin, arrived last, tossed down his pack and collected orders for the bar.

An impromptu yoga practice in the grass, several bug bites, lots of photographs, and many drinks later, dinner was served. And I mean served..."Have some wine, try this soup, now try this one, have some chicken, want some pork, more wine, more water, try this dessert, coffee?" Everywhere, a male hand offering something, a happy smile, and a laugh.

Jakob, looking like a handsome elf with gingery sideburns running around jawline as a narrow beard, sat next to me speaking English and *ein bisschen Deutsch,* while Spanish and Catalan swirled around us.

"Yoga? I think my mom does some of those stretching classes," said the twenty-five-year old German before going on to discuss the martial arts training he did for much of his childhood and teens.

Later, the first aid kits came out and both Mónica and I found our feet encased in warm masculine hands to pierce and disinfect our blisters. Palm fronds, peeled grapes...anyone?

My own feet were in the capable hands of young Jakob. When someone handles your wounds so gently and holds your feet so firmly in his muscular lap, it's impossible to keep him out of your dreams. And it just so happened that the dear boy was lying directly above me in a bed in the loft.

We started walking the next morning with our new group of friends, but it became apparent by the second break that our pace did not match theirs. Finally arriving at a bar housing another green oasis, the group exclaimed, "We've been waiting for you for an hour!" and prepared to leave immediately. We made arrangements to meet at a specific albergue in Carrión de los Condes, and the men set off after first noticing that Jakob remained behind to do some yoga with me.

Barefoot in the grass, I gave him some basic instruction on physical postures and energy cues before taking him into wide-legged mountain pose and forward bend to open his lower back and hamstrings. "I feel the energy," he said excitedly, as I instructed him to pull it up through the grassy earth. "My legs feel stronger."

A sun salutation or two later, we finished our midday practice and he headed out for the next town.

The day progressed through many kilometers, a three-course lunch with bottle of wine and a trip into the mystical realm in a thirteenth-century Knights Templar church. The afternoon sun blazed through the Rose Window, converting it into a moving vision of my personal meditation symbol and transporting me to a place of deep peace.

On the fumes of spiritually infused fuel, we stumbled for the last of twenty-six kilometers into Carrión. Turning the corner into the stone town, we spotted Josep, one of the Catalan twins, milling about. He hailed us, took over a backpack and led us through the medieval streets. Immediately, Jakob appeared around a corner and a handsome Madrileño we'd met at the last stop strolled out an abbey entrance. Plans had changed! Apparently we were to come to a different albergue so our new friends could cook a community meal for just about everyone we had met so far on the Camino.

Surrounded by Catalans at one end of the table, I was served assorted plates of gluten until I could shyly remind my new friends that I had allergies and didn't eat pasta or bread. The non-edibles were whisked away immediately and replaced with salad, eggs, and potatoes, and the wine was poured.

Time once more for blister care, and there were new ones. Coming up the stairs as I came down, Jakob pouted, "Now will you sit with me?"

"Will you take care of my feet first?" I asked.

Lucky guy, drawled a man from D.C., as Jakob placed my bare calf in his lap and took hold of my foot. A pair of grandfathers closely supervised his technique and offered suggestions in Spanish, as the German became more and more testy, tickling my soles when they finally moved away.

Later in the dark, down the cobbled lane in a stone plaza by an ancient church, the younger pack of pilgrims who were our friends shared stories, laughed, and drank Spanish wine. Finally on a hard surface for yoga, I indulged in some seated stretches by a male set of American and Mexican pilgrims, while Mónica sat sandwiched on a bench between two Germans and the Italian *hospitalera,* or volunteer worker at the hostel.

For the first time on the Camino, I spoke about the yoga philosophy that had guided me through my life changes, and took my new friends on a mini-journey through the koshas. "Well done," said the droll American, with a long considering look.

"You look like Sigourney Weaver in *Alien*," a drunken Jakob burst out a little later. Very interesting. I had heard that before from another admirer in Costa Rica. I needed to watch that movie again to better understand the comparison.

Even later in the dormitory bed, I finished my daily practice with some energy work and chakra clearing, while Jakob tossed and turned on the bottom bunk below me.

"E-e O-o A-a U-u," I grunted with each of my final steps into the first town after eighteen kilometers on the old Roman road. A row of recently planted trees no higher than a tall man had provided narrow stripes of shade on the gravel path, and the imagined echo of Roman sandals marching had been the only hint of civilization encountered. Reaching the town's one bar and hostel, I threw down my pack declaring, "I go no further today."

"But it's too soon to stop," Jakob said reasonably from a table in the sun, sockless feet up on a chair and an empty beer bottle in his hand.

I sank down at the next table. "Nope, no further...you could stay here and watch the stars tonight with Mónica and me," I tossed at his table with a grin. He froze to consider the proposition even as his friend prepared to leave.

"No, it's too soon," he said again reasonably and resumed pulling on his socks then lacing his boots. "I feel very sad," was his last comment before heading out on the road.

"He'll be back," I said to Mónica before the first wave of nausea rolled over me.

Several rounds with the toilet bowl, as well as sweaty, dizzy hours in bed feeling close to death and moaning for my mommy, ensued before Mónica reported Jakob's reappearance in the hostel lobby below.

"El Camino is breaking you down," said the friendly hostel owner, as he patted my cheeks and head and spoonfed me a special soup. My droopy head was propped on Jakob's shoulder, his muscular arm around my knee bolstering me against his side and in the chair, as yet another masculine angel tended the broken skin on my feet.

The next morning we traded emails so we could meet up again on the Camino later. Then Jakob took to the road and I crawled into a taxi to go to the health center in Sahagún.

"If I stay there tonight, I will come to your hotel room," he threatened before he left, staring meaningfully into my bleary eyes.

(Week Two)

As my second week on the Camino matured, I reflected how fate sometimes stepped in to save you from making easy choices instead of holding out for what you wanted. I recognized when young was too young for my forty-something self, but had enjoyed the easy energy exchange with Jakob despite his youth. I was glad that we had not taken things further in a moment of weakness.

However, several days off solid food, three infected toes, and many friends met and lost left me feeling lonely for a familiar face. While we had reconnected with many from the group in Leon and Astorga, there were only rumors of Jakob's whereabouts. In Villafranco del Bierzo, I sent him an email to let him know our location and check on his. It came back undelivered. "Oh well," I said to Mónica, "I put the energy out there."

The next day, we began the longest and hardest climb of the journey to O'Cebreiro. Twenty kilometers went by beautifully under lush green trees reflecting sunlight along a clear wide mountain stream and through tiny stone villages, passing and being passed by a group of four beautiful Spanish brothers we'd slept next to at the last albergue. The climb then began in earnest at the point we would usually stop for the day, and continued vertically through the last ten kilometers. The first bar appeared at a level spot on the mountain about four kilometers up, and we filled our tanks with *café con leche* and chocolate for the next segment in the rain, which had begun softly falling.

Almost up to the next town, I abruptly ran out of steam, red-faced and panting by the side of the road. "You go too fast," commented my new friend Jose Manuel, "charging ahead when you should pace yourself." *Wise words to keep in mind,* I thought.

Dragging myself the remaining 500 meters up the hill, I turned the corner into the small stone barroom that was our destination for the next break, and came face to face with a wooly bearded Jakob, sitting weary and defeated at the table by the door.

"I thought I would never see you again," he said, managing a bright smile.

"Hah!" I laughed. "Where did you come from?"

A Fanta Limon for me, some hot tea and energy work on hands and wrists for him, and we were both restored enough to complete the climb. The three of us—Mónica, Jakob, and I—crossed into Galicia together, boosted by the sun's reemergence, the soaring air and the magnificent green-carpeted mountains rolling around us into the distance.

We stuck to each other like glue through the heavy mist that blanketed the mountaintop village that night, despite Mónica and me claiming the last two beds at the albergue and Jakob staying elsewhere. The four beautiful Spanish brothers with whom we'd been keeping pace completed our dinner party in a cozy warm restaurant, and looked on curiously as Jakob and I caught up in English and German. Chakras, energy meridians, meditation, and martial arts dominated the multi-lingual conversation when two of the Spanish brothers, who were aikido teachers and black belts, lingered after the meal.

After-dinner drinks brought us to another bar, and then Mónica and I dashed to make curfew at our albergue, as Jakob disappeared into the mist.

I thought of him frequently the next few days, wondering if we would meet again or if we had served our purpose by lifting each other up the last mountain.

(Week Four)

Travel companions shifted again, and we walked with a fun pack of Spaniards from all over the country the rest of the way to Santiago. Hoping to reconnect with friends who had outpaced us, we arrived only to learn that most of the group, including Jakob, had set out just that morning for Finisterre.

A friend had also reported seeing Jakob the day before sitting on the steps above the cathedral outside the entrance to the viewing room for the St. James statue and relics, looking utterly lost and alone in the crowded city. I wished that Mónica and I had been able to arrive one day earlier, so that I could have offered him support like he had given me during my early journey and illness.

The old town of Santiago had a damp and dark feel to it, as if the stones retained an echo of its violent history of brutal battles to expel the Moors from Spain. Arrival at the pilgrimage's Christian end was anti-climactic for many, walking the last few kilometers with hordes of tourists who showed little respect for those of us who had been on the path for months. After so much time spent among fellow travelers walking without walls, and being supported by the community on the road, the frenetic tourism of the city felt harsh and abrasive.

Everyone walks the Camino for his or her own reasons, and the end often sneaks up with an abrupt reality check. Jakob had been cryptic about his reasons for walking, but had expressed no hurry to get home to Berlin when he was done, having described for me his possible plans to cycle all the way back through Spain, the Pyrenees and Alps, and Southern Germany. His consumption of large quantities of alcohol each day, his vague allusions to not being able to drive until the following March, and a lack of clarity on what to do after university pointed to possible reasons he was not in a hurry to end his own particular Camino.

Walking barefoot on the beach our second day in Finisterre, the traditional pagan end of the Camino at the western most point of Spain, I basked in the warm sun and slipped into my Nosara morning chakra meditation. Looking up at a figure walking across the sand towards me, I recognized Jakob, who was once again sporting a wooly beard. We walked directly into each other's arms and stayed there, heart to heart. We had made it. Separating, we sat in the sand catching up on our journeys while he and his friend drank from liters of beer.

"Have you been in the water yet?" Jakob asked. "It's an important ritual, you know. But be careful if you do go in; this is the death coast," he dared with a cocky smile.

I walked to the water, determined to rinse and release the journey and its pains. *Don't think. Just dive under,* I thought, and did, finding the cold shock almost pleasant as I allowed myself to be tossed around for a moment.

Streaming water across the sand, I rejoined the group and Jakob offered his snowboard jacket as my blanket to dry in the sun. Mónica joined us, stoutly refusing the dunking and opting instead for the drinking.

As I dried, I snuck in a mini-yoga practice while the others in our party drank beer and rolled cigarettes and told stories of their three-day adventure between Santiago and Finisterre.

With laughing eyes, Jakob reminded me of my offer of Pranassage in thanks for his blister care during the Camino. Arranging him on his back, I gave him a session in the sand, his freckled legs and torso relaxed and loose, his breath in sync with mine.

While his friend meticulously carved bread, tomatoes, and cheese for sandwiches, Jakob reciprocated my attention. He flipped me on my stomach, face down into his jacket and straddled me with his knees. Long firm strokes up my back and around my neck and shoulders caused him to lie nearly prone on top of me. Thoughts of our age difference, the others on the beach, and just about everything else fled as I was pressed into the sand by his hands, the weight of his body, and his intensely focused energy.

When he was done, I hungrily ate a sandwich from his friend, not caring what the gluten would do to my body.

Later that night, Jakob and his friend appeared at our albergue, which they had moved into during the day. One by one the other pilgrims went to bed, leaving Jakob and I alone in the moonlight outside the front door. The next thing I knew, we were body to body, hugging in the street, and I felt him twitching and growing hard against me.

I pressed my lips to his shoulder before we pulled away from each other. "No," he said, "this is friendship, not sexual. Not on the Camino."

"I know," I said and began to cry as I told him about an intense love affair I had during the last week of walking and how I had parted abruptly with my lover two days before in Santiago.

Jakob pulled me close again and held me. Held me for days, it seemed—for all of the time I needed to let the pain and heartache bleed out of me and be replaced by his strong, clear energy. We both understood that this was the release I really needed, and we cared enough about ourselves and each other not to make the easy choice.

❦

Two days later, Mónica and I were ready to move on and begin our journey back to the "real" world. A last trip to the lighthouse point the night before, another round of goodbyes, and the arrival of a new group of pilgrims bewildered by the journey's end marked our departure.

Jakob appeared early that morning, puffy faced and hungover, and hung out on the bench in front of the albergue until I finished up inside.

We hugged again, and I thanked him for his part in my Camino. "You have a good heart," I told him tapping the center of his chest.

"What? But my heart is over here," he replied with a cocky little smile, as he pointed to the left side of his chest.

We separated, I hoisted my backpack and waved at him over my shoulder as I walked off with another friend.

32.
Sisters Having Fun

"Music touching my soul, something warm, sudden cold, the spirit dance was unfolding."
—John Lennon

(Week One)

I watched in amazement as bag after bag of toiletries came out of Mónica's backpack. "How much does your pack weigh?" I asked, appalled.

Day cream, night cream, undereye cream, toner, exfoliant, facial mask, body lotion, sunscreen for face, sunscreen for body, deodorant, perfume, essential scented oils...it went on and on. And that doesn't even mention the cosmetics. Never mind just the weight for her, the amount of time it took to apply her beauty products in the mornings before heading out on the road was what affected me.

The first few days were all about compromise. We had always known that the New Yorker and the Latina had very different concepts of time, and now we were finding out just how much accommodation was necessary. Living the yoga and surf lifestyle in a basic and somewhat primitive part of Costa Rica, after shedding most of my belongings in Manhattan, had tempered this ex-city girl's concept of what was necessary. Lipstick and mascara, moisturizer and conditioner were my essentials.

Mónica, on the other hand, had lived in one of the most built-up, westernized, and tourist-ridden parts of the country's coastline in a luxury condominium.

After a particularly brutal day on the Camino during which we were caught on the high desert under the glaring mid-afternoon sun, because we (she) couldn't seem to get out of the albergue until mid-morning, I put my foot down. "You do your daily facials after we walk. I'm leaving by seven each morning." Mónica, also suffering from a slight case of sunstroke, agreed to the schedule.

While living in Costa Rica had also mellowed my walk into a more natural gate, years of city living and minimizing time between Point A and Point B meant that my pace greatly exceeded hers. I could walk about two kilometers in the time it took her to walk one, and that presented a challenge to our commitment of taking the Camino journey together. Eventually, I began to leave her in the dust and we'd meet at the first bar in the next town.

And then, there were the sounds.

For two days in a row, ominous grey clouds had blanketed the sky before opening into a distant bright blue that we never quite reached. Could it have anything to do with that strange Native American chant Mónica had been grunting for most of both days? Tap tap tappedy tap went her two walking sticks, punctuating certain grunts for emphasis.

I stepped on my accelerator and sped forward to have room for my own thoughts, and the strange song that had overtaken my mind. *It's raining men, hallelujah! It's raining men, every specimen...tall, blond, dark and lean. God bless Mother Nature, she's a single woman too...*

There were other times, however, when we did walk together and gave each other strength.

Grounding the four corners of each foot into the earth, drawing energy up through the legs, lifting the knee caps, tilting the tailbone, lengthening the abdomen, shoulders up and back, top of the head to the sky, I cued us into mountain pose. Re-energized and aligned under our packs, we began walking again for Villalcázar de Sirga where we would take a long lunch break, visit a Knights Templar monument, and decide our next steps.

The last six kilometers into Carrión de los Condes were torture, but we had decided to press on to meet up with a group of new friends we'd made.

Carry on my wayward son, there'll be peace when you are done, lay your weary head to rest, don't you cry no more, dah nah NAH NAH...the old '70's song from Kansas attached itself to my brain and carried me through the first kilometer or two.

Later, Mónica and I amused ourselves by chanting the beej mantras, specific sounds used to clear each of the chakras. "See that red farm equipment in the field on the crest of the horizon? We'll clear the first chakra until then. Ready...LAM...LAM...LAM...See that orange sign on the top of the hill in the distance? Second chakra until then...VWAM...VWAM...VWAM..."

"How long have you two been together?" asked our fantastic South African friend, Marc, before the group of pilgrims hanging out in the cobbled street. "Oh, we're just friends," we both replied laughing.

The hardest adjustments for this autonomous single woman were dealing with the complications from partnering on the journey with a friend locked in a codependent marriage. Mónica had taken to speaking for me in some instances, and relating stories of my life experiences as if they had happened to us both. A very irritating development for someone like me, who had just recently discovered and was still guarding my own voice.

"Sorry, I thought...," Marc said. "Are either of you married?"

"No," I answered truthfully.

"No," Mónica lied.

I did a doubletake. *If she lies so casually here, what else does she lie about?* I wondered. The coach in me took over, recognizing a breakdown of the agreement to speak the truth. The next day while walking, I brought up the conversation.

"Oh," Mónica excused herself, "I just didn't want to get into the whole mess in front of everyone."

"That's understandable," I replied, "but there are ways to address a question about something sensitive without hiding or lying about it. What do you think it does to the potential for a deeper relationship when you've started out with dishonesty?"

"I guess I could have said I was separated, and that I didn't want to talk about it," Mónica said after some thought. "I'll do that next time."

(Week Two)

"O sooole mio, Sta 'nfronte a te," Gabriella crooned as we plunked down next to her in the rest area. She was a crazy Italian woman Mónica and I had met and fallen in love with our first night on the pilgrimage. Our paths crossed repeatedly during the first week on the road, usually at the point when Mónica and I started to forget that the Camino was about having fun. Shouting Italian and gesturing dramatically, Gabriella always found a way to infect us with her *joie de vivre*, and be understood without sharing any other common language.

I was back on the road again after my two days spent in bed and at the toilet bowl. Yogurt and bananas had been successfully stomached that morning and I was maintaining energy by choking down the fluorescent orange drink for dehydration that the pharmacist had given me.

After a rest and recharge, Mónica and I parted company with Gabriella, saying that we would see her in the next church. It seemed that we could spontaneously summon her by entering a religious monument, where she had an uncanny way of springing from behind pillars or through doorways the moment we went solemn in the stone palaces.

The path to El Burgo Ranero was quiet and windswept, bordered by broad open fields with dark brown earth, trampled corn stalks, and blinded sunflowers missing their center. I was walking for the first time without my pack, having shipped it ahead to accomodate my weakened condition. My body and I gloried in the freedom, walking erect and in alignment for the first time since beginning the Camino. *Ahhh...this was why I chose to do the pilgrimage,* I thought gratefully as I dropped into moving meditation, my body relaxing into its own rhythm and my hips swaying naturally. The screaming pain in my right hip that had been building since the first day under the pack's crushing weight, finally began to release and dissipate, and, along with it, the vague sense of despair that I was undoing almost two years of healing the joint.

"I would love some white rice and chicken," I said longingly to Mónica as we walked together, our paces evened out by my invalid's status. Being gluten free on the Camino was once again proving to be a challenge, especially with my tortured stomach, and I was ready to attempt some solid food.

Checking into the albergue, the Canadian hospitalero, whose daughter who was also a yoga teacher, offered me a private room to sleep soundly and recuperate. Despite my alarming pallor, I was feeling much better, I assured him as I declined the room in favor of someone else more in need.

Entering one of the two restaurants in town, Mónica approached the hard-faced woman in charge behind the bar. With her own unique charm and persistence, she cajoled the owner into instructing the kitchen to make a special meal of *arroz blanco y pollo* for her wan, sick friend. This was a town full of angels already, it seemed, as I blissfully ate the bland food and felt better than I had in days.

"Oh my," breathed the fatherly hospitalero, as I came down the stairs with my journal later that afternoon. Nothing like some solid food and a shower to change your outlook. I lay on a sunny bench outside the door catching up on my journaling, feeling clear and peaceful in the same way I had following the cleanse retreats in Costa Rica. My adopted father passed by frequently, affectionately tickling my feet with an empty beer bottle each time.

I am ready for whatever comes next, I thought gratefully.

Well, two infected toes were not exactly what I had wanted to come next, but it was what it was.

Mónica took one look at the chorizos that had replaced my pinky toes, and informed me that we were going directly to the medical center in Leon. After a prolonged and thorough scolding by the doctor, who unleashed his frustration with all pilgrims on poor little me, I resigned myself to two more days off my feet. Mónica resigned herself as well. It seemed that now she was the one waiting on me.

We took the opportunity to stock up on much-needed supplies with a new friend from the neighboring bunk in the albergue. Laura, from Toronto, was walking the Camino slowly and coming to grips with some life changes of her own. Upon hearing I was a life coach and yoga teacher, she offered me the perfect outlet for doing some good of my own while dealing with my body's weaknesses.

Roaming around the city in search of Tiva sandals to replace the yoga shoes that tortured between each infected or blistered toe, I shared my story with Laura and listened to hers. "Yoga is scientifically shown to help with depression," I told her, and described various styles that she might try instead of the fast-flow classes she had tried and disliked.

Trading phone numbers with her, Mónica and I left Laura the next morning to take our first bus ride of the Camino. With all of my health-related delays, having sufficient time to complete the journey was becoming a concern. My second enforced day off my feet would be spent in Astorga, where we hoped to have more success in finding supplies for the changing terrain that lay ahead of us. We were about to leave the wide-open plains and head into the mountains, where temperatures dropped and rain fell frequently.

Astorga was a time for female bonding. At the bus station leaving Leon, we first encountered Franziska, a German Swede just beginning her second time walking the Camino, who was a beautiful kindred spirit. At the homey little albergue, I was introduced to Emerald, an Australian, who was a fellow life coach and yogini. She had just discovered that she was pregnant. We spoke for hours tucked under blankets in the common area, both of us hungry for another like-minded person to hang out with, someone in sync with our spirituality, life philosophy, and language.

"You have chia seeds, too!" I exclaimed, as I saw the package Emerald pulled from her pack.

I had been carrying a full eight ounces of the superfood along the Camino, and heavily relying on them for natural energy and nutrients. I figured if the Mayans, Aztecs, and Incans used them for nourishment on their long-distance journeys, they would be beneficial for mine.

Finally, someone else who understood. I had loved my time so far along the pilgrimage, but was beginning to feel that old familiar Catholic restriction, as steeped in the tradition as we were at times. Spending time, even briefly, with another like-minded person brought back some balance. Mónica, who had been raised in Mexico among devout Catholics, had jumped whole-heartedly into the religious spirit and traditional doctrines.

Then there was Ann from Belgium, last seen walking away under her giant blue backpack, short brown hair pushed back by a red bandana, just moments before illness had overtaken me the week before. Much of our first few days on the Camino had been spent with Ann, sharing rooms in albergues, drinking wine at tables in the sun while she rolled and smoked her cigarettes, laughing along the path and passing around chocolate, almonds, and anything else from the grocery store of her pack. Whenever we encountered Ann, the comedy team of Mónica and Robin expanded to a trio and the fun level increased exponentially. Our time spent together lifted us all.

With laughing eyes and a warm Belgian accent, Ann called out to us from her perch on a rock under a tree off the path, sheltered from the heavy drizzle. "Would you like a tomato?" She asked as we crouched below the leaves and settled in for a break before the final four kilometers to our evening destination.

After a soggy but quite enjoyable night by a cozy fire with a fun group at the albergue, we departed Rabanal with a Maxi-Pad in my shoe well after the albergue had cleared of pilgrims. Upon finding another toe borderline infected, the *hospitalera* instructed me in the finer arts of padding the hiking boot to cushion the toes.

A thick fog shrouded the landscape as we left town and entered a field of tricolor ferns throwing vibrant red, yellow, and green into contrast against the white mist. Trees coated with hairy green moss, looking like a strange form of muppet, escorted us through the lonely hills. Eruptions of rose quartz thrust in chunks through the dirt trail, calling me to periodically stop and feel their smooth surfaces.

The familiar feeling of slipping through the mists into another world came over me, not a soul in sight. I had a conversation with God and forgave myself. I recognized that I had finally woken up and was learning my lessons this time around. I could manifest my heart's desires if I just believed.

Mid-morning, we reached the deserted town of Foncebadon, rumored to house a population of wild dogs, particularly by those who had read Paulo Coelho's book about El Camino. I sat munching on a huge plate of jamon, my second breakfast, when Ann wandered in from the fog.

"I've been lost in the mist for over an hour," she said. "The yellow arrows disappeared."

"Have some *jamon,*" I suggested, "it will cure anything."

I had just checked email for the first time since setting off almost two weeks before. A series of encouraging notes had lifted my spirit from my Inner Quest family, who had reunited a few months earlier for a weekend we called "the Abbey Mela." Our group had formed a special bond during the yoga teacher training with Don and Amba Stapleton earlier that year in Costa Rica. A dear friend from the program was a Catholic nun who taught yoga for her monastic community, which had hosted our gathering at their abbey in Southern Connecticut. I had sent out an email to the group before departing on the Camino, since the decision to walk had been very much on my mind during our reunion. While there, I had received two commemorative stones to place along the way from a friend whose son had died.

I told Ann of my friend from the reunion whose son, Sam, had been killed in car accident, and of the stone I carried to place at the Iron Cross, which we would reach in several kilometers.

"I saw your Sam stone and heart," Ann said later in the day climbing down from the monument. We had reached Monte Irago, the highest point on the Camino at almost 5,000 feet above sea level, and home of one of the abiding symbols of the Camino, el Cruz de Ferro. Since Roman times, travelers have left stone offerings at the foot of the simple iron cross mounted there atop a weathered pole, resulting in a mountain of intentions and loose rocks. Pilgrims traditionally bring stones from home, pouring their grief, pain, and regret into them along their journey, and then symbolically release all these emotional burdens by leaving the offering of the stone behind at the cross.

I had placed two offerings at the base of the monument. The first stone was in honor of my friend's son, Sam; it symbolized my hope that he might be at peace and share that peace with his family. The second was a red, heart-shaped stone with a vein of quartz running through it, which I left behind with the intention of releasing all that was keeping me from opening my heart. The red stone had jumped up at me on the beach in Costa Rica and had been on my yoga altar for the last year as part of my trio of intentions for love, abundance, and fulfilling my life's purpose.

As we were leaving the monument behind, the sun broke free of the clouds, and Ann, Mónica, and I felt as if we had released the past and were moving forward into a brighter future.

The next few days were spent in sisterhood with the group of women we had connected with over the past several days, nourishing and nurturing each other through our various physical challenges and life changes. I celebrated the new moon with Emerald, my fellow life coach and yogi, on a dark night in the town of Acebo, and then we disbursed again to our individual journeys around Molinaseca the next day.

I had picked up a new walking stick leaving Acebo that felt as if it was an old friend, a gift from the new moon along with the powerful dream that preceded it. In my dream, I was standing on cliffs high above the ocean, the wind whipping my hair, a fire blazing on the ground, and a powerful staff in my hands. I was leading some type of ceremony and power surged all around.

Unfortunately for me, Mónica had also picked up some new walking poles in Acebo—of the artificial variety. Clickedy-clack, clickedy-clack they reverberated through the quiet mountain air. I couldn't seem to get far enough away to silence the sound.

The disbursement of the ladies heralded a period where I went internal as I released old friends and dealt with my period and its hormonal surges. I craved quiet and solitude, hiding out on my bunk in the albergues where we spent our nights and walking far from people during the days.

Nerves on edge for most of the morning after leaving the town of Ponferrada, we passed through a more modern town, over a major highway, and suddenly entered a vision of heaven: a sunny autumn vineyard washed in reds, golds, and greens in the rolling hills of El Bierzo. I sighed in relief and slipped into meditation until an older French couple speeded up to pass me and then slowed down to my pace once ahead—and then chattered incessantly, barely stopping to catch breath between their dramatic and nasal dialogue.

No peace for the weary, I sighed to myself, stopping to sit in a grove of willowy trees by a stream and letting the world pass me by. The calm place nourished me enough to walk with Mónica once she caught up to me through the beautiful stone town of Cacabelos, where we stopped for a delicious pilgrim's menu and excellent wine. *Are you my home?* I silently asked the town, as I had asked one or two others along the route. Marking it for future consideration, we floated out of town and right into the group of four beautiful Spanish brothers just as they were beginning a shortened Camino over the long holiday weekend. Smelling strongly of fresh laundry, they asked us to take a picture to mark the beginning of their walk.

Charging up the long hill out of town, the brothers kept pace with us and followed as we took the detour suggested by the guide-book through vineyards, despite strong recommendations to the contrary by a local driver. If only we had listened!

The detour added many kilometers to the day's walk.

Again foiled in my search for a quiet contemplative walk, we first encountered The Whistler, a red-suited gentleman from somewhere in France. His knee-length breeches through his tee-shirt, fleece, jacket, and backpack were all a shade of red, as was his rosy mouth, which would not desist from whistling off tune. The only thing that did stop the whistling was when he tried to make conversation in his only language. No amount of *"Je ne comprends pas"* would stop him from trying to be understood.

Somehow finally eluding him, I walked for a while in blessed quiet until a herd of footsteps approached. Ah, the four brothers again. One separated himself from the pack and joined Mónica and me to chat. I bared my teeth in an attempt to be polite and pulled ahead and away.

When we were finally settled into the albergue in Villafranca del Bierzo, freshly showered and doing my bunkbed yoga practice, I wondered at myself. These brothers were all very attractive, interested in getting to know us better, and sleeping in the beds next to us. *What is up with me?*

(Week Three)

"No puedo darte la luna que tu esperas...," I sang over and over to myself, swaying from side to side and exulting in the freedom from my pack. Our first thirty-kilometer day ahead, and the toughest climb of the Camino, meant that my backpack was being transported separately and would be waiting for me on top of the mountain. Walking between the concrete barrier blocking the roadway and the beautiful mountain stream, I poured all of my attention into the flowing water and green trees. We were crossing into Galicia that day, the region of my grandfather and ancestors. I had been looking forward to arriving there since before the journey had even begun.

Like when a big sister and a little sister spend way too much time together, I needed some freedom from the bond with Mónica. Little things from the past few weeks had begun building up. As we each went deeper into our own experience, our objectivity began to disintegrate. Our clearing conversations became few and far between. Mónica's codependency, which in the beginning I could view with compassion, had expanded to include the claiming of whole aspects of my life. All of a sudden, it was Galicia that she, too, had been waiting the whole trip to see, and that she, too, felt a special kinship with. I knew it was all part of her search for identity, but to me it felt like the all too familiar constriction of not being seen or having the room to be myself.

Needing space for myself, I told Mónica that I would meet her in the next town and pulled ahead. Passing the beautiful brothers, I managed a cheery smile and wave, declining their friendly invitation for a picnic lunch.

Mónica and I met up at midday, ate a lunch of fresh vegetables, and then began the climb together before my customary charge uphill separated us. Walking up the steep and leafy path, I was distracted by a strange commotion in the branches high above me. I stopped to investigate, and spotted a pair of birds making love in the green carpet of leaves in the sky. *Thanks angels,* I thought, as I finally snapped out of my funk.

"Mónica look!" I said when she caught up, sharing the magic.

"Tell me, why are you ladies walking El Camino?" asked the wise man. We had run into the young Mexican photographer from our night in Carrión again, who was walking with his father for a few days to celebrate his birthday. Pablo, the senior, gave off an air of wisdom, power, and openness that inspired confidences. Come to think of it, so did the junior.

Once again, I described my transition from a depressed corporate woman in Manhattan to a happy yoga teacher, coach, and writer. When questioned, I explained my belief that life is a choice between fear and love, and that only by choosing the latter can one ever hope to find happiness.

When it was Mónica's turn to share, she began mouthing some bland generalities about life changes of her own and moving from Costa Rica back to the U.S. Both Pablos looked on politely. "Now might be a moment to share what's really going on," I said to her quietly when their attention began to drift.

She took a deep breath, switched to speaking Spanish, and explained that she had been married for ten years to a man who was bipolar and had frequent devastating manic episodes. She took her wedding vows very seriously, but didn't want to remain married to a man who couldn't do his part to make the marriage work and pulled her down instead of helping her grow. Pablo immediately offered wisdom from his own painful divorce, and the two shared and supported each other throughout the remainder of the evening.

By being honest and open, Mónica was able to deeply connect with another human who had shared similar circumstances and learn from his wisdom and experience. Her own burden became much lighter.

I beamed like a mother whose child has taken her first steps. This was what I loved about coaching.

33.
Cupid's Gift

"Your task is not to seek for love, but merely to seek and find all the barriers within yourself that you have built against it."
—Rumi

(Week Three)

Something flared in his eyes. It grabbed and hooked me, prompted me to comment to his friend as they passed my table.

"USA?" I said pointing at letters on the shirt.

"No, Italiano," said his friend, Franco.

"Española?" Gerardo asked me, eyes twinkling greengreybrown, shaggy black hair tucked behind ears.

"Nueva York," I replied, smiling back.

The men went off down the road, or so I thought. I sat in the sun making idle conversation with an older American from Milwaukee and a thirty-something from Peru. Mónica arrived after about ten minutes, made her hourly bathroom break, and then we decided to move forward immediately. Standing to go, I spotted the Italian man and the very interesting Spanish man, just finishing their pack adjustments at the wall across the way, also making ready to leave.

The girls fell into place behind the boys, just as the lane narrowed to single file over an uneven bridge of stones bordered by deep puddles. A group of cyclists in bright blue bounced by, dragging their bikes. The pedestrians crowded together to let them pass.

It was the most natural thing in the world, then, to form pairs and begin walking together as the path widened again.

"*¿Tu novia y tu tienen...?*" (Do you and your girlfriend...?) I began.
"*No,*" Gerardo broke in, "*mi* ex-novia."

Oh. We had spent the past hour going over the basics before diving into more philosophical matters. There had been the moment when the girlfriend was casually dropped in, and I had immediately resolved my thoughts on friendship. Not available.

My Spanish had a way of breaking down around cases and tenses. His was remarkably easy to understand and his English was excellent.

Turns out the ex, a recent one, was also American, but of a very different variety than me. She was from Kansas, and her family was staunchly Republican. This New Yorker squelched an automatic disavowal of any affiliation. The two had broken up because neither was ready to give up their own country, and the idea of marriage had not been seriously considered after two years together.

Very interesting. I was exploring dual citizenship through my grandfather, and contemplating a permanent move to Spain.

Mónica made a strangled cough behind us. Looking back with concern, I watched as she distorted her face to point to the ground ahead of me. Directing my eyes to the road, I witnessed my boot and Gerardo's stepping simultaneously into a giant yellow heart painted on the pavement.

A phrase from last night's dream floated across my mind—*if not today, then tomorrow*—as I began again to hum the silly jingle plaguing me since O'Cebreiro: "Look for the union label."

Shaking myself out of it, we turned into a bar where the friends fought over who would buy the coffees. A tiny Buddha head smiled serenely out of the stone wall above our table.

Four hours later, we crossed the modern bridge to Portomarín over verdant and mossy emerald banks and the base and arch of a medieval bridge that was its precursor breaking the water far below. Flat land by the river stretched like empty shelves since all historic buildings were moved stone by stone to the top of the hill housing the town. A reservoir had been built in the 1960s and the Rio Miño flooded the old village land, according to a useful tidbit from Gerardo.

While walking companions had shifted among the four of us, Gerardo and I spent the majority of time paired in conversation. His twinkling hazel eyes and ready smile, fair skin, and black hair, combined with his air of accessibility and curiosity to charm me as we walked. Clever in either language that he spoke, the energy that was sparked during our first contact burned brighter as our intellectual connection grew.

The men led us up the steep ancient and arched stone stairway and through the modern town to the albergue they had reserved. When there weren't beds available for four, they decided to change to one that could accommodate all of us.

An exchange of phone numbers, showers, naps, and a brief walk around the small hillside town brought us to a tapas bar off the main square. Engaged again in discussion, Gerardo and I strained across the table toward each other while glasses of wine were drunk and refilled and other pilgrims joined our group and moved on.

Alberto, our dear friend and sage counselor from the Dolomites, whom I had met and immediately loved during my cozy evening by the fire in Rabanal, joined us. He bought us his customary round of *hierbas* liquor and informed the men, "You are with *las muchachas mas bonitas del camino!*"

Back at the albergue in time for curfew, Gerardo decided that more wine was needed. Making clandestine arrangements for building reentry, he grabbed my hand and pulled me out the door to accompany him on his mission. Waiting in the near-empty bar while two bottles were procured, our eyes caught and we gazed into each other across the pulsing air.

Please kiss me, I thought, right before he did so hungrily holding my head in his hands. And did again in each dark corner back up the hill to the albergue.

"How is it possible that you are not taken?" he asked in wonder.

Seated at a table in the kitchen while the rest of the pilgrims slept, the four of us drank both bottles and took turns answering questions about love and attraction. "You must come to Madrid!" exclaimed Gerardo, repeatedly wagging his index finger excitedly in the air, "You are coming to Madrid!"

Barely waiting for the door to close as Mónica and Franco retired to the dormitory, he tackled me on the couch. Simultaneously melting, moaning, and trying to maintain a layer of clothing between us, we rolled off the couch and around the floor like teenagers in my parent's basement. The sound of a pilgrim in the hallway making his way to the bathroom brought an abrupt end to our activities. I crept into the dark dormitory and onto the top bunk with my heart pounding and was dreaming before he climbed up to his bed sometime later.

"Remember that scene in *The Truman Show,* when Jim Carrey's character comes up against the edge of his world and realizes that his life is just a movie set?" Gerardo asked me as we walked through green fields, forests, and mountains the next morning. "That's how I feel now, understanding that it's not all about me."

Just like me, everything he had wanted in life had come pretty easily for Gerardo until now. He was highly educated and had based his career and his life to date on being in control: understanding patterns, drawing conclusions from data inputs, predicting behavior, and solving analytical problems. He was proud of his mind and his intellect, and had been very successful in his life using these skills.

Also like me, he had come face to face with a situation that taught him, despite all of his abilities, that he really had no control over the outcome regardless of how much he analyzed it. He had been an economist for the national bank of Spain until the innovative program to which he had only recently transferred was cancelled due to the country's economic decline, leaving him jobless for the first time in his career. Combine that with a recently failed relationship, a return to his parent's household, and the overwhelming sense that life, including a family of his own, was passing him by. In his depression, he had also let himself go physically, black hair long and shaggy, and body carrying extra weight. His innate confidence appeared shaken at times. A crisis of faith had led him to walk El Camino.

However, unlike me, all this had just happened and he was still clinging by his fingernails to the illusion of control. For me, almost identical scenarios had played out at the same time in my life, around the ripe old age of thirty-three. Ten more years of life experience, including the past two of intense healing, surrendering control, and believing in intuition as a guiding force, had brought me to a place of finally forgiving myself for decisions I had made then. As a result, I currently had more faith, peace, and happiness than I had ever hoped for.

"In Spain it is different," he said. "You can't just walk away from your career for a year or two and expect to be hired again." He listened, fascinated as I told him of my time in Hollywood and in Washington, D.C., and of my corporate life in Manhattan. I explained that I wasn't going back to that career, and described my plans as a writer with a new career combining consulting, coaching, and teaching.

"Do you want children?" he asked me. "I want them so badly, I think about getting a surrogate mother. Other men have done it. What if it doesn't happen for me?

"Are you afraid to die?" he asked me. "I'm terrified. Where does the mind go? How does your mind just cease to be?"

Dark trunks anchored branches like the giant gnarled fingers of a witch stretching long in all directions and lacing together in a high arch above my head. Vibrant leaves flickered in greens from deep, earthy darkness to a golden glow as the sun shone against and through them. As I walked, my attention was drawn deep into the forest to my left, expecting to see Arwin, Elrond, and other woodland elves from *The Lord of the Rings* appear in jewel-colored clothing within the beams of light breaking through in patches.

Unable to resist any longer, I detoured off the path and strode into the vault of old trees, hungry to be enfolded in their green energy. I grounded myself in mountain pose, reached high to the sky, opening my heart in a back bend, and then folded forward in worship of the powerful place. Breathing in, I absorbed the vitality into my lungs and through my pores. Galician magic.

"I'm having visions," I said later, rejoining Gerardo after concluding my private ceremony and walking a while on my own.

"Visions?"

"Yes, visions of you pressing me up against a tree." I grinned at him and kept walking.

He quickly caught up, shaken out of his existential crisis.

I stretched my leg into the air to better massage lotion into the aching muscles, while Gerardo reclined on the adjoining bunk fiddling with his things. We had a semi-private room in this albergue, so far only the four of us in a room built for sixteen.

Marking the large empty floor space between his bed and the door, I asked if he'd mind if I did some yoga. As I folded into a much-needed forward bend, he dropped all pretense with his electronics, exclaiming, *"Espectacular!"* I had his undivided attention as I continued through the Sun Salutation, pausing in Plank position to properly align my shoulders, and then continuing through Upward Dog to Downward Dog.

The door abruptly opened, admitting two new women to join our room party. Sighing, I continued with the bunkbed practice I'd adapted of side twists, Reclining Butterfly, Happy Baby, and Snail. Mesmerized, Gerardo gravitated to the bunk just one foot away, until his phone rang, startling us both.

Walking to dinner, we spoke of family and of how different relationships were in Spain and in the U.S. He had just hung up with his mother, and explained that he spoke with her and his aunt every day. "They love me," he said simply, shrugging his shoulders, sweetness shining out of his eyes. I immediately resolved to call my mother more just because I knew it would make her happy.

Then I told Gerardo of my father, and the reconciliation we had that summer. For the first time, I was able to communicate that the hardest part of leaving my career behind had been the pride my father had always taken in my successes. It had been the one place where I hadn't worried about measuring up during our long years of strife. But spending time together over the summer had shown my father how happy I was now, and by being myself I was able to shift our relationship to one filled with love and understanding.

Escorting me like his prize into a seat at the restaurant, Gerardo advised me through the menu and queried the waitress on gluten-free options, demanding at one point that she check with the kitchen.

Dear Alberto joined us again for *hierbas* after the meal, and we exchanged contact information since it seemed likely we wouldn't meet again. After hugging and patting our Camino father goodbye with sadness and affection, I looked up and met Gerardo's soft eyes for a long moment. Mónica and I then left the men to walk back to the albergue.

Laundry, a short email to my parents, and catching up on a few days worth of journaling were finished quickly before preparing for bed. I returned to our room to find the two new ladies had moved out and Gerardo sitting alone. He stood, we stared, and he closed the distance, kissing me as if he were starved before tearing abruptly away and leaving the room with his toothbrush. Breathing heavily, I grabbed my own toiletries and went in search of a free sink.

Back in the room, Mónica and Franco completed their complex and lengthy evening rituals in the top bunks above us while Gerardo and I throbbed. Facing each other and leaning against pillows on opposing walls, we grinned as he patted the bed beside him. Sensing that Franco was just about finished, he stood in his red briefs to turn off the lights and waited and waited, while I drank in the view.

Finally Franco was done, and the room plunged to a pulsing darkness. I breathed, wondering what was next. Suddenly, my sleeping bag was ripped off me and onto Gerardo's bed. I rolled off mine and onto his, bag quickly tucked around me as I was tucked into his chest. We lay for long minutes as the energy built, and then began kissing quietly and slowly. Catching flame quickly, he rolled on top of me and began incursions under my clothing as we writhed against each other. Rising above me, he grabbed hold of my pants. *Ahhh...* until reality crashed in and I rose against him to whisper in his ear, "*Stop* I can't forget there are others in this room."

Clasping me to him, he immediately rolled us onto our sides, his chest hairs tickling my nose, our hearts booming together, legs entwined. THUMP, THUMP, thump, thump...*Where am I?* I wondered dazedly as the word *"home"* floated through my mind. Gradually our bodies calmed, our hearts slowed, our positions shifted, and he spooned me tightly the rest of the night, his nose nestled in the nape of my neck.

(Week Four)

"Are you a saint, as well?" Gerardo queried as I tenderly drained and bandaged Franco's blisters for the second morning in a row.

"No, just an angel of mercy like many who have helped me," I replied, slightly irritated with the comment. I thought of Jakob and others who had cared for me when my feet were really bad, no questions asked.

After several delays, we set off on the day's thirty kilometers. We started off together, and then gradually drifted to our own speeds and thoughts, Gerardo plugging in his earphones and charging ahead.

The first morning alone again with my thoughts, and I meditated on a phrase from the guidebook as I walked through the enchanted green landscape: *All of my ancestors are behind me. Be still, watch and listen, they say. You are the result of the love of thousands.*

Inspired by the words, at peace, and completely open from the energy of the past few days, I quickly slipped into an altered state. When I arrived at the first small village, and bar, after about five kilometers, I was dazed. Even second breakfast couldn't quite stop the bubbles of laughter from rising sporadically.

Off again to the town of Melide, where we were promised the biggest *chuletones* we could ever hope to see. Our group of four arrived early enough to sample *pulpo* (octopus) fresh from the pot, clipped, seasoned, and served before our eyes in a traditional Galician *pulpería*. At the steak restaurant, we were seated next to a large group of Spanish pilgrims who walked together every year.

Spontaneously, the grandfather at the end emoted verses of flamenco and at one point broke into a duet with a lady from the next table who began weeping mid song.

"Are you okay?" Gerardo asked as I gazed out the window pensively. "Yes," I replied, "just very sensitive from my walk this morning."

"And," he said, "because the Camino is coming to an end soon." Smart lad.

Restored by a clay bowl of wine, half a pound of steak, and as many *patatas fritas,* Gerardo and I started the afternoon's walk together out of town and back into the countryside. He pulled ahead when I stopped behind the bushes for a bathroom break and we lost each other. Many kilometers passed before the next bar, and he wasn't there waiting for me. My feelings were hurt.

As I walked truly alone for the first time, no one in sight, no one waiting for me, my demons one by one began to rise. *Where am I going? What am I doing? Am I doing the right thing? Will I ever get what I want?* Overtired and afraid, always alone, an endurance test, the damn climb. I worked myself up to quite a state before reaching the outskirts of ugly and industrial Arzúa. I sat on the stone ledge of a bridge to collect myself before calling Gerardo for the name of our next albergue.

"I've been lost for hours," said an anxious Gerardo when he picked up the phone. "I got off track and walked for many kilometers before realizing I had made a wrong turn. Where are you?"

Arriving at the albergue, frustration flared as we opened the door to the dormitory and noted the fifty-plus beds. Sinking down onto bunks across from each other, I sighed, "Will we ever get to be alone?"

"I think it will have to be in Santiago," Gerardo replied regretfully. Knees touching, we began our unpacking routines, pulling plastic bags of toiletries, and then fresh clothes, out of our packs.

"Can I ask you a question?" he said looking at me earnestly. "Do you promise you will answer honestly?"

"Yes, of course," I replied, my mind flashing to a vision of us checking into a private room, shedding our clothes, and rolling around on the bed. "Ask me anything."

"Do you think my English is good enough to work in the States?" *Huh?*

"Yes," I replied, "your English is great."

Something inside me closed. *He is still thinking about a future with his ex-girlfriend,* I thought to myself. *He is not available. He is not the one.* I let disappointment shut me down, and I walked away from him and out of the dormitory.

A hot shower and a long yoga session in an empty room downstairs brought me back to myself, and I joined Gerardo at the little table by the washing machine. He had been planning out our next day's walk, and asked if I would be okay with walking another thirty kilometers so that we could make it to Santiago in time for the pilgrim's mass on Sunday. Agreed, we found a pension for the four of us just ten kilometers outside our destination.

When the others left the room, we finally addressed our intimacy the previous night. "Did you know that you snore?" I asked him with a grin.

"I do not," he teased. "It must have been my compressed lungs from sleeping in the tiny space you left me."

A long, sleepless night wrestling even more demons ensued and left me very cranky in the morning. The recognition of how susceptible I still was to making other people's actions be about me, and how in that way I closed off possibilities and killed relationships, had kept me alternating between weeping and balancing myself with affirmations through the long, dark hours.

Desperate to start moving the next morning, I hurriedly nursed Franco's feet, gave a brusque kiss to Gerardo, and said we'd meet at the first break. Then I grabbed my stick and dashed out the door.

By the first stop seven kilometers out I had released most of my crankiness and aggression into the earth by slamming my staff. Mónica and I sat eating eggs with our friend Jin from South Korea, a woman from Berlin, and a man from Barcelona who lived in Iceland. Glancing up, I saw Gerardo walking with his friend. They grinned at us and waved as they cruised past, and we grinned back.

"I think he likes you," Jin observed.

Over lunch, Gerardo quizzed me about my past experience and the project I was currently working on. I told him about how it had evolved, was structured, what remained and about the business plan Mónica and I had just written in Barcelona. He smiled and nodded in approval.

Sporting a towel fresh from the bath, I peeked around the door to gaze at the outstretched foot clothed in bloody sock that he presented. "Look, my toes started bleeding along the walk. Wow, your room is much nicer than ours!" Gerardo was very chatty after the long day. I, on the other hand, needed a nap desperately. *Shoo!*

During dinner, my tired brain refused to understand any of the Spanish spoken. After a glass of wine, it was a struggle for all of us to keep our heads elevated. We crashed into bed early that night, a wall separating the boys from the girls for the first time, sleeping soundly despite the fiesta blaring outside in the square.

Mónica and I left early the next morning, to walk at our own pace and finish the journey into Santiago together, as we had started it. We met up with Gerardo and Franco again in the line for our Compostela certificates and confirmed directions to our adjoining rooms in the four-star hotel they had arranged.

Freshening up in the beautiful hotel room after the short day's walk, I felt the return of my mojo. Mónica and I had deferred attending mass, having already connected with several dear friends from the walk. Laughing, we set out to explore the city, passing Gerardo and Franco on the way and agreeing to meet up with them later.

Following a nap, Gerardo and Franco joined us at a wine bar and proceeded to drink rapidly, catching up to our celebratory state and drowning any nervousness. Mónica and I spoke of our plans to proceed on to Finisterre, and were excited about being there for the full moon. Pagans, we were called, due to the yoga we practiced and our belief in magic and the moon cycles. "My Camino ends here with Saint James," said Gerardo, a traditional Catholic.

Later, walking at a snail's pace with his injured toes, Gerardo and I fell back into our easy private connection, letting the other two walk ahead.

"You are so positive! Do you ever get angry?" he asked me, back in the hotel having drinks in his room. "Yes, but not much anymore," I responded, looking at him soberly.

The energy was starting to build nicely between us with some Pranassage to open his lower back, when Mónica abruptly sliced the mood. Stuck in her own drama, she declared she was leaving us alone to "get down to business." Gerardo laughed awkwardly, and I felt myself shut down inside. Masking my feelings, I attempted to hide from him the internal melt-down I was experiencing from ongoing tensions with Mónica and the journey's end. I wanted my grand romantic ending and she had turned it into being just about sex.

Lights off, except for what came in from the courtyard beyond the window, Gerardo and I lay on the bed together reestablishing intimacy. It didn't take long, given the intense energy of the past week. Clothes off, sexy lingerie not even noted in the haste. Slowing it down, I recalled a few things he had mentioned liking during the first night's drunken conversation. Why yes, he did seem to enjoy that very much.

Rough with his hands, he pushed me down and slid home. Yes, he remembered I liked that, too. "That feels so good," I breathed.

Later, pressed together under tightly tucked sheets, still needing the feel of body against body, I thanked him for his role in my Camino. I described a moment in Costa Rica earlier that year during an intense meditation exercise, when I was frustrated about not being able to visualize my home and how I had suddenly popped into a vision of it. In the vision, I was laying in bed with my nose pressed into a man's chest hair, hearts beating together, in a white room full of sunlight and flowers. As I walked the Camino searching for my home, that vision returned to me during our night together in Palas de Rei. I realized again that the specifics of my home do not matter, what was important to me was the intimate connection. I could be at home anywhere with that.

The beauty of the connection between Gerardo and me was that he understood what I said was about the revelation and not based on an attachment to him. He knew I understood he was at a lost place in his life, and looking only to find some solid ground.

"Feel free to wake me if you'd like to again," I teased much later as we drifted to sleep, "or I will wake you towards morning." Immediately he began again with long, slow kisses. "Do you know what a good kisser you are?" he murmured. "Can you feel what you do to me?" I sighed. "Yes," he moaned, hands moving to my hips holding me down.

Scooting out of bed with the alarm the next morning, he was in the shower before I realized he was gone. *Ah, there it is again,* I thought as I recalled his apology in the dark warmth of last night for the times when he was cold and preoccupied in the mornings. He was all business as he dressed and reviewed his list of petitions, nervous about having time to complete his personal Camino with the statue of Saint James before he and Franco left later that day.

"I've always wanted to come to New York," he began tentatively as we ate breakfast together in the empty dining room. "Maybe…"

Bam! We both startled, jumping as Mónica slammed her bag down on the table between us, again slicing the energy connection between us. She dashed over to the breakfast bar. Franco followed more cautiously, placing his things at a nearby table.

"You might as well join us," Gerardo sighed wearily. "Mónica is already here."

Nervously checking the time, he prepared to leave for his appointment with the saint.

"Robin thinks it's ridiculous to hug the saint," Mónica said to Gerardo. "She doesn't understand why anyone would do that."

Huh? I looked at her in shock, wondering why she would say such a hurtful thing, putting her words in my mouth. Once again, she had severed something important between us.

Silence around the table, and then Gerardo rushed off to the saint barely looking at me, hurriedly saying we would meet up later.

On our way to the pilgrim's mass after showering, Mónica and I ran into Franco hurrying back to the hotel. He and Gerardo were leaving for the train station in less than an hour, he said as he hugged us goodbye.

"So this is it?" I said sadly. "Gerardo and I won't get to say goodbye in person."

Franco stroked my cheek saying, "I will send him to meet you outside the cathedral."

Reeling with the sudden severed connection, I sat in the plaza outside the cathedral journaling and crying, knowing in my heart that he would not come. *What should I do? Go back to the hotel to say goodbye in person? Go into the mass?* I floundered painfully for ten minutes, not able to decide. *Surrender,* I finally thought, and taking a deep breath entered the cathedral and found Mónica.

Midway during the mass, a text came from Gerardo saying he was sorry that we couldn't say goodbye in person and a few other wonderful things about me. Anger flared as a deep hurt pierced me with the impersonal communication. Surely he will call me later for a more intimate goodbye.

In the line for communion, I meditated again on surrender. Praying afterwards, I cried freely and accepted the experience as another lesson, another step towards being with the right man by experiencing what was possible and getting clearer on what I wanted. Falling in love, even if only for a few days, was a major opening for me. I would release the pain in my heart as needed, in addition to releasing the experience and the man.

But please, universe, God, Grandpa, my ancestors, and angels, I prayed, *I'm tired of the damn climb, show me that the end is in sight and transport me there soon.*

34.
Downhill from Here

"What are regrets? They're just lessons we haven't learned yet."
—Beth Orton

(Week Three)

Midway through the second climb after leaving O'Cebreiro, I was cursing the author of my guidebook, who had once again left out vitally important information. I had been promised a downhill walk the day after the big climb. Nowhere had it stated that two major climbs happened before the eventual descent. My legs, already tired from the challenging day before, were like deflated rubber as I collapsed against the stone wall of an old cemetery. Shuffling to stand under the broken tile overhang, hoping for some shelter from the heavy drizzle, I burst into tears.

Please, Grandpa, ancestors, and angels—I'm so tired of the climb, please show me that the end is in sight, I sobbed dramatically.

The zip of tires on wet pavement distracted me from my misery and I looked up to see a roadway twenty feet above eye level. *Oh, thanks. That is the end of the climb there. Let me rephrase the request: Oh please, transport me easily to the end of the climb.*

In no time at all, I was ensconced behind a table in a warm barroom, plate of *huevos y jamon* (eggs and ham) in front of me and a grande *café con leche* in hand. The room was packed with the rumble of raised voices, laughter, clanking cutlery, and about twenty damp and virile Spanish men. I was *really* loving my ancestors and angels. And judging by the size of Mónica's grin, I think she felt the same.

Back out into the cold rain, we walked through landscape that was rumored to be the most beautiful on the Camino. We, however, could only see the misty sides of buildings just before running into them. When it finally did begin to clear, it was like passing through the mists into Avalon, revealing a charmed land of green fields, sloping hills, and slate villages.

This was a magic land, where nature was a living force. It was a place where man lived with nature as he had for many centuries past, and would for many to come. Galicia was the Shire, the pure land.

"Look for the union label!" I sang, punctuating each second syllable with a stamp of my staff. It was a '70s jingle about supporting the women's labor union that had been popular during my childhood. It had the cadence of a marching song, and it had certainly moved me for the entire day.

Roaming around Triacastela before sunset, I wandered into the small churchyard and began idly looking for my family name on the gravestones. Memories of Tom and me finding the grave of my ancestors in my grandfather's village torpedoed to the surface, and I began to cry. Many, many years ago, that was the last time I had been in Galicia.

Tom had first surfaced on the Camino after my illness, when I forgave myself for adopting the belief after him that I would never find someone who loved and accepted me. He popped up again while walking on another misty day to the Iron Cross on Monte Irago, when I released my old beliefs and replaced them with faith that I was learning the lessons this time around, that I had broken the cycle and would be united with my right man.

If you want it, you got it, you just got to believe, Lenny Kravitz sang in my head as I made my way back to the albergue.

Look for the union label! On the second day it possessed my mind, I began to make a game out of it. What was the Spanish word for "union"? The German one? French, Italian, Portuguese? I began searching for labels everywhere, on clothing and backpacks, on signs in the towns we passed, and messages written on the rocks.

I needed a diversion that day. A wrong turn leaving Triacastela meant that our walk was seven kilometers longer than planned. Yes, we would get to visit a beautiful eighth-century Benedictine monastery, but I was tired, really, really tired. When fellow traveller pointed the route on a roadside map, casually demonstrating that we were on the road to Samos not San Xil, I had a mini-meltdown. How was that possible? I was the Navigator, I always steered us in the right direction! I always knew where we were going! Shades of disbelief, doubt, guilt, and shame crashed through my tired brain, along with schemes for correcting the situation and calculations of the kilometers we would need to retrace.

Finally, I took a deep breath and reminded myself that my practice was surrender. There was a reason we were on this path.

The land then immediately enchanted me and the images from that segment are still etched in my mind: a giant spider web stretched between two rails of a rough-hewn wooden fence with diamond-sized drops of dew sparkling on the delicate white fibers, glowing green fields with morning mist rising from the ground, mossy irrigation streams channeling water over a mini-waterfall of slate rocks, narrow rich brown earth and rock tracks enfolded by ancient trees dripping leaves and dappling the ground with patches of sunlight.

Despite the detour, we arrived in Sarria in time to meet up with the joyful group of Spaniards from the north, south, east, and west of the country that we had been bunking with the last few days. The Spanish soccer team was playing Scotland that night, and we watched the first half drinking *hierbas* with Alberto, part of the second with Jose Manuel and a few others, and then I stayed up to watch the rest with the *hospitaleros* at the albergue.

I really enjoyed Spanish football, but was also not looking forward to a night in our smelly room. When we had checked into the albergue, we were overjoyed at the small rooms: only two bunkbeds and four people instead of the customary dormitories ranging from twenty to over one hundred beds. Perhaps this would be a night without earplugs and the constant background symphony of snoring? When we opened the door to our room, we recoiled from the wall of body odor that assaulted us, baked into the clothes and belongings of our roommates, the French couple who had so annoyed me in El Bierzo.

Mónica and I thought we had become old pros at life in the albergues by this point, but we had never encountered something quite like that. We could maneuver quietly in the dark along with the best of them, skillfully dressing and undressing under cover of sleeping bag, fearlessly using blankets and laying on bedding regardless of the threat of bedbug bites, and efficiently hanging our laundry on every available hook, slat, and bar to maximize drying for the morning. But what to do about the smell? Perhaps Mónica still had some of her essentials oils for under the nose...

Look for the union label! By the third day, I took a more philosophical approach to the phrase. Perhaps this was a message to begin looking for the right man, to use my Right Man BATNA to assess whether there was a union label and not waste my time if there wasn't one.

Ah...let me review my list, I thought as I turned the corner, came upon a bar, and caught Gerardo's eye.

"You're wearing army boots to walk the Camino?" Mónica and I looked at each other in dismay. Peeling off Franco's socks, I took a first look at the blisters covering the balls and heels of each foot. Ouch. Pulling out my disinfectant and needle, I said, "This may hurt..."

Somehow, we had changed from a twosome to a foursome without conscious effort on any of our parts, and ending up walking with a male me and a male Mónica. I had never noted the similarity before between an Italian Man and a Latina: both traveled with enormous bags of toiletries, had elaborate pampering rituals, considered perfume an essential part of hygiene, and took half the morning preparing for departure if you let them. My male counterpart (Gerardo) and I, both big city dwellers for most of our lives, walked and talked quickly, packed lightly, stayed one step ahead of the program, and smoothly analyzed each situation for the most beneficial and efficient outcomes.

"We thought we'd stay in this albergue tonight," Gerardo and Franco told us. "What do you think? How do you feel about walking this far tomorrow?" they asked us. Mónica and I both thought it was just wonderful to be taken care of.

(Week Four)

Less than a week left to our journey, and we were still mostly having fun despite more frequent breakdowns in our agreements and ground rules. The natural flipside to Mónica being more open about what was happening in her life was that it began to consume her. She began swallowing things instead of expressing her truth, building resentment instead of clearing away small annoyances. Avoiding conflict was a deep habit for her, and she let it override her commitment to our agreements.

I became involved in my own experience, too, and stopped actively reminding her about our commitments, thinking by this time in the journey we were on the same page with them.

As Mónica went deep into herself, her role as victim in her marriage began to take over and direct her behavior. She began transferring more and more of her husband's qualities to me, as well as her passive-aggressive patterns of dealing with him. She began to undermine rather than to support. Her behavior brought back remnants of old patterns from my relationship with Tom, when he played victim to my angry woman.

For the most part, I tried to address each instance as her coach, proud of the way I was managing my own triggers and firm in my commitment not to be an angry person again.

However, things really broke down when we began speaking predominantly Spanish. Mónica started to (s)mother me, not seeing that it was the last thing in the world that I wanted. She stopped seeing me, she stopped listening to me. Driven by her own demons, she began taking away my voice. Uh-oh.

"He's asking if you would like coffee," Mónica said slowly in English.

"Yes, Mónica," I sighed, "I understood him. Again, please don't translate unless I ask you to."

My Spanish was at least good enough to get my meaning understood and have a decent conversation, except when she was around.

She had also taken to interrupting me when I was speaking Spanish to tell people what I was trying to say before she even knew what I was trying to say. In addition to this, and her habit of claiming things I had said or done as her own, she began telling stories about me. "Robin says this, she thinks this..." *No, I don't!* screamed the frustrated storyteller in me, *You are not me.* Ancient triggers flared: *Give me room to be me! Let me have my own voice!*

"Mónica tells me you healed your hip," Gerardo mentioned one morning when we were walking. A small pocket of anger exploded inside. I had made the conscious decision not to talk about my hip with anyone other than Mónica on the Camino, looking forward to the freedom from my birth defect being an issue here. Many people, I had observed over the past several years, changed the way they related to me after they learned about it.

As the tension began to build between Mónica and me, I told myself that the Camino was offering me an opportunity to choose differently under similar dynamics. It was okay to feel the anger, recognize it for what it was, and find a constructive method to release it. It was important to be compassionate to the struggle that Mónica was going through, to recognize the thwarted mother in her, the woman who desperately needed to control uncontrollable surroundings, and to coach her to be the best she could be.

In her pain, I could see that Mónica had become unconscious of the impact of her actions.

Finally, the Milky Way! Mónica and I left well before the men our final morning, wanting to complete the journey into Santiago the way we had begun with just the two of us. Leaving Lavacolla in the dark, we asked some drunks still hanging around following the evening's fiesta where the yellow arrows pointed, and walked quietly through the dark town. Looking up, we lost ourselves in the starfield that had given the Camino its name.

The sky gradually brightened towards dawn as I approached the climb to Monto do Gozo, the mount of joy where pilgrims got their first sight of Santiago.

Flickers of other men who had impacted my life raced across my mind and then faded away.

*I'm free to do what I want at any old time...*the old Soup Dragon's song exploded in my mind. Laughing with joy, I leaped into the air, forgetting about the heavy pack on my back. It was worth it, despite the uncomfortable landing. I sang and danced the rest of the way up the last climb of the Camino.

I slowly walked around the top of the mountain and the strange modern monument erected there, looking for a place that called for my last two offerings. I found it in the form of a stone basket held by St. Francis of Assisi as he gazed at Santiago in the distance.

Placing the second of my Sam stones in the basket, I sent up a prayer for my friend's teenage son who had been killed. *Let him be in a place of joy, and let that knowledge bring his mother peace.*

Next, I took out the quartz stones and spiral shell, which symbolized my life's purpose on my yoga altar, and placed them in the basket. I prayed for the courage and strength to joyfully fulfill what I was placed in this life to do.

I stood in front of the basket and began a sun salutation to release my offerings, calling on the magic of my yoga time in Costa Rica.

"ROBIN! ROBIN!" Mónica interrupted my flow of postures, shouting with jangling nervous energy, not paying attention to anything other than her own immediate needs. "There's a bus full of tourists coming, let's go!"

Blocking her out, I finished my ceremony, walked past her into the little chapel and prayed in the other way I was taught. Surely she wouldn't intrude in here.

The remaining walk into Santiago was an abrupt confrontation with reality after the peaceful magic of the Galician countryside. Tourists and day-walkers crowded the hillside, roads, and sidewalks down and into the city limits, jostling for space and showing little courtesy to pilgrims carrying heavy packs who had been walking for weeks or months. Moving with the crowds, there was no time for personal reflection on the journey's end, just a sense of urgency to be done mixed with some anticipation on who we might encounter upon arrival.

Passing through the darkness under the pilgrims' arch, we entered the large, crowded plaza and stood looking up at the massive cathedral of grimy, aged stone. We had done it, we had arrived. Time for pictures, to climb up the steps of the cathedral, to find a quiet place against the rail overlooking the plaza and to absorb the scene.

Now what? It was too early to stop walking for the day and I had too much energy left to burn.

The line for the Compostela, the certificate stating you had completed the Camino, was uncharacteristically short and we were advised to go directly there or it would take hours at another time. More jostling and lines, and we received official documentation of our accomplishment from the Catholic Church. A plenary indulgence was granted, and all our sins were now forgiven. We were saints for the moment, at least.

Now what?

We reunited with Ann leaving the pilgrims' office, and met for drinks in the main plaza above the cathedral, where a long line of tourists and pilgrims waited for the opportunity to petition the statue of St. James.

"Relics," I said, "I don't understand them. Why honor a piece of dead body when the spirit has departed?"

Drinking glasses and then a bottle of wine to celebrate, we filled each other in on news from our separate journeys, shared pictures and laughed over our adventures. Ann was leaving for Belgium the following morning.

Familiar faces popped up here and there. *"Felicidades!"* The Italian man from El Burgo Ranero who tried so hard to communicate but only the word *"bella"* could be understood, the Canadian ladies from the albergue in Astorga who commiserated on my infected toes, the Irish and Finnish ladies with whom I had walked the beautiful, but endless road into Samos, the smelly French couple from our room in Sarria and the vineyards in El Bierzo, the mother and daughter from Marbella who were our bunkmates for several nights starting in O'Cebreiro. Jose Manuel from Salamanca, Patricia from Madrid whose husband joined her for the holiday weekend in the mountains with her dog, Sergio and Miguel, business consultants from Barcelona and Madrid, all of whom we had met leaving Ponferrada nine days before.

Our community, all the faces that were so much a part of daily life were now being seen for the last time ever. For time on the Camino did not pass according to regular measures. Lifetimes were lived in each phase of the day, each segment of the walk, each break, and each meal, and then another lifetime at the albergue, and yet another during the evening meal and social time. Time passed very differently when planted firmly in the present moment, heart wide open.

Sadness crept up from the ancient cold stone of the city and settled in my heavy heart. It seemed that there was a price to pay for walking without walls, for opening my heart.

A bit tipsy with the wine and the nostalgic energy of the place, I left Mónica and Ann to prepare for the evening ahead with a long hot soak in the tub. We would meet for an early dinner before celebrating with Gerardo and Franco, whose morning departure I couldn't even begin to process.

"The wine is on me," I said, leaving Mónica money to pay for it. Later, walking to dinner, I asked Mónica if there was any change. "I decided to keep it," she said. "I figured you probably owed it to me." I had been the accountant on our trip—instant calculations came naturally to me after twenty years of working with numbers and statistics. This was the first I had heard she was concerned with our system. "That was a petty thing to do," I observed, "after I had just bought all your drinks this afternoon."

My heart was a lead ball.

Following dinner, we ran into Daniel at the bar of the restaurant. We had met the German our fourth day on the road, and he was part of the bigger blister pool group of Jakob, Mario, Pere, Cesç, and others. Thankfully, he was also going to Finisterre and we didn't have to say another goodbye just yet. The Brazilian man with whom he was traveling caught Mónica's attention, and I had to keep reminding her of our plans with Gerardo and Franco.

When our foursome finally reunited at a wine bar, Gerardo and Franco agreed to speak in English, since I had not spoken my own language in over a week. Mónica barely joined the conversation, declaring she couldn't think in English anymore. Her aggressive energy began to build as she focused on every attractive man who entered the bar.

Can my heart get any heavier? I wondered. I was determined to enjoy this last evening with Gerardo and what had been building between the two of us for five days and nights now. Whatever was happening with Mónica could wait until the morning. I was taking this evening for myself.

Back at the hotel, she lay sprawled on Gerardo's bed, her sexual energy spraying the room. My own nerves felt frayed.

He lay on the floor with his feet on the bed, trying to open up his lower back, which had cramped from walking with his injured toes. On the way back to the hotel, we had agreed on some Pranassage to see if that would help. I knelt on the edge of the bed and began working with his extended legs. I was also hoping to ease the cramping around my heart by opening a healing connection with him.

Mónica made her rude sexual comment. I shut down completely, as she sauntered out of the room, drawing him after her on the pretense of getting ibuprofen for the following morning.

"What's wrong?" asked Gerardo when we were alone. I had allowed Mónica's actions to extinguish my own energy like sand thrown over a fire. My ability to open up and enjoy my private time with him was limited. "I feel shy," I replied, swallowing my truth.

I couldn't believe my friend would insert herself that way on an evening she knew to be vitally important to me, no matter what she was going through internally. I thought she was my sister, there to support me in reaching my Camino intention. Instead, she had treated me as the enemy, as many women do when in competition for a man.

In the morning, she carelessly inserted herself yet again. Claiming to be speaking as me, she ridiculed something that was very important to Gerardo, and that was the last I saw of him.

Perhaps worse, I allowed my "friend" to sabotage the manifestation of my Camino intention. Instead of responding to her actions from a powerful place, I let them to flip me into being a victim, too. And that made me a very angry woman.

Not exactly the best I could be.

35.
A Gallego, a Catalan, and Two Italians

*"Take this soul, stranded in some skin and bones
Take this soul and make it sing"*
—U2

(Week Two)
"There are four kinds of pilgrims," Cesç sneered on a park bench across from the Palacio de Gaudi in Astorga. "Those who walk, those who ride bicycles, those who ride horses. And then there are the ones like you, who take taxis and buses."

Ouch. I wasn't expecting that on the Camino. Or was I just being defensive?

Es más importante seguir adelante, to keep moving forward. I had been practicing the phrase all day on the bus to Astorga, feeling some shame about the way my Camino was unfolding. During the first ten days, I had learned a valuable lesson about accepting help with all of my unforeseen physical ailments. The blisters I could handle and walk with, and was grateful for the help in treating them. The gastroenteritis, well there's nothing better to teach you about surrender than losing control of all your bodily functions. I had to get to the health center and a taxi was required. The infected toes, given the fact that I could not stomach (haha) antibiotics, necessitated a certain level of caution and obeying doctor's orders. The bus had been the only way to keep moving forward.

I had come into the Camino with a firm resolution to walk the entire way. No shortcuts for me, my feet would connect with every inch of the earth along the path. But even with firm resolutions, some flexibility is needed when faced with reality, and yoga certainly does

- 259 -

help develop that quality. I surrendered to necessity of motorized transportation, and recommitted to walking the rest of the way.

It seemed, however, that more surrender was needed to accept having to accept help.

"Mónica! Don't spit or blow," I hissed. "I think that's Mario coming."

The two men came abreast as we stood casually by the side of the path, quickly disguising the post-start adjustments we had been making.

"It wasn't just Mario, it was Carlos, too." Dreamy sigh.

It was a grey day coming out of Astorga, and I had clearance to walk again after my medical hiatus. As usual, our pace was such that the fast walkers, the medium walkers, the slow walkers, the infirm, and then the extremely aged passed us. We kept in sync with the two men as far as the first village for coffee and fruit. Leaning into the bar, I stretched out my shoulders and upper back with some surprise hands-on assistance from Carlos, who then proceeded to knuckle my shoulder away with his fist several times during our short conversation.

After mentioning I was a yoga teacher, he replied that he was not surprised, those he had met shared the same positive energy and beautiful minds.

Again, the knuckle. What did it mean? Was it a sign he wanted to touch me? Or a gesture of pushing me away?

He and Mario were moving quickly, and weren't sure if they'd meet Pere, Cesç, and the rest in Foncebadón or stay where Mónica and I were stopping. Carlos recommended a good albergue in Rabanal for us, and then took his banana and nectarines back on the road.

I had decided that Carlos was a definite yes just hours before I became violently ill the previous week. We had met on the old Roman road when I had stopped to drain a new blister.

"Can I help you?" he asked walking up with concern and goodness shining out of his beautiful blue eyes. His head and jaw were covered in dark stubble framing a kind and masculine face, his strong body clothed in knee length pants, a bright blue athletic shirt, and a dark sleeveless fleece. His backpack appeared weightless as he strode along.

We walked together for about an hour or so that day. We could understand each other well, with both of our supply of English and Spanish. His father was from La Coruña in Galicia, close to where my grandfather was born, and he visited family there frequently from his birthplace and current home of Madrid. Hungry for more information about the region and my ancestors, I drank in his words and his manly presence.

I was nearly a week into the Camino at that point, and while my mojo had been awakened by flirting with young Jakob, no serious candidate for my affections had yet presented himself. It would be another week or so before I met Gerardo.

Yes, thank you very much, I said to my ancestors and angels, *I will take this one.* For not only did Carlos appear to have many attractive qualities on my Right Man BATNA, he was also universally regarded by other pilgrims as perhaps the nicest guy on the Camino. And I am a sucker for a nice guy, particularly a Spanish/Galician age-appropriate nice guy.

Illness intervened and then luck reestablished itself when we arrived in Leon and ran squarely into our entire group of men in the lobby of the albergue. Carlos and I gazed soulfully at each other, agreed to speak later once Mónica and I had settled in. Later never came.

We spent the afternoon joyfully engaged with our blister pool group from Boadilla and Carrión, celebrating a local festival with traditionally costumed folk dancers up on stages nestled against crumbling stone walls, and party tents serving regional wines and blood sausage. Huddled together on the steps of another mounted cross monument, we watched the festive crowd gathered in the large cobbled plaza and tried to remain dry in the rain that had begun falling. The Terrassa twins (Jaume and Josep); the handsome Madrileño; Marc from South Africa; and Cesç, the Catalan funny man with a razor sharp tongue rounded out our party.

But where was Carlos?

It was here that I was officially introduced to Mario, from the Piedmont region of Northern Italy, and previously only an attractive face in the crowd. Shaggy dark hair framed a mobile face and brown eyes that emoted laughter, merriment, and passion as his moods changed. Turns out he was the apparition that I passed on my way into Boadilla, looking remarkably like my last lover and shooting a blast of heat at my sunstroked and already overheated body. Even in my delirium that day, I had registered the moment as the awakening of my Camino mojo. "Well, hello, Mario. Nice to finally meet you."

"I no speaka English," he joked, as we stood mashed together in the wine bar where we had moved for shelter from the rain. "I no understand." We pieced together a conversation in basic Spanish and laughed along with Cesç, while I gazed longingly at the wine they were drinking and avoided the scent of the blood sausage that made my tortured stomach curdle. Mineral water was the only menu item suitable for this recovering pilgrim, until Mónica and I departed in search of bland food.

Later, the Terrassa twins were our companions as we roamed the gloomy city in the rain, splashing through the dark and narrow streets before ending up at wide open plaza of the tenth-century cathedral. Coming through the giant wooden doorway into the gothic stone masterpiece, I shook off my umbrella before looking around. A rainbow washed over me. I raised my eyes and was absorbed into the magnificent round window of chakra colors shaped in circles, petals and detailed mosaics high above the entrance and shedding its radiance even on a grey and monochrome day. The rose window was flanked by rows of arched stained glass marching up the main hall and vibrating hues into the dark church so vividly that I could only see color and not the religious scenes depicted. My heart sprang open.

I wandered down the hall until an alcove drew me in with its beautifully carved statue of the Virgin Mary. I stood and prayed, throwing all of my being and offering my illness to the fulfillment of my Camino intention of finding home. Tears flowed freely as I released the past few days of physical weakness.

On cue, our crazy Italian friend Gabriella popped from behind a pillar, spreading her laughter up to the vaulted ceiling and cheering my heart.

But where was Carlos?

Even with its pockets of fun and beauty, it had been an exhausting day trying to be all the places I thought he would be. Returning to the albergue, I felt cranky and exhausted and cold and wet. When the group reformed for dinner, I declined in favor of a hot shower and fresh laundry. Oh, if only I had known that Carlos was now joining the party...

Later that night, the pilgrims assembled for a multilingual blessing and vespers in the convent/albergue chapel. Waiting outside the entrance, Cesç grabbed a camera and shot photographs as I played model in my stylish pilgrim clothes. Tonight, as well as most others, my ensemble included a black fleece, black tights to my ankles under knee-length waterproof pants, and bare feet in yoga sandals with blistered toes wrapped in white bandages.

Mario hovered close as we waited, held the chapel door open for me and made a smiling comment in Italian-accented Spanish in my ear as I passed. *"No entiendo,"* I grinned at him over my shoulder and was rewarded with another blast of heat. Mercy.

But where did Carlos go now?

We filed into the chapel pews as the nuns glided into the choir area and assumed their positions. The chaplain read greetings in five languages, blessing the pilgrims and the twenty-two countries we represented. As the beautiful voices rose in song, I was transported back to the sunny spring retreat at the Abbey in Connecticut with my dear Inner Quest yoga friends, and listening to Sister Cecilia and her community at prayer. I grounded myself in mountain pose, remembering the weekend's revelation that true Catholicism supports the principle of one love, one world. Joy and peace followed me out of the chapel and into the dormitory bed for a restful night's sleep.

Two infected toes manifested the following morning and blocked the path to further time spent together with Carlos. I had hoped to catch up with Carlos and the rest of the blister pool group in Astorga, but apart from a long distance sighting of Mario down a cobbled street, the critical Cesç was the only one we had seen there.

Singin' in the rain...Mónica and I spent the rest of the route to Rabanal crossing paths with Franziska, walking her first full day, and Ann, our partner in comedy from Belgium. Following several carafes of wine and another excellent pilgrim's menu, Ann and Mónica ferried me and my wounded feet across the stone village to the albergue that Carlos had recommended.

Entering the cozy little common room next to the albergue bar, I waved at the long table containing Mario and Carlos and went to journal near the fireplace at a table with Franziska. Yes! The men had chosen to stop here instead of meeting the larger group in the next town.

Journaling complete some time later, I slipped onto the bench across from the two men. A big-haired, blond Irish lad I had met in Astorga quickly slid next to me and attempted to chat me up while his dark-haired comrade grinned down the table. "Yes, yes, and what do *you* think, Carlos?" batting my eyelashes. Soon the laddies left us to our own conversation. Progress, as he got up to get another drink and slid onto the bench beside me upon returning. The energy was starting to work nicely when Mónica fetched me for my massage.

Fire blazing in my chest, body loose and tingling from the massage and energy work, I returned to the cozy little room after two amazingly therapeutic hours on the table. Rejoining the group, Alberto, a silver-haired ex-footballer and wise man from Italy, eyed me admiringly and graciously stood so I could slide in across from the younger men. Glowing like a lamp, I described my life change and my search for a home in Spanish and English, while Carlos helped with translation for the two Italians.

"Nooo," Mario sighed tragically, when I admitted for the first time that I didn't think I could go home to New York after my experiences the past two years.

"You must live someplace small in nature," advised Alberto, as he bought us a round of *hierbas*.

Carlos spoke of his own life changes with Spain's economic decline and being out of work. He had worked as an accountant for several international companies and didn't think he wanted to go back to that life. He had done the Camino before, once on bicycle and once walking from Leon, and found it useful in clarifying his next steps.

He spoke of entering Galicia, his excitement to have the regional foods he had grown up with, and how his accent changed the closer he came. "Demonstrate it," I requested spellbound, watching his mouth closely, firelight glinting off his stubble as he articulated his Madrid versus Galician accent.

Ahem, back to the group...the war, September 11, world citizenship, the plight of the worker, and many other topics graced our hours together until the tired walkers started to retire.

"Are you sleeping in our room?" Carlos asked as he stretched and stood to leave. "No, the other one," I shrugged regretfully.

Buenas noches were exchanged with the remaining Italians as I announced my intention to retire soon after. I stood to leave. *"Buenas noches,"* Mario said again, standing as well and flashing more heat from his big brown eyes. *"Buenas noches,"* I responded smiling. Five feet towards the door, I was stopped for another round of goodbyes. Reaching the door, I turned to wave. *"Buenas noches,"* he called again. *"Duerme con los angelitos!"* (Sleep with the angels!)

"I think another toe is infected," I said tearfully to Mónica after a night of jarring awake whenever the offending digit touched the bed.

"Ah, she has a blister under her toenail," the matter-of-fact *hospitalera* told Carlos in Spanish, and described the signs of infection to watch for. "I'll need to drain it," she warned as she pulled out a large needle. Carlos winced and I turned to my breath, once again offering the pain towards my Camino intention of finding home.

Feet properly bandaged, I sat with my *café con leche* and rice cakes, considering the next steps for the day. Carlos climbed over the high-backed bench to sit across from me with his breakfast, and suggested that maybe I should take a taxi. "No," I said passionately in Spanish, "The Iron Cross is close and I must place a stone offering for my friend whose son had died." I would walk. "Yes, then of course you must walk," he agreed solemnly.

He gave me his email and asked for mine. I gave him both my email and Spanish cell phone number. "I will write you," he said.

Mario bounced into the room, took the guidebook from my hands, and said, "Meet us here tonight!" pointing to Molinaseca nearly twenty-seven kilometers away. "Yes?" Looking into his happy eyes, I thought to myself, *Yes, of course, I'll make it somehow.* My feet, however, had other plans that did not include that much walking with a borderline toe.

"No," I replied sadly, we would stop in Acebo, ten kilometers closer. We gazed at each other mournfully and kissed goodbye, knowing that we probably would not meet again. I assured him that I would remember him and Carlos.

Later while packing, I saw Carlos geared up to walk outside the dormitory window. I moved toward the door as he came in to say goodbye, kissing my cheeks then grasping both my hands saying, "I *will* see you in Santiago."

"I prefer Mario, the Italian, for you," Ann said as I limped with her and Mónica out of town and into the misty mountains. "He has more spark, more fun to him."

"Mario?" With my crush on Carlos, I had not even considered him as an option. True, on more than one occasion Mario had vividly reminded me of my last lover and the powerful and oh so satisfying connection we had in Costa Rica. Was I so attached to the idea of Carlos that I overlooked such a strong and pleasurable association? Very interesting.

Shrouded by the heavy drizzle, walking among the red, orange, yellow, and green ferns, I reflected on the two men and what they represented in my life. Part of Carlos's attraction was his challenge, his ambiguity trap. I had chosen him because he had all of the right qualifications at the right time, and decided that he was the one I wanted. But did he want me or not? Hmmm...this was beginning to feel a lot like an old pattern. Was I reliving behaviors that had kept me trapped for years with Tom? I could make Carlos' actions and words mean whatever I wanted to, but the fact remained that he was not claiming me. *Release him,* I decided, *and free yourself so the right man can choose you.*

Two sides of a coin, I mused. *I want a man with both quality and kindness* and *a powerful energetic connection. I don't have to give up one for the other. Attachment to one leads to closing off opportunities for it all.*

Besides, both Carlos and Mario had disappeared into the mist, speeding ahead down the Camino and out of my life. I chose not to struggle to keep up with them.

Sighing, I focused the remainder of the walk to Foncebadon on releasing them both, believing that I could have it all and accepting the lesson to walk at my own pace. When my right man appeared, there would be no ambiguity.

(Week Four)

Many adventures later, we arrived in Santiago on a Sunday morning and eagerly sought out signs of lost friends. Outside the cathedral, Pere materialized almost immediately and gave us the news that Carlos, Mario, Cesç, Jakob, and a few others had set off just that morning for Finisterre after two days in Santiago. Mónica and I had our celebrations and completed our rituals in the tourist-filled city.

On Tuesday, we left by bus to Finisterre, our final Camino destination, bringing with us Alberto, the Italian, another Carlos from Mexico, and Daniel from Southern Germany. Our hope was to celebrate the end of the journey together with all our friends on El Faro, the lighthouse point considered to be the end of the known world in centuries past.

Walking the long road by the sea up to the lighthouse point buoyed by the fresh open air, I meditated on surrender yet again and called on all my angels and ancestors to fulfill my Camino intention. The Atlantic Ocean stretched down the coast in looping coves as far as the eye could see. The pale full moon rose over the distant shoreline of the first loop to the south, as the sun sank to the same level over the hills to the north. The sound of the wind and the tapping of my trusty walking stick were my only companions as I once again pulled far ahead of Mónica.

Earlier in the day, I had prepared my offerings for the burning ceremony, practiced on El Faro since ancient times when pilgrims would burn their clothes in celebration of a journey completed. I had selected three items to burn. My socks would be burned to offer the pain of my journey to the fulfillment of my Camino intention to find home. The little bag that had carried my special symbols throughout my two-year adventure would go to releasing the energy of my offerings along the way. And finally, my walking stick, which had been my support and meditation tool, symbolized accepting help when needed and believing in my own strength with or without it.

I had such hopes and expectations for the night in that magic place. Still reeling from farewells and the journey's sudden end, I was hoping that the ritual would help me to release some pain and ground myself again in the present. And that reunion with other friends would give me the closure that had been lacking in Santiago.

I was curious to see Carlos again. How would I feel about him after all of my experiences on the Camino? Was he still a yes? Would we finally have time to connect?

It seemed, however, that the universe had yet another lesson for me and it was a big one. The funny thing about life is that you keep getting new opportunities to learn the lessons that elude you.

Breathing in the ocean air, I arrived at El Faro, eagerly looking around but seeing no familiar faces. I sat on the rocks and absorbed the scenery alone until a friendly Scot from the albergue offered me food and beverage. His lively group enfolded me as I waited for Mónica.

Boulders tumbled down the triangular point to the sea, a strong wind ruffling the pilgrims scattered in crevices all over the rocky promenade. Fishing boats bobbed on the water fall below, clustered together under the setting sun. Rose, peach, and orange washed the heavens and was reflected back. Pale ghostly moon and fiery glowing orb played in opposite ends of the sky, changing intensities as the balance shifted to the lunar.

Gradually, our party expanded first with Mónica, then Alberto, and then Daniel. But still no sign of the walkers as the sun sank lower.

A fire was lit in the moving air. I flashed back to my dream in Acebo of being a powerful woman leading a ceremony with fire, earth, sea, and wind, past-life readings along my two-year journey of being a priestess in Celtic times and Atlantis, my deep desire to fulfill my Camino intention.

Red-faced and panting, Carlos, Mario, Cesç, and a German girl appeared at the lighthouse. They had just completed their thirty-kilometer walk to Finisterre, dropped their packs, grabbed some food and raced up to El Faro in time to make sunset. Carlos spared a moment to describe their predicament during a quick greeting before the foursome dropped down in their own nook on the rocks.

Cesç scowled at our presence, once more making pointed comments to Daniel, Mónica, and I about taking the bus instead of walking. A bit of the moment's magic faded as I absorbed the judgment. I was a bit shocked by the negativity at the very end of the Camino.

Giving them a chance to settle in after their day of forward motion, and the closeness of their walking group, Mónica and I respectfully left them their space. We returned to our new albergue friends and their festive party, as they tended the fire for the burning ceremony.

"Yeah, I guess I could 'do' a forty-year-old," Cesç sneered loudly to Mario, the ocean and everyone else around, after observing Mónica and I laughing with some men from the albergue.

As Cesç's ongoing volley of negative comments hit my trigger points, I withdrew deeper and deeper into myself. Gone was the open, light, and smiling Robin, replaced by a stormy cold front. The magic of the scene was lost for me. Cesç's words were the third strike that I allowed to topple me, already feeling bruised and highly emotional after the impersonal break with Gerardo, shaken and insecure with Mónica's continued passive-aggressiveness.

Slam, down came my wall, and I blocked out the whole group.

Cesç's nasty energy continued throughout the beautiful sunset and his judgments amplified and expanded to our broader group during the burning ceremony as I set fire to my three items. I plowed through the ritual, trying to focus on my intentions and celebrate with the firetenders.

El Faro slowly emptied of people and the last rays of sunlight, until it was only our two foursomes that remained. Mónica and Alberto said a pleasant farewell to the group, while Daniel and I stood off to the side.

"*Espero que estes contento, espero que seas feliz en tu vida,*" I said to Cesç, wishing him a happy life when he came up to say goodbye. "*Yo soy feliz,*" he snapped back, "I am happy."

With earnest eyes, Carlos stepped up, kissed my cheeks, and said again that he would email me. He explained that they couldn't seem to stop walking, and were continuing on early the next morning to Muxia.

Mario came over cautiously, and eyed me warily as a stranger until I reached out and initiated a warmer goodbye.

Then both groups climbed the rocks up to the road and began the long walk down. Cesç and the German girl walked fast, pulling away from us quickly, while Mónica and Daniel dropped behind. I linked arms with Alberto, feeling sad and lonely behind my wall, and he began singing songs and prompting me to join in.

"I don't sing, remember?" I laughed. He kept trying. Looking for an escape from my self-imposed prison, I jumped the wall and sang loudly in public for the first time in thirty years. The magic began to come back.

First Mario and then Carlos dropped back to walk with Alberto and me. "Amazing grace, how sweet the sound, that saved a wretch like me, I once was lost but now am found, was blind but now I see... this land is my land, this land is your land, from California to the New York island, this land was made for you and me..." I belted them out, not caring when my voice cracked off tune.

"*No puedo darte la luna que tu esperas, mañana yo partiré sin tus flores...*" I sang then, as I had so many times to myself during the last two weeks of the Camino. Carlos walked next to us, ears straining for the words in Spanish. I stopped short and laughed to Alberto, "That's all that I remember." Carlos laughed, too, then visibly shook himself and walked ahead.

We arrived at a crossroads. Carlos looked at us, and Alberto made for us to keep walking with him, Cesç far ahead.

I pulled back, choosing to wait for Mónica and Daniel who had dropped out of sight. Carlos stopped for a moment, then waved and followed his friends out of my life. I had received my answer, and accepted that he wasn't to be.

Somehow, with a mixture of Italian, Spanish, English, and hand gestures, Alberto reminded me of the importance of conscious choice. "We all share the same energy," he said, "and we affect the group energy by who we are being." Yes, Cesç was very negative, but it was my choice how I reacted to it and that impacted the situation. I was a writer, a woman of the Camino—why did I give my power away? Why did I let nasty comments affect who I was?

The light bulb over my head lit up the night. In a flash, I saw how I had influenced the dynamics on El Faro, just as I had created a "disconnect" with Gerardo when I withdrew into my own pain. My light, all that attracts others to me, gets cut off when I do so. My energy becomes cold and defensive, and pushes people away, not allowing connection. I do that by becoming a victim to outside forces, allowing them to change who I am being.

Cesç had only been acting as he was, with all of his own history and humanness influencing his behavior. He had his own Camino, his own path to walk, and he had been placed in my journey so that I could learn something vitally important and practice compassion for myself and others.

"Thank you, Alberto," I said with all of my heart. "Life is a choice between fear and love. Tonight I chose fear and I see the impact. I will consciously choose love going forward. And love starts with extending it to myself. For this, I will always be grateful, my dear friend and angel."

36.
Implosion

"I know there's nowhere you can hide it, I know the feeling of alone.
Trust me and don't keep that on the inside,
soon you'll be locked out on your own.
You're not alone."
—Jude

(Week Four)

We arrived on the Island of Misfit Toys on a bright and sunny Tuesday morning.

For that's what Finisterre felt like, with so many pilgrims arriving with only parts of themselves intact, the rest still propelling out in space after so much time in forward motion. The magic of walking the Camino is in how it opens you up and takes you apart. The hardest thing about ending the Camino is putting yourself back together—especially when many of the parts have changed while walking.

In our beautiful little Albergue do Sol y Luna, we found the perfect halfway house to do just that. Pilgrims arrived there and stayed, some for days, some for weeks—however long it took to feel ready to face the outside world again.

Mónica, Daniel, and I settled into the bottom bunks in the sunny little room with six orange beds, absorbing the quietness of the place after all of the activity among the damp stones of Santiago. Finally back to nature, with the salty sea air washing over the small town and the weary pilgrims, we each visibly dropped a weight from our shoulders.

Lucky to have so many days of clear bright sun, as we had repeatedly been told since entering Galicia, we dispersed to explore the town. Then we met up again mid-afternoon on a sunny terrace in the harbor to begin the watch for arriving pilgrims.

We had met Daniel early in our Camino, climbing with an American man up to the high *meseta* (desert plateau) after Castro-jerez. He was friends with Jakob and our blister pool group, and had been the other German in our plaza party in Carrión. "That was my favorite night on the Camino," Daniel told me as we drank beer and watched for Jakob, Carlos, Mario, and the others to arrive. He had travelled with the group from the beginning until the last week or so, when he had fallen ill and behind.

Our group expanded as the afternoon shadows lengthened. Matteo, a beautiful man from Switzerland, was enjoying his last day in the town and preparing for return in the morning. His home near the Bodensee sat right on the Camino, and he had stepped out his door one morning three months ago and had been walking ever since. In Switzerland, he worked with the severely handicapped, teaching them a profession, and needed the personal recharge that the pilgrimage provided. We found many pilgrims with similar professions healing in Finisterre.

Another Carlos, Mónica's surrogate father and compatriot from a neighboring state in Mexico, joined us for a farewell meal as he waited for the return bus to Santiago. Alberto stopped by to say hello, and we made arrangements to meet him at sunset on the lighthouse point.

No sign of the walkers, we headed back to the albergue to rest and prepare for the walk to El Faro.

"That's lovely, what's it from?" asked the pile of clothes and sleeping bag on the top bunk, which then resolved itself into Lizzie from Australia.

"Oh, it's from me," I replied. "Sorry to disturb you, I didn't know you were there." I had been reviewing my intentions aloud and organizing my items for the burning ceremony that night on El Faro.

"No worries," she replied, good nature shining out of bright blue eyes under a mop of tussled ash brown hair.

Lizzie, a veterinarian with a sweet, open, and matter-of-fact demeanor, was recovering from the flu and had already spent several days in the nurturing albergue, resting and reading. It turned out that we had met on our second night on the Camino in the tiny pueblo of Hontanas, when Ann had tried to arrange a morning yoga class with me as teacher. She had travelled most of the pilgrimage with Emerald, my fellow life coach, until the other Australian had slowed her pace considerably upon learning she was pregnant.

While not interested in walking all the way out to the lighthouse, Lizzie was up for drinks afterward.

Returning from El Faro later that evening, we regrouped at the albergue and collected Lizzie, Matteo, and a few others for drinks. Wandering through the deserted town, we heard signs of activity down a dark street and found our rowdy friends from El Faro making their own party in a café. A few more Germans, a few more Australians, a couple of Catalans, and the friendly Scot livened up the evening until Daniel and I ran out of gas around the same time.

Walking back to the albergue through the quiet town, Daniel told me that the word from Cesç was that Jakob would be arriving the next morning. He was disappointed to be missing him, his main traveling companion for most of the Camino, but had to leave on the morning bus to catch his flight back to Germany.

Sitting at the breakfast table the next morning, I met Nici, a German-South African, who wrapped recovering pilgrims in warmth and caring as a volunteer *hospitalera,* in exchange for room and board. Tall, tan, and broad with blond hair pulled into a tight ball at the back of her head, she was a powerful woman, strong enough to show her vulnerability with ever-present good humor. She had been in Finisterre for over a week and was unclear about her next steps, only knowing that she had to be in Barcelona by the end of the month for her flight home. I mentioned that Mónica and I were flying out the same day from the same airport and were considering a cross-country drive back. "Maybe I will join you," Nici said. "I will, too, if that's okay," said Lizzie, who had joined us at the table.

We chatted casually about our Caminos, the trouble we were having with the ending, and how glad we were to have found this place instead of ending in cold Santiago. Nici shared some personal stories about important moments in her journey, and the others joined in.

Then I opened up. I described the end of my brief intense love affair, and began to cry as I described needing some kind of closure for the lost connection. Mauricio from Verona embraced me with his beautiful blue eyes, and reached out and took my hand while Nici held the other.

"I know that he's not the right one for me," I said, explaining my Right Man BATNA and the vital things missing. "He did not have the union label," I laughed through my tears, but the severed connection was painful especially on the Camino where everything was felt so intensely. Gerardo's text and the lack of personal closure had left me feeling devalued.

I shared how Mónica had inserted herself into the last night and morning with him; and the sense of betrayal and hurt that I felt. I told the group about how, when I tried to express my feelings about what had happened to Mónica, she discredited them, scolding me for feeling pain over something that had lasted such a short period or reminding me that he thought we were pagans anyway. She had refused to take any responsibility for her actions.

As I thanked this group of new friends for their support, their caring, and their listening, I began to realize just how angry I was with Mónica.

Time for yet another round of *Auf Wiedersehens,* as Daniel and Matteo departed for their respective sides of the Alps. To compensate, the day also brought a joyous *Hallo* from Franziska, whom we had lost after Villafranca del Bierzo, and from Jakob, last seen in the mists of O'Cebreiro. The two arriving Germans were there to stay a few days, and apparently so were we, as each day passed and we stayed lodged at the albergue.

"You are so beautiful now!" Franziska exclaimed to me upon our reunion, "El Camino has changed you." *Now?* I thought, puzzled.

"I can't stop kissing you!" I exclaimed to Franziska each time I saw her, smooching both cheeks soundly before joining her for yet another *café con leche*. She was a dear, wise woman, who had left her home country over fifteen years before to settle and raise her family in Sweden, a place more in line with her values and lifestyle. From the moment we met, she inspired me and made me laugh, and we commiserated on experiences in looking for the right man.

Sharing with friends new and old, walking on the beach, listening to the waves, and practicing yoga in the sand, I slowly began to put myself back together. I had no definitive answer about home, but I had plenty of faith in the process and trusted that the answers would come. I was getting pretty good at surrender, I thought.

And then, one morning, I woke up and felt ready to move on.

"I found a cheap car rental, and we can pick it up in La Coruña tomorrow. How do you feel about taking the bus there, driving to Mera, my grandfather's village, and then starting the drive back?" I asked Mónica.

"I'm ready, too," she said. Nici and Lizzie jumped in, and we began planning a reverse Camino along the northern route. We would stay in albergues to keep the cost down and slowly reacclimate to the mainstream world over the course of our road trip.

Arriving at the lighthouse in Mera, I walked to the platform edge and looked down at the rugged coastline stretching out in either direction. I pictured my grandfather as a young man walking that coast, dreaming of his life ahead and considering the opportunities that lay on the other side of the ocean. I felt the fear and sorrow as he considered leaving his own country behind, settling in a new land where he didn't speak the language yet and would be marked as a foreigner. I imagined the hope he felt about the possibilities that were open to him in a place where a man could make himself. I visualized the voyage that he made and the hardships he faced during that era. I wondered if he would recognize what the country he had chosen had become, and what he would think if I decided to reverse his decision and leave my country to return to his. And I wished that I could sit down and talk with him.

Returning to his baptismal church after so many years, I felt no remaining trace of Tom. I took new pictures to replace ones that had been thrown in a box with all the other photos of our time together.

Then I asked the ladies if they were ready to go, and we began our journey back to the real world.

"Listen as your day unfolds, challenge what the future holds, try and keep your head up to the sky...," Des'ree sang as we merged onto the highway.

Each day we talked through our memories and highlights of El Camino, laughed and cried, and remembered. We watched the country unfold in reverse, exclaimed over the scallop shells we saw, and pictured ourselves out there walking, and we honked and offered support to the few pilgrims we did see along the northern route.

At Bilbao, we took the highway going south and spent the night in Ventosa at the albergue that Nici's friends had marked as their favorite. As we spoke with a group of pilgrims in the kitchen, I almost handed the car keys to Lizzie, wanting to walk again and see it through without taxis and buses now that I was toughened up. I wanted to walk and keep walking until I had a clear answer, until my home was presented to me on a silver platter. It was there that I made the commitment to myself that I would walk the Camino again, within two years, as Pere had recommended, and I would take the journey on my own or, preferably, with my right man.

The last day on the road, we drove to Monserrat, a beautiful monastery set on top of a strange, jagged outcropping of mountains like a giant coral reef close to Barcelona. On the site of an ancient shrine to Venus, the monks had erected a statue of the Black Madonna, who was revered in a way similar to the statue of Saint James in Santiago. As we slowly moved forward in the line to visit the shrine, I recognized many of the symbols adorning the walls, hallways, and door arches from other natural religions. One love, one world. At some point in history, religions had recognized that oneness before man made them a method of separation.

Recognizing this place as the end of my Camino, giving honor to the Goddess, the Sacred Feminine, I requested space and quiet from Mónica to meditate and prepare my petition.

"Robin, ROBIN! Do you want to eat after this?" She broke in before five minutes had passed, jangling energy once again inserting itself into a private moment.

"Are you conscious of anything other than yourself?" I snapped at her. Three-part breathing and yogic focus were required to regroup and then we were upon the statue.

I had been avoiding spending any time with Mónica on the return trip, beyond sleeping in the rooms we shared each night. Nici and Lizzie were both native English speakers, and I was glorying in having my voice back. We would eventually need to resolve our conflict, but I needed some space for understanding and forgiveness before facing that challenge.

Back in Barcelona, we sprinted the five narrow flights up to the apartment in Barceloneta. *This place feels like home,* I thought, dropping my pack and opening the windows. Later, at our neighborhood hangout, Bar Ké, the feeling of home grew stronger and continued to intensify as the week went on. Was it the place, or was it me?

Reclaiming our luggage from friends the day after our return, I gratefully slipped into a pair of loose jeans that had not walked El Camino with me. I tossed my hiking boots out of sight into the back of the closet, and took off for a long stroll by the beach alone.

And then, later, I was finally reunited with my yoga mat. Practically pushing Mónica out the door to meet with Elena, another pilgrim she had connected with in Finisterre, I spread out my mat in blessed privacy. First, the chakra clearing practice that I had developed. I wept as my tight muscles and emotions began to release, reminding myself to keep breathing. Next, Downward Dog, Squat, Dangling, Lunge, Triangle, Wide Leg Forward Bend, deep side twists, Pigeon... creak, pop, crackle, this was better than sex. Well, some sex.

Two hours later, Mónica called to see if I wanted to meet them for a drink. "No," I said, blissed out. "I'm still at it."

Half an hour later, she called back. "Elena would like to see you, we're coming up."

"Please be mellow," I requested, feeling my body start to clench immediately at the thought of her frantic and unwanted mothering filling up the tranquil space.

When they arrived, we kept it low key in the flickering candlelight. Elena was sad over a German guy that she had parted with in Finisterre. As she described his behavior and her reaction to it, I dropped easily into coach mode. I asked her if she had a list, and explained the process as the best way not to waste your time and energy on a guy if he's not right for you. You have to know what you want, and having that knowledge makes it very simple when you are presented with options.

I showed her my Right Man BATNA and told her briefly about the men of my Camino. Jakob, my young German friend, had taught me about allowing open connection, flirting just for fun, and about not making the easy choice when emotions and needs seemed overwhelming. With another ten years, he might have developed into a good match, but he simply did not have the maturity at twenty-five. Despite his attractiveness and the strong energy between us, he was simply like a dear brother to me.

Carlos was a clear example of my mind choosing a candidate, in the absence of any clear signs, just because he materialized at the right time. He was a mystery, an enigma. Despite several indications that he was attracted to me in some manner, he had not acted to claim me as anything other than a friend. That characteristic—a clear claiming of me—was non-negotiable. I would not fall into the ambiguity trap again, and was grateful to have seen it in action and break its hold on me. Challenges had always been very attractive to me, but would no longer be tolerated in the romantic arena. I was interested in a real relationship.

The chemistry and communication were amazing with Gerardo, and he had many characteristics of my right man. His personality, smarts, openness, and wit charmed me in a way that not many men had, and he taught me a wonderful lesson about what was possible with a good match. He also taught me the absolute necessity of being with someone who was emotionally available, clear on his purpose and open in his spirituality. I was very grateful to have had the experience of opening up with him, and also of being able to release the attachment to him while allowing myself the room to mourn the lost connection. I felt sad when I needed to, and reminded myself to hold out for what I wanted. It would manifest, experience had taught me that.

"Can I copy your list?" Elena asked. "I need to do this."

Back in the United States, Mónica and I went our separate ways to begin building our new futures.

As I described my journey to friends, I realized that El Camino was indeed one of the most powerful experiences of my life and the perfect closing chapter to my two-year period of self-discovery.

The beauty and power of El Camino lies in its simplicity, in the absolute necessity of taking life step by step, day by day until you reach your goal. Walking, you are in the present moment with few distractions in a way that is very difficult to duplicate in modern society. It's just you and nature, living in community with your fellow travelers, who are all walking with purpose, but without walls, and moving in the same direction. The only decision you need to make is your goal each day, and then the path is laid out ahead of you clearly marked. You just have to trust and to surrender.

The longer you walk, the deeper the lesson becomes a part of you.

37.
Forgiveness

"The weak can never forgive. Forgiveness is the attribute of the strong."
—Mahatma Gandhi

There is a common understanding among those who walk El Camino de Santiago: that walking the path gives you exactly the experiences you need to be able to manifest your intention. It will clarify that which needs to be clarified, and if you are open to the lessons, you will fulfill your intention by making the journey. Like most things in life, you need to pay attention, be open, and not be attached to the way it is unfolding. Above all else, you need to have faith.

My intention in walking the pilgrimage was to find home, which for me was not only a place; it was also intimate connection with the right man for me. To be able to manifest it, I had an important lesson to learn about myself that kept presenting itself in different scenarios until I finally paused and recognized it.

My lesson was to accept responsibility for the impact of my own actions, regardless of the environmental causes that may have influenced them. Ultimately, the way I behave and appear in this world is a direct result of my own choices. When someone else's actions are negative or attacking, I still have a choice as to whether I will allow them to influence who I am being or whether to continue being true to who I am even in the face of adversity. Alberto clearly demonstrated this lesson to me at the end of our first night on El Faro in Finisterre. Mónica further illustrated it in during our time in Santiago.

When the actions of others hurt us, we have a choice. In our pain, we can choose to be in integrity with ourselves or we can choose to indulge in self-pity and blame.

For myself, by recognizing that pattern of changing who I am based on external stimuli and seeing how it played out in many areas of my life, I could begin to consciously make a different choice. Learning this lesson enabled me to be my best in all situations. As I saw on my journey over the past two years, it was now simply a matter of putting it into regular practice.

There is another common understanding about the pilgrimage: that the process doesn't end when you reach Santiago de Compostela or Finisterre. Much of the true work of El Camino takes place after you have returned to "real" life, and you begin to integrate and understand your experiences.

For me that process took many months to unfold and provide clarity.

I had a highly developed defense mechanism of camouflaging unpleasant information and direct attacks, burying their message and wounds deeply without experiencing them. Why I buried them made no difference, whether out of compassion for the attacker or in disbelief of the ability of one person to treat another in such a way. The important thing was to bring the pattern into my awareness.

I had deeply buried the events that played out the last week of El Camino and in Santiago between Mónica and me. I allowed my desire not to cause her more pain as she went through a difficult separation and divorce to dictate what I acknowledged about my own experience. I limited the expression of my own truth based on her reaction to it, and my own fear of being unfair.

I made allowances for her and suppressed my own experience. That behavior did not serve either of us.

What Mónica did, regardless of whether it was done unconsciously in the depths of her pain, was to deal one of the worst blows that one woman can direct at another. Knowing me to be within reach of my heart's desire, my Camino intention, she passive-aggressively sabotaged through her actions and her energy. All she could see was herself and her pain, and she struck out without thought. That is precisely when the most harm can be inflicted upon another.

With each of the three strikes that Mónica dealt in Santiago, I could have chosen to act differently than I did. When she was pure sexual energy striking out during our last night with Gerardo and Franco in Santiago, I could have stood in my power and the strength of my own connection with Gerardo, to neutralize Mónica's attack instead of allowing it to extinguish my energy. When she physically broke between us during our intimate moment at the breakfast table, I could have handed her things to Franco and thanked him for giving Gerardo and me a private moment. And when she made a hurtful attack on Gerardo's beliefs and attributed it to me, I could have spoken up to properly identify the comment as her own or to clarify the more general statement I had made about relics. I chose not to do any of those things.

The last climb of the Camino for me was to open fully with a man I allowed close to me, and let him see my vulnerabilities. It was an essential step in fulfilling my intention, regardless of whether Gerardo was my right man or just another lesson. It was a time when I needed my "sister" to support me, to build me up for it, and to help me be so confident that I shone.

Instead, my sister acted against me in her pain, passive-aggressively cutting down my supports and weakening my foundations with her subtle warfare. I allowed her underneath my defenses because I was feeling fearful and sad at the journey's endings. I was feeling doubt, and self-doubt had cut me off from my power.

The impact of her actions needed to be addressed to serve both Mónica and me. I knew I must be able to express my truth. She needed to learn to take responsibility for the impact of her actions, especially as she struggled to let go of her marraige. It was the only way for us both to heal ourselves.

By finally speaking my truth about the experience, I was able to see the very clear and painful example of my own shadow and the way I had allowed it to sabotage me in my life. Because of Mónica's actions, I was able to begin the process of forgiving myself and making a different choice going forward.

My shadow is the victim. She is an angry woman, who strikes out in blind pain when feeling vulnerable and powerless. Not so unlike Mónica on El Camino.

My angry woman was very powerful, and she also wounded with words and energy. She was a razor instinct on a hair-pin trigger for much of my life. She has caused me great shame.

Who I was in the world had been too often influenced by her, so much so that I suppressed her and the expression of my anger. I was afraid that I would not be able to express my truth in a kind and feminine way. Going forward, I choose to believe in my ability to express my emotions with clarity and compassion.

We are the only ones who can make ourselves a victim. When we let fear begin to define us, we become the victim.

Our other option is to choose love. Knowing that we cannot control the experiences that life deals us, we can make a choice to love ourselves by being in integrity with who we are. The only behavior that will serve both us and others is to speak our truth. It is a conscious choice and a practice we can adopt for every decision.

I realize that there are many sides to every situation. Mónica's world on El Camino, I'm sure, looked very different from mine. She had come from a destructive situation and was just starting the process of separation and healing. She was deep in a place of fear.

We all do things we are ashamed of, things that in our balanced state we could never imagine ourselves doing. Certain transitions in our life can send us there: a life change, a divorce, a death or even just a constant state of overwhelming stress.

It is our choice how we handle those things, too. We can use them as excuses for all kinds of behavior, but unless we stop making excuses and accept responsibility for our actions and their impact, we cannot heal. The healing process begins with forgiveness.

I know Mónica to be an exceptionally good, loving and caring woman, who in her balanced state, would not have acted as she did. I have seen and loved that other side of her; she is my sister. Knowing that woman to be present and trapped under the pain, I chose to forgive her. And to feel grateful to her for the important lesson she taught me.

Seeing both sides in her, I could own that I have also been both those women. Knowing myself to be a good woman, I could forgive myself as well.

And I could choose to be more conscious in my choices going forward.

That was the gift El Camino de Santiago gave to me. Having learned that lesson, I was open and ready to go home.

"Love is not the easy thing
The only baggage you can bring
Is all that you can't leave behind."
—U2

Connect

"If you cannot see God in all, you cannot see God at all."
—Yogi Bhajan

Bliss Body *(Ananda-maya-kosha)*
The innermost layer, the bliss body, lies closest to our experience of the divine. Having balanced our physical, energetic and personality layers and developed our ability to witness life for the lessons it provides, we begin to see that we are all interconnected. Our separateness is the true illusion. We are an essential part of something bigger, and the way that we act directly impacts the health of our greater "organism". This could be our family, our community, our country or our planet. Like the heart is a vital organ pumping blood to sustain life in the rest of our body, we play a vital role in the health of our world. Imagine if the heart refused to direct blood to the liver or even to the toes—how quickly that would impact the rest of the body's ability to function. When we make unhealthy choices for ourselves, our whole community suffers because we are not living to our potential. When we follow our bliss—with all our bodies balanced and in alignment—we are infinitely powerful and can create a life and a world that sustains us in joy. We are not alone.

38.
Conclusion

"So, what will you do next?" It's a question I heard frequently from friends and family along my years on the road.

"When are you going to get back to work?" That was another one I heard a lot, especially as my journey stretched into year number three. "It must be nice to have your adventures, but you have to eventually come back to the real world."

The real world. How do you define that?

My answer to the first question was usually to describe long-term goals and to say that life is a journey that unfolds each day. I had a vision of where I wanted to go, and projects that were important to complete. The rest, I told them, would become clear as I walked the path.

My answer to the second question was: I have been working very hard. It may not have looked like it to some because I found a way to accomplish a lot while having a really good time at it; nonetheless it was so. Since leaving my corporate career, I have had more fun *and* worked harder at more meaningful things than ever before in my life. For example:

- I totally reshaped my body and my spirit
- I healed a hip destined for replacement through natural and holistic methods
- I reinvented my life and discovered my life's work by going through the process of truly to getting to know myself
- I fulfilled my life's dream of writing a book
- I completed more than 400 hours of inter-disciplinary yoga teaching training, combined with over one hundred hours of teaching
- I walked El Camino de Santiago

None of that was easy stuff, but I sure enjoyed the journey. I made the conscious decision to stop living life according to external rules following a certain prescribed path. I followed what felt true and important to me.

Better yet, I did accomplish my major goal in setting out: I found happiness. It was not a blissed out state all of the time. There were ups and downs, and challenges to keeping balanced and happy. They were many periods when I lost my equilibrium and felt like I would never regain it. But I always believed it was possible as long as I stuck to my practice, even in the most difficult parts of my journey. I always found balance again by setting goals, holding my boundaries, and just getting into action.

Even in the midst of those challenging periods, I never seriously questioned my decision to change my life or the direction I was headed. I had chances to go back, to cling to security when things felt really unstable, but I made the conscious choice not to, and held out for the vision of my life that I created.

I ended this segment of my journey feeling gratitude for the realization that true happiness was sustainable and accessible for everyone. I wouldn't trade my experiences for anything. Whatever happens in the future, it is my choice. I know I can face anything, learn my lessons, and manage to have fun in the process.

I am woman, hear me roar.

Though I didn't find my right man at the end of El Camino, I opened my heart to him by releasing the past and learning my lessons. I gained clarity on what I was looking for, and made smarter decisions about the men I did let into my life. Some really beautiful men appeared, and with enough regularity to give me faith that the right one was on his way.

I regained faith in my future, in my dreams, and in a higher power. Isn't that a better way to live than to be angry at the world?

Along the way, did I think I would break? A doubt or two may have crept in, but overall, not a chance.

How did I come into my power as a woman? By following the science of yoga, I was able to create a new now for myself.

Healing my physical body set the base for further growth. For many years, I believed that my physical health just happened to me, that I had no power to influence it, and that some things just were the way they were. My weight had fluctuated for most of my adult life, as did my level of physical fitness. Exercise and diet were the first things to go when my life got out of balance, and that in itself knocked me further out of balance. A vicious cycle. Nutrition and physical movement were essential for my well-being and I learned that they cannot be allowed to slip if I am to live a happy and healthy life. Again, my choice.

The healing of my hip was a dramatic testimony to the power of intention and the value of nutrition and exercise. We are provided with everything we need for health and healing, if we are open to seeing it. Rehabilitating my hip was not an easy process, and I had to work through a lot of physical pain. I was always able to balance that effort against the pain and recuperation that would have been necessary if I had gone through the trauma of a replacement surgery. Some things in life take effort, and your results are directly linked to how strongly you are committed to the outcome. I was committed to healing.

Developing my understanding of energy and allowing myself to receive was the beginning of opening my heart. Trusting, sensing, and intuiting enabled me to use my heart as the guiding force in my life rather than my brain, which could spin itself in endless circles trying the find the best analytical solution. I found that the heart will rarely lead you astray once you develop the skill to listen to it with discrimination.

A major element of developing and managing my energy came with the process of defining and setting my boundaries or BATNAs. Taking the time to define what I wanted and what supported me in life enabled me to devote my energy to creating situations with those characteristics versus reacting to what life presented me with constant questioning. I could focus my energy in more productive ways.

Another key element to my healing process was recognizing that there are no wrong choices. Releasing the deeply instilled belief that there is a right way and a wrong way was essential. Forgiving myself for decisions made in the past, and actually consciously learning the lessons from those experiences was the turning point in my process. To do that, I had to become aware of the behavioral patterns that had been running in my life—in many cases, I had to be slapped in the face a few times by them before I could begin the process of making a different choice. It all came down to responsibility—accepting that the choices I myself made were the reason that for the results I got, and actively making a different choice to get a different result in the future. Key to it all was forgiveness, releasing self-judgment (which is the basis of judgment of all things), and offering compassion to myself and others while holding my boundaries.

The ability to shift out of the reactive mode created by my beliefs came with the understanding that I was not my mind or my emotions, I did have a choice as to how I would respond to a situation. In yoga terms, this is called *witness consciousness* or discrimination. The ability to see life for the lessons it teaches, and each experience—regardless of its painful or pleasant effects—as a valuable part of my life journey is what gave me the freedom and ability to find true happiness. I shifted out of being a victim of circumstances to being a powerful student of life. I could then live in integrity with myself because I had done the work to know who I was, and gained the discrimination to see experiences objectively rather than personally. As the Buddha said, "Pain is unavoidable, suffering is optional." Internalizing that key learning enabled me to live life from a more powerful place.

All of that leads me to now. I created a new now for myself by taking a healing journey through the koshas or layers of the self. The science of yoga was my medicine. I move forward knowing that there is nothing that I can't handle in life. I put the practices in place to remind myself of that when I will inevitably fall out of balance for a while.

From this place of confidence and health, I could now look beyond myself and explore the ways in which I can serve. Just as each layer of myself needed to be functioning in a healthy manner, so do I need to participate as a healthy and essential part of my greater "organism" or community. The world needs help: It is seriously out of balance.

I have created miracles in my own life. It's time to create some for my world.

Acknowledgments

Gratitude and heartfelt thanks go out to all who helped me bring this book to life:

Mayra Alvarado Driessen, my sounding board, story reviewer, collaborator for practical exercises, partner in fun, teacher and student, and most of all, my sister.

All of my teachers, but especially Don & Amba Stapleton, Ann Hunt, Erika Luna, Joy Burch, Jane Fryer, Menlha Bruneau, Ruth Fellner, Silver Kim, Elena Brower, BJ Galvan, Paulette Bodeman, Katrina Abrams, Krishna Kaur, Sho Albert, ZaChoeje Rinpoche, Guy Sengstock, Alexis Shepperd and Karen Walch

My editor Stephanie Gunning, my launch strategist Michelle Price

My dear friends who respectfully provided feedback and support while the book was incubating: Dana Courtney, Sandra Kirkland, Asil Toksal and Lori Falk.

All those who helped me find a home during my journey: Agnes Pinheiro, Steve Geon, Mary Flynn Bruhn, Alexandra Lorraine, Pat & Brendan Flynn, Betty & John Patino, Etelka & Damir Franekic, Humberto Faraco, Will Pflaum, Cathy & Brian Kane, Quentin Koetter, Mayra Alvarado Driessen, Janice Ashby, Anna Sokolova, Jan Thompson, Anne & Damir Franekic, John Patino & Nikki Mintrasak

Resources

For a list of resources cited in the book, as well as other materials that guided my journey and healing, please visit my website: www.robinpatino.com.

About the Author

Robin Patino has devoted most of her life to understanding human behavior, with a profound curiosity about what inspires and motivates people. Both an empathic and logical person by nature, one of her key strengths is the ability to see the world through another's eyes, while at the same time observing the patterns formed by behavior. Patino credits the union of her parents for the skill—one a logical engineer, the other a creative artist. For nearly twenty years, that curiosity was funneled into selling ideas and products, as well as into developing the employees she managed in the political and corporate worlds.

In 2007, the author chose to begin the process of creating a new now. Patino became certified as a life coach and transformational workshop facilitator through an intensive year-long program consisting of over 500 hours of training, which she fit around the edges of her busy corporate lifestyle. Her world started to shift.

By the time she left the corporate world permanently in 2009, to move to Costa Rica and become certified as a yoga teacher, Patino was clear on two overarching goals. She wanted health and happiness for herself, and she wanted to devote her energy and curiosity to helping women find balance in their lives. Since then, she has seen miracles unfold in her own life.

During the first 20 years of her professional life, Patino built a career in the business world based on understanding and predicting market and customer behavior, utilizing that information to drive communications, marketing and business strategy. She spent over 10 years providing insights and data for shaping political strategy at two of the largest lobbying groups in the US and globally: the Motion Picture Association and the American Bankers Association. In addition, for 10 years she provided strategic research and competitive intelligence for multi-national corporations and major consulting clients in publishing, software, and financial services, as well as for entrepreneurial and startup efforts. In the process, Patino devoted over 15 years to mentoring, coaching and developing employees in the many departments that she managed, emphasizing teamwork and empowering her staff to set and meet goals. Throughout her career, she was consistently recognized as a valuable part of the management team, and a key asset for problem solving, process development, change management, and facilitation.

Like most graduates of the Thunderbird School of Global Management, Patino considers herself a citizen of the world. While studying with colleagues from 70 different countries, she earned an MBA combined with international and language studies at the school, which has been top ranked for over 20 years in international business and focused on responsible and sustainable global leadership. Her undergraduate work earned her a Bachelors of Arts in communications and journalism with a minor in psychology from Shippensburg University in Pennsylvania.

On a personal note, Patino is a risk-taker who has never been afraid of change if it presented the opportunity for growth and an improved quality of life. She has traveled extensively throughout Europe, Latin America and parts of Asia, absorbing unique aspects of other cultures and adapting them into a lifestyle most suited to her needs. She currently divides her time between Costa Rica, New York and Spain.

CPSIA information can be obtained at www.ICGtesting.com
Printed in the USA
LVOW090815040212

266963LV00019B/157/P